THE SEARCH FOR JUSTICE I

The Search for Justice in a Media Age

Reading Stephen Lawrence and Louise Woodward

SIOBHAN HOLOHAN

Routledge
Taylor & Francis Group
LONDON AND NEW YORK

First published 2005 by Ashgate Publishing

Reissued 2018 by Routledge
2 Park Square, Milton Park, Abingdon, Oxon OX14 4RN
605 Third Avenue, New York, NY 10017

First issued in paperback 2021

Routledge is an imprint of the Taylor & Francis Group, an informa business

A Library of Congress record exists under LC control number: 2004021039

Notice:
Product or corporate names may be trademarks or registered trademarks, and are used only for identification and explanation without intent to infringe.

Publisher's Note
The publisher has gone to great lengths to ensure the quality of this reprint but points out that some imperfections in the original copies may be apparent.

Disclaimer
The publisher has made every effort to trace copyright holders and welcomes correspondence from those they have been unable to contact.

ISBN-13: 978-0-815-39821-9 (hbk)
ISBN-13: 978-1-351-14540-4 (ebk)
ISBN 13: 978-1-138-35753-2 (pbk)

DOI: 10.4324/9781351145404

Contents

List of Figures and Tables

Figures

Tables

Acknowledgements

I would like to thank David Bell and Ellis Cashmore for their comments during the earlier stages of this project and Staffordshire University for the funding that made the research possible. Thanks also to John O'Neill for his continued advice and direction and everyone at Ashgate Publishing.

I am indebted to Mark Featherstone for his dedicated support and inspiration throughout this project.

Acknowledgements

Introduction

Society, Regulation and Representation

In the late 1990s the two criminal legal cases that form the locus of this study came to dominate news media narratives. The varied portrayals of the death of baby Matthew Eappen in the USA, reputedly at the hands of British au pair Louise Woodward, and the murder of black teenager Stephen Lawrence, by five white men named in the UK popular press, but never found legally accountable, have fuelled dramatic public debate in addition to conferring legal authority upon particular socio-political ideas.

In many ways this mixture of law and rhetoric has become a central feature of modern judicial process. As the mass media preserves its prime position as a daily forum for public dialogue on issues of social, political, economic and legal significance, many authors argue that it is possible for it to define legal agenda as well as report it (e.g. Ericson, Baranek and Chan, 1991; Hariman, 1990; Howitt, 1998). Such consistent intervention of the media into private and political life necessitates renewed interest in light of the changing socio-cultural landscape. While there has been a long history of the exposure of such events (and of writing about why they are transformed into media spectacles) it is essential to continue to consider contemporary examples in order to provide a critical appraisal of public spectacles surrounding the operation of legal process in multicultural western societies.

Although the cases in question will inevitably fall from popular awareness in time, I have focussed upon them in order to offer an in-depth analysis of debates that I argue were as particular to the late 1990s as discourses surrounding the AIDS pandemic were to the 1980s or stories of economic crisis were to the 1970s. That is to say, while at the end of the twentieth century many have argued that the boundaries of gender, race and class have fallen away in favour of postmodern notions of inclusive identity relations, such accounts reveal a continued concern to bind subjects to a particular set of structural relations.

Media Spectacle and the Search for a Scapegoat

Like many authors writing about media discourse on law, order and deviance, I suggest that the focus of media enquiry transforms over time in order to confront issues that may concern the current dominant ideological structures within a particular society. In this regard, the two cases that I have chosen to study – Louise Woodward and Stephen Lawrence – reflect social concerns in Britain and the United States of America that are universal, insofar as they keep re-emerging over time, i.e. family, work, and education, and in particular because they are discourses that are filtered through specific time/place rhetoric on class, nation, gender, and race.

While I am concerned to examine the effects of both media and legal discourse on the objects of scrutiny, I also want to analyse how these discourses reflects back onto the society in which the cases occur in a way that acts to stabilize existing structures. Consequently, the aims of this book are (1) to examine the function of media representation in criminal legal cases. That is to say that it aims to explore the possibility that the objectivity of legal cases may be structured by media representation and symbolization. This possibility is especially important given the central role of the mass media in dispensing information or contributing to public sphere knowledge in contemporary society. Taking into account the media's central role in articulations of criminal legal cases my second aim is (2) to consider what makes some criminal legal cases prone to scrutiny and spectacle. Following my examination of the public sphere focus on criminal legal cases, and an assessment of the way that such cases foreground wider social, political, economic and cultural issues, I also aim (3) to politicise legal authority. In other words I want to draw out the political content of legal decisions by presenting a deconstruction of the representations surrounding the Woodward and Lawrence cases. Insofar as this strategy will illuminate the presence of power relations within legal decisions, the final aim of this study is (4) to suggest a more inclusive form of social and legal judgement that can take into account social inequalities. Here, I want to put forward an ethics of representation, which, I argue, can be formed from the model of the Macpherson report[1] that gives voice to the abject subject/object of power relations articulated through media and legal discourse.

The above themes highlight the concerns of an academe that has for years questioned the role and intent of media institutions when dealing with law and order issues. The technological advancement of media communication over the last part of the twentieth century has meant that more and more people have access to exceptional events as if they were close at hand. Throughout this period of change theorists have been concerned to analyse the effects of the mass media amplification of real life events on the public perception of the world. For some authors the result of this increased access to information has been to make media audiences better informed about the world we live in, whilst for others it has demonstrated a 'dumbing down' of political debate as stories compete for discursive space in an overloaded marketplace (Scannell, 1992; Sparks, 1992). Upon entering the twenty-first century the arrival of new media technologies such as the Internet and digital communications have provided even greater means for global interaction. As a result of such enhanced possibilities for public sphere communication, postmodern theorists argue that media technologies could provide the possibility to enhance democratic global interaction and micro-political debate as they level the field of social interaction (Lévy, 2000).

---

[1] This was the report of the inquiry into the investigation into the murder of Stephen Lawrence.

Despite such frequent interventions, for many years academic debate in the field of media communication and social relations has been strongly influenced by the work of Adorno and Horkheimer (1944/1997) who perceived that mass culture or the Americanization of disparate societies would have a detrimental effect on our cultural and intellectual life as we sink further into a homogenized existence. This neo-Marxist argument runs through much of the later work on media and society as theorists have attempted to understand how representations of the world are produced and how audiences might negotiate the increased bombardment of images and discourses in terms of their own culture and identity. One of the most contested aspects of the relationship between media and society concerns the way that media forms pursue issues of crime and deviance. Following on from theories of stigma and labelling highlighted in the work of Howard Becker (1963), Stan Cohen's (1972) work on the moral panics generated by the media coverage of 'dangerous' youth cultures in 1960s Britain, raised the debate about the relationship between press constructions of social 'problems' and the maintenance of social order. In this regard, Cohen sought to unpack and problematize the ideological work of the media.

Further to Cohen's enterprise, the Glasgow University Media Group (1976; 1980) succeeded to shatter the myth of objectivity that surrounded British news production, Steve Chibnall (1977) specifically examined crime journalism in the British press, and Hall et al (1978) put forward a thesis that saw the media as unwitting agents of hegemonic social regulation (Kidd-Hewitt, 1995). It is probably this last piece of work that relates most closely to my objective. In *Policing the Crisis*, Hall et al extend previous work in the growing field of sociology of media by exploring the inter-relationship between various state regulatory and cultural institutions. Their contention was that the media promote the emergence of a kind of false consciousness, whereby those at the bottom of the social hierarchy become scapegoats for deteriorating social conditions. Not only does this take the locus of blame away from structural authority, but it also legitimates increased legislative control in the development of a law and order society.

The literature on the construction of tales of morality in the news media has also been extended in the work of Toronto based academics Ericson, Baranek and Chan (1987; 1989; 1991). Theoretically informed by previous studies, in these texts the authors systematically examine news representations of crime, law and order, as channels for describing deviant behaviour. In their study, *Visualizing Deviance*, Ericson, Baranek and Chan detail the importance of news organizations and individual reporters as 'authorized knowers' (1987: 18) in determining social knowledge. While their later studies refine this distinction by stressing that the place of these producers of knowledge is paramount to maintaining a dominant law and order perspective in the public sphere, here they show that perceptible deviance is the essential component of any story because it allows for the visible organization of insider/outsider identities.

Yet it is also vital that these representations appear neutral; that they are legitimated by the public's 'right to know'. Here the reporter can claim a privileged position; they can claim autonomy from the institution through the popularity of notions of the truth-seeking investigator who is willing to go beyond the narrow demands of the institution in pursuit of 'the facts'. Thus the journalist provides the link between public sphere and private citizen. Reminiscent of Antonio Gramsci's (1971) concept of intellectual leadership, whereby hegemony is achieved via the relationship between political and everyday life, within this framework the journalist is converted into an agent of social order through their apparently neutral position in the public sphere.

Thus, according to Ericson, Baranek and Chan the idea of journalistic impartiality is an image. However neutral they appear, journalistic and editorial decisions about content, language, and the juxtaposition of images, made in the newsroom are subject to structural regulations. Yet, regardless of any real or imagined political motive or influence that the media may possess, many still argue that decisions made in the newsroom are only ever important in direct relation to decisions made in the living room (Corner, 1996). The latter idea would seem to agree with many media effects studies which state that what is newsworthy is also generally that which might give the audience vicarious pleasure (Barker and Petley, 1997). Such theories would ostensibly seem to suggest that producers of crime knowledge are dependent on the whims of the audience rather than acting to support any ideological imperative of the dominant strata of society. According to this perspective, whilst continually accused of sensationalism and the construction of scandal, the mass media would be right to claim that they simply report issues and events that reflect the interests of the public. Minimal effects studies and the dominant ideology thesis have thus butted heads since concerns were first raised about effects of violence shown in various factual and fictional media forms (Reiner, 2002).

It is precisely such conflicting academic debates about the public's relationship with the media which suggests that the media present an ideal space for the cultural construction of social order. In accordance with this idea Dennis Howitt adds to the growing consensus in areas of sociology of media and criminology that the media function to stabilize society rather than to subvert or question authority. He states that:

> ...the media, along with many other social institutions, act as agents of political control with society. That is, the media are so allied to the power structure of the state that inevitably they serve to support and maintain power structures and dominant ideologies (Howitt, 1998: 13).

Here, once again, we need to understand the idea of the media as 'agents' of political control in the Gramscian sense. Whilst Howitt's model of cultural ratification seems to suggest that the media somehow represent the interests of the state, it is arguable that because newsmakers are part of the same organizational system as the audience they are therefore subject to the same social influences (Scollon, 1998). Consequently it is important to imagine the production and consumption of media messages within an institutionalized context. That is to say that although the mass media relies on individual journalists and editors to mould messages to the requirements of their perceived readership, the actual messages should also be read in terms of the specific socio-political factors that shape the social system inhabited by both media producers and consumers.

Evidence of this relationship can again be observed in several key studies into representations of deviance. In one such example Peter Golding and Sue Middleton (1982) examine the function of the press in its response to the economic crisis in the mid 1970s. They consider how it reproduced negative stereotypes about the poor and unemployed, those popularly perceived to be welfare state 'dependent'. Situating the crisis within an historical framework, Golding and Middleton suggest that in response to economic hardship the media discredited an element of the community in order to legitimate neo-liberal reform of the welfare state. Much like the 'muggers' presented in Hall et al's (1978) study, who were used to justify more punitive police powers, Golding and Middleton reveal how the unemployed were discursively turned into 'scroungers'. This move quickly took them from deserving to undeserving poor with the effect of diminishing public sympathy for those living in poverty.

Past accounts on representations of law and order allow us to understand how the media fits into a larger ordering system that structures meaning around agreed norms and values. Ericson, Baranek and Chan (1991) explain that both media and legal institutions fit into this system of representation by organizing actions/events that seem to work against the accepted moral agenda of the time and place in which they occur. In other words the legal system and the media normalize events which seem to transgress the bounds of social acceptability. This strategy of normalization magnifies the moral agenda, which sets the norm as that which is good for the majority, and pathologizes those who are understood to be deviant (Goode and Ben-Yehuda, 1994). The effect of this process of normalization and demonization is that the voice of those represented as deviant – usually those who are already marginalized in terms of ethnicity, religion, poverty, gender etc – is muted or disregarded as irrelevant to the wellbeing of society.

Hall et al make a similar point in their study when they show how politics demonizes certain groups in order to legitimate certain policy routes. Drawing on a discussion about how the 'new' crime of mugging was amplified by the media in the 1970s, Hall et al's study makes links between public sphere debates on law and order and the construction of racial stereotypes that are suggestive of scapegoat theory. Referring to Gramsci's work on ideology and Michel Foucault's theories of regulation, the authors develop a discussion about these manufactured discourses, i.e. the way the media frames an event to give it a certain meaning. Where I seek to differ from my predecessors is via the theoretical treatment offered in my discussion of these cases. Therefore, I attempt to extend this argument by drawing on the work of another writer of scapegoat theory, René Girard (1979; 1986; 1996). While Golding and Middleton, and Hall et al provide in-depth analyses of the relationship between media mechanisms and constructions of otherness, they concentrate on how this association informs the content of poverty or race relations. That is to say that although their work considers a *particular* case of the construction of outsider identity, it does not interrogate the symbolic structures of dominant ideology and the legal system that generate the outsider position in *general*. It is by undertaking this project of generalization that I want to deepen their analysis. I do not only want to consider the construction of otherness as it appears in the public sphere, I also want to explore the formulation of the law and social norms that determine the place of otherness in the social system. In this regard, the works of Girard will allow me to explore the construction of the social order that creates deviant individuals or scapegoats in order to stabilize its own ideological integrity. Unlike Hall et al, who analyse contemporary culture from within contemporary culture, Girard is an anthropologist and literary theorist in communication with authors such as Freud. In this respect his work is able to offer us a historical perspective on contemporary processes of scapegoating. The advantage of this approach is that it can render strange taken-for-granted practices for the creation of insiders and outsiders.

Consistent with this perspective my argument is grounded within the theoretical framework of Girard and Foucault. In their respective socio-historical studies of deviance and social control, both authors emphasize how the dangerous individual (Foucault, 1988) or the scapegoat (Girard, 1986) is key to understanding how social order is constructed around a conflictual relationship between self and other. Foucault's version of social discipline describes how the individual deemed to be deviant is often physically contained, but always symbolically reinvented, as a docile body. Under the gaze of authority (and moral society) the docile body becomes a container for regulation. Regulation is written onto the aberrant individual via discourse in order to act as a warning to wider society about the consequences of their actions; the deviants figurative or literal expulsion from the community. Girard adds to this by emphasizing the mythologizing function of story-telling, which is enacted in order to reiterate the story of deviance over time and place. Here, the story of the scapegoat is repeated in different guises and different places and internalized as a tale of morality and correct legal order.

In line with this thesis Alison Young (1996) suggests that today's media functions as such a symbolic system. In this respect media articulations of crime and deviance repeat the dominance of law by textually expelling the rule-breaker. Challenging Durkheim's idea of the *conscience collective*, whereby the rule-breaker remains part of society and actually acts to bond society based on the fact that we can recognize similarities between our own actions in their more extreme behaviour, Young asserts that we still retain a kind of prehistoric desire to literally expel the outsider from the community. She states that 'such an outlaw can never belong to the community, in that the community's very existence is founded upon her prior and continuing symbolic expulsion from it' (1996: 11). Following this point, I would argue that the media also acts as a re-ordering tool. In order to create a scapegoat that the collective can unite against, it must remove any traits that make the outsider recognizable. Meanwhile, the scapegoat must also remind us of the consequences of rule-breaking. Consequently, drawing on Foucault (1977/1991) I suggest that the deviant individual contains the seeds of regulation. Here, one can argue that in a world drawn closer together by media technology, regulation is written onto the deviant body through the constant reproduction of images of abjection.

It would, therefore, seem logical that the evolution of media technologies would affect the institution of the law – itself a sign system. In this respect media technologies can affect the law and ask whether the expansion of the media (whereby closed sign systems break down, e.g. national boundaries) means that the apparent objectivity of legal decisions is always under threat from the wider sign systems of the media. For postmodern theorists like Jean-François Lyotard (1984; 1992) this dialogue between previously static institutions (where structural dominance is problematized by interruptions from many alternative sources) provides the promise of a fractured public sphere where there is no one dominant discourse. For Lyotard the idea of the fractured public sphere means that no agreement can be reached. Thus we have no alternative but to accept plurality in society. In contrast, Jürgen Habermas (1992) wants us to understand postmodernism as an attempt to avoid coming to a social agreement. His idea of the ideal speech community asserts the need to complete the Enlightenment project whereby 'human and civil rights, and democratic self-determination remain realizable goals, the struggle for them governed by the conventions of communicative reason and consensus' (Brooker, 1992: 21). For Habermas, then, we should strive to create a democratic space within the legal and political system articulated in his idea of the ideal speech community whereby media institutions could be used as a resource to this effect.

In an attempt to reconcile the structuralist and post-structuralist positions occupied by Habermas and Lyotard, Canadian political philosopher Charles Taylor proposes a 'fusion of horizons' (1994: 67).[2] In his essay *The Politics of Recognition* Taylor emphasizes the need to broaden structural law – to make it more inclusive – rather than discard it all together. In this regard, the post-structuralist position occupied by theorists like Lyotard fails to provide a proper answer to the problems of inclusion because it falls back to relativism. Because he says that nothing is more important than anything else, everyone must compete equally for discursive space. Unfortunately, this fails to take into account existing social inequality – not everyone starts from the same structural/ideological position. Still, Taylor also finds fault with the Habermasian position, which he regards as too rational, leaving little space for micro-debate and plurality.

Akin to Taylor's assertion for the need to reconcile the two positions inhabited by Habermas and Lyotard, human rights theorist Costas Douzinas (2000) suggests that breaking down traditional institutional boundaries could in some way promote a more democratic social order. This position perhaps interprets the intervention of the media into the law as a way of asserting some kind of natural law. In this sense there is a higher power or natural right and wrong that compels us to correct institutional judgments that might be technically right, but *seem* somehow wrong. However, I believe that it would be wrong to say that the media occupies the role of objective arbiter. It does not comment on what is right or wrong and attempt to modify the law in some kind of natural, objective sense, but rather works according to the rules of its own particular symbolic context, i.e. it might be British, American, capitalist, black, white, male, female.

---

[2] Taylor is referring to Hans-Georg Gadamer's use of the term.

A Case Study Approach

It is fitting to suggest that these two cases captured the press and public's imagination if we consider the significant amount of coverage that surrounded both Louise Woodward and Stephen Lawrence in the run up to the millennium. News coverage of the Woodward case spanned two nations (UK and USA) and lasted from a few days after Matthew Eappen's death to a few months after the end of the trial, when Woodward was still subject to media scrutiny upon her return to Britain.[3] Coverage of the Lawrence case was much more significant in the UK, but particularly intensified over the time of the inquiry in 1998 and publication of the Macpherson report in 1999, which examined the apparent failure of police and judicial procedure. Indeed, the story of Lawrence's murder ranks fourth in *The Times* index of homicide stories between 1977 and 1999 with a total of 264 articles. It came only after the Dunblane primary school shootings, the Yorkshire Ripper, and the Tottenham riots (where PC Keith Blakelock was killed) in some 22 years, but was the top ranked story in 1999 with 139 articles (Soothill, Peelo, Francis, Pearson and Ackerley, 2002).

In this study I want to follow the methodological principles enacted by writers such as Derrida, Foucault, Girard, and Hall in order to excavate the political content that remains hidden within my cases. Previous work cited on the relationship between the media and law and order enables one to develop an argument around other cases that have captured media and public attention. Whilst these studies have been concerned to explore the important link between representations of crime and deviance as a response to economic and political crises, I take the deconstructive approach to look at how the Woodward and Lawrence cases were amplified in terms of the micro-political concerns that face today's multicultural societies. As such my reading of the Woodward and Lawrence cases is concerned with the apparent crisis of identity facing affluent western countries.

Following this interpretation I want to explore whether current trends in media communications have tended to continue to follow the logic of the dominant ideology thesis. This is against the idea that new technology, and a greater recognition from media audiences of the mechanisms at play in communication, has provided more room for micro-political debate. In line with theorists such as Baudrillard (1995), who asserts that the simulated effects of media messages reduce our real association with political culture, I want to suggest that media representations of crime and justice fall back on stereotypical constructions of otherness which routinely fail to fully engage with the political motivations of the story. In order to unpack this process the two cases that I have chosen illustrate different aspects of socio-political debate. However, additional cases are drawn upon in order to further consider the social, political and historical conditions in which these stories occur.

---

[3] For this study I traced newspaper coverage of the Woodward case between 7 February 1997 and 23 June 1998 in the US and UK newspapers in which it was principally covered.

In part one the study looks at the case of British au pair Louise Woodward, who was tried in the American courts for her involvement in the death of her eight-and-a-half month-old charge, Matthew Eappen. In the USA the case was bound up with debates about working mothers and the collapse of the nuclear family, but also contained an underlying narrative of patriarchal order that framed the main protagonists – Louise Woodward and Matthew's mother, Deborah Eappen – in terms of their particular gendered attributes. According to this perspective in chapter one I aim to explore how each woman was re-ordered from within dominant ideological discourse. Here, I closely explore British and American representations of the events surrounding the trial and reveal the competing discourses in relation to national identity, gender, and the family.

In order to contextualize the writing of the case and the main characters, chapter two then examines the specific socio-political climate in which the case unfolded. Part of the chapter is concerned to unravel the effect of the UK/USA divide on the case and show how the changing parameters of the insider/outsider binary was dependant on the actors' relation to this cross-cultural communication. Following this discussion of the actors and their social context, chapter three seeks to theorize the idea of the scapegoat. Here, I explore the psychoanalytic ideas of Freud (1950/1994) and Lacan (1977) and discuss their relationship to Girard's anthropological theory of the evolution of law and social order. The purpose of this exercise is to consider the legal construction of Woodward and to show how Judge Zobel's decision to find the nanny guilty of manslaughter, rather than murder, upheld the symbolic order of American society, despite the complaints of those who suggested that Woodward had escaped the rule of proper justice.

After my discussion of gender and nation in the Woodward case, part two is concerned to expand upon this reading of media rhetoric and the politics of exclusion through an analysis of the legal events and media representations surrounding the murder of Stephen Lawrence. While ethnic difference is an important aspect of the Woodward situation, it is central to the discussion of the Lawrence case. As such, the second part of my study aims to examine media discourses surrounding Lawrence in order to reveal how processes of exclusion can focus on racial signifiers as their proof of difference, thus revealing inequalities in modern liberal society. In this respect, and following the work of authors such as Edward Said (1978/1995), I am concerned to argue that contemporary depictions of race in the west remain bound to colonial assumptions about identity attributes. Thus chapter five explores the construction of the western self and the non-western other through a consideration of post-colonial thinkers such as Frantz Fanon (1952/1986), Albert Memmi (1957/1990), and the author of *Orientalism*, Said. The central purpose of this chapter is to trace the history of thinking about the representation of the racial subject and show how particular conventions are at work in the textual construction of the other. For example, when reading Fanon it becomes clear that the author of *Black Skin, White Masks* believes that the black man is *constructed* as the other that supports dominant European identity. It is not that the black man *is* other, but that, as Said argues, he is made abject in relation to the colonial master.

Following this model of colonial self/other relations, chapter five shows how Stephen Lawrence and his family were constructed by the British media. However, in the post-colonial age of multiculturalism, it is clear that the black man can no longer be easily understood as exotic or dangerous other. This is not to say that racial signifiers have necessarily collapsed and that contemporary society has become truly inclusive. In order to explain this position, the purpose of chapter five is to show how the scapegoat mechanism, which creates others, marks primitives and designates the place of the self, is able to impose identity characteristics upon different actors depending on the demands of any given situation. Thus the media is able to make Lawrence middle-English, while his alleged killers become the modern primitives that are cast out of society for their transgressive behaviour. Insofar as this process projects the traditional stereotype of the violent, animalistic, colonial other onto the working-class white man we can begin to see how the scapegoat mechanism is a formal construct that is more concerned with finding *any* other than a particular individual transgressor.

This interpretation of the case shows that the object of debased representation is moveable. While Lawrence, the black man and traditional other, can become white after his death, his alleged killers, white men and traditional centre figures, are also written through racial stereotypes often associated with the socially excluded. This shows how the scapegoat mechanism creates insiders and outsiders to fit the particular circumstances of the age. To critique the systematic nature of the creation of the other, and explore the possibilities for a more inclusive mode of justice that can order society apart from the construction of ideal types, the final chapter of this section addresses the relationship between social construction and legal justice. To this end, I intend to discuss the implications of the Macpherson report as a policy document that suggests a form of multiculturalism that takes into account the subjectivity of other ethnicities. This allows me to consider whether it may provide a model for a form of institutional decision-making that can cut through scapegoating practices that objectify otherness.

PART I

GENDER AND POWER

Chapter One

The Family as Moral Centre of Social Organization

In the autumn of 1997 the British public were alerted by a television documentary[1] to a murder case being tried in the Massachusetts courts. *The Big Story: Presumed Guilty* featured the story of Louise Woodward, a British teenager working as an au pair for Sunil and Deborah Eappen in their suburban Newton Highlands home, just outside Boston. In February that year Woodward had been charged with murder after the suspicious death of the Eappens' eight-and-a-half month-old son, Matthew, who together with their older son had been in Woodward's care. The broadsheet press in this country and the American news media had been following events since the case began. However, the airing of *The Big Story* a few days before the trial commenced ensured that the British tabloid press and their readership (presuming her to be innocent) championed Woodward's cause with a zeal that provided a nationalist backdrop to a case that had already engendered debates about the state of working families, childcare, and perhaps more surprisingly the apparent divisions between a British and American sense of justice. The ensuing trial that played out in the courts, in the American and British news media as well as on *Court TV* (known in America for its live coverage of the O.J. Simpson trial two years prior to this event) for a time captivated two nations caught up in the unfolding drama.

In much the same way that the O.J. Simpson trial took place under the constant glare of the media's gaze, the Woodward case began to take the form of media spectacle discussed by writers such as Debord (1967/1994), Baudrillard (1983), and Postman (1986).[2] For example, in *Amusing Ourselves to Death*, Postman shows how any socio-political motives underlying an event discussed by media institutions become subsumed by the spectacle that claims to represent them. As a consequence the audience is far more aware of the narrative of the story than the political debates surrounding it. This highlights a fascination with the judicial process in media-saturated cases such as Louise Woodward's trial, which

---

[1] The documentary *The Big Story: Presumed Guilty* (Carlton television) was screened on 2 October 1997, five days before the trial commenced. It followed the defence team's argument that the medical evidence, which made Woodward the only possible perpetrator of the crime, had been badly misinterpreted by the police and prosecution.

[2] These theoretical perspectives introduce the idea (to be elaborated on in later chapters) that media manipulation distorts reality to such an extent that the representation itself becomes more important than the original event.

underlines an understanding of the fictional mechanisms at play, rather than any concern with the notion of truth content. Thus, much like the on-going storyline of a soap opera, as the case unfolds parallel narratives develop, characters emerge, and allegiances are formed.

In this chapter I will read the Woodward case against narratives of familial fragmentation that developed in its wake. Referring to media articulations of the case I want to present a picture of how the Woodward case became subject to symbolic re-ordering. In terms of a theory of the spectacle it is necessary to outline the events that led up to Woodward's trial and subsequent conviction for second-degree murder. As such, I will elaborate on the socio-political significance of the media representations in greater detail in the next chapter. In this section I will show how the media representation does not articulate a debate in the process of being decided but rather an argument that has been given meaning retrospectively. In other words, the debate is 'closed off' to certain readings because its outcome has already been decided (Baudrillard, 1995). Furthermore, I will describe the public sphere debates that emerged as a direct result of the media exposure of the case and relate this to Judge Zobel's reduction of the charges and sentence – these being the events that, I will argue, became pivotal points in the 'shaken baby' media spectacle.

Here, my suggestion is that the subject's guilt or innocence is an inconsequential aside to a mechanism of regulation and sacrifice (Girard, 1986). Therefore, this chapter aims to outline the events of the Woodward case and discuss them in relation to the discourse that dominated media coverage and contributed to the public understanding of the case (i.e. family values and domestic labour). Chapter two will consider how these symbols were discursively reordered in order to resume a dominant ideological perspective. The final chapter in this section will analyse the events and debates against a theoretical framework based on a model of mimetic desire discussed by Girard. This thesis will be read against a Freudian interpretation of the structural violence of the mechanism which necessitates the obscurity, or apparent absence, of the originary sacrifice (in this case Matthew Eappen). Importantly, chapter three will show how these two perspectives illustrate the process that saw Matthew Eappen become the symbolic sacrifice through which the dominant social order was able to reassert its own self-identity.

'The Nanny Murder Trial'

The case began on 4 February 1997 when Louise Woodward made a frantic telephone call to the emergency services. A taped recording of the telephone call later revealed that she was concerned about the erratic breathing of one of her charges, Matthew Eappen, the younger of Deborah and Sunil Eappen's two children. Woodward was 18 at the time and taking a gap year between school and university. By the time the story broke she had been with the Eappens for only two months since late November 1996. Her duties were normal to the job: taking care of the children and home during the day while the Eappens went out to work as doctors in local clinics. Prior to her appointment with the Eappens, Woodward had been employed in the home of another family since June 1996. This couple had decided to 'let her go' because of differences of opinion about the late hours that she kept. The Eappens paid Woodward $115.00 (£71.00) per week to look after their two children, Matthew, and two year-old Brendan.

According to various newspaper reports in the UK (e.g. Goodwin and Wark, *The Times*, 26 October 1997 and Kettle, *The Guardian*, 31 October 1997) and evidence from witness testimonies during the Woodward trial, the Eappens were also concerned about the late hours that their nanny kept and how it might affect her ability to look after two young children during the day. They became concerned that after late nights out with her friends she would be too tired to care for the children. As a consequence the Eappens initially wanted to impose a curfew upon Woodward, but this suggestion was met with resistance. After an unsuccessful trial period, where both parties agreed to see how things went without a curfew, on 30 January 1997 Sunil and Deborah Eappen gave Woodward an ultimatum. Through this ultimatum the Eappens imposed a written list of conditions that Woodward would have to abide by or else leave their service. It was the prosecution's contention that this incident was instrumental in Woodward's actions on the 4 February. They argued that Louise was so angered and frustrated at having to live in the suburbs and take care of two young children, rather than being allowed to stay out late with friends, that when confronted with a crying baby she intentionally – that is with malice and forethought[3] – shook him and banged his head against a hard surface. The prosecution claimed that this action caused Matthew's death a few days later, in hospital on the 9 February 1997, from a brain haemorrhage resulting from a two-inch fracture to his skull.

After a trial lasting 24 days, on 30 October 1997 Woodward was found guilty of second-degree murder. She had been on remand since her arrest in February and now faced a mandatory life sentence, serving at least 15 to 20 years. The trial proceedings had not only been covered by the British and American press, but were also subject to *Court TV* treatment, where it was being showcased as 'The Nanny Murder Trial'. Over the course of the trial the jury and media audience heard prosecution and defence lawyers battle it out for discursive supremacy. But this was not a clear cut case. Woodward denied harming Matthew. There were no witnesses to the alleged assault and no physical evidence to prove that Woodward was responsible for the child's injuries. Her defence team argued that Matthew's injuries could have been caused at a much earlier date, and attempted to attribute the skull fracture, together with an earlier undiscovered break to his arm, to a genetic disorder which causes brittle bones. They continued by arguing that this

---

[3] This was the distinction between 'accident' (manslaughter) and 'intent' (murder) provided by Judge Zobel in his decision to reduce the charges against Woodward from second-degree murder to manslaughter. Here, the former charge can be used to argue that the defendant acted without intention. Whereas the latter definition implies some degree of motive or planning was involved (Jackson, 1998; Solan, 1998).

medical pathology could result in undetected accidental fractures.[4] In contrast, the police and Eappen family lawyers concluded that as Woodward was responsible for the children and the only person around when he appeared to have suffered his fatal injuries, she must ultimately be responsible for Matthew's death.

The initial outcome was met with horror by the tabloid press in the UK. They wanted to know how the American justice system could get it so wrong. Headlines in *The Sun* screamed: 'Off to Hell for 15 Years' and 'We Wept at Her Screams' (Coles, 1 November 1997). However, ten days after the trial had ended, Judge Zobel stunned many by overturning the jury's original verdict to guilty of involuntary manslaughter and commuting the sentence to time served. To add to the spectacular nature of the case, Zobel's decision was initially posted on the Internet, at the time a novel medium. It would seem that this decision would appease both camps: Woodward remained guilty, but it also acknowledged her victimary position. So, what was it about this case that made it hit the headlines in two nations and cause the breakdown of proper legal practice?

The Family Values Debate

Of the competing narratives being played out across the Atlantic, and between various media sources, the family values debate was prominent. The police officers who interviewed Woodward after Matthew's death were widely seen to condemn her for her part in the death of a child. One of the arresting officers, Detective Sergeant William Byrne, later sent an open e-mail to the *BBC News Online* Internet site stating his assertion of what he saw as 'absolute child abuse'. He wrote:

> Why is it so hard for many people to realize that this is absolute child abuse? It happens every day here in America and in England. If this girl (Louise Woodward) were a big unattractive woman with no teeth and tattoos, would the public have had a different opinion as to whether or not she was guilty? (Byrne cited on *BBC News Online*, 1998).

In this e-mail sent to the website after the airing of Woodward's *Panorama* interview (which took place upon her return from Boston in June 1998) and in his earlier trial testimony, Byrne was adamant that Woodward was guilty of murdering Matthew Eappen. Like Byrne, many commentators from the American press felt aggrieved that she could walk free after being found guilty of crimes against the family. For many it seemed that this case justified fears that the absence of mothers from the home does harm to children (Robertson, 2000). Here, one can see how

---

[4] The medical evidence presented at the trial showed that Matthew Eappen had died from massive intra-cranial bleeding. The prosecution argued that this could only have been caused by 'extraordinarily violent shaking and overpowering contact with a hard surface' ('shaken-baby syndrome'). In contrast the defence council argued that the haemorrhage was caused by a "re-bleed", inferring that an earlier undetected injury was to blame (Commonwealth v. Woodward, 1997).

Woodward became an expendable figure in the debate about family structure that has dominated the end of the twentieth century. The competing debates that surrounded the Woodward case developed into an ideological discourse that in one way or another bemoaned the breakdown of the family. It is my suggestion that for the American public the Woodward/Eappen case became a matter of civic concern with fundamental family values.

To family researchers Rosalind C. Barnett and Caryl Rivers (1996), the public's attitude toward Deborah Eappen came as a surprise because it controverted much of their research on dual-income families. This research showed that public opinion was becoming much more lenient towards mothers going out to work. In an article in *The Boston Globe*, one of the authors of the study was asked to comment on the Woodward/Eappen case. In response to the public's undeniable hostility towards both Woodward and Deborah Eappen, Rivers stated that the backlash against working mothers was directed at both parties because it "was about more than working parents. It was class, it was who pays for what, it was how much child care should cost" (cited in Canellos, *The Boston Globe*, 17 June 1998). In other words, although Woodward was often represented as the evil perpetrator of child abuse, the Eappens were also condemned for economically exploiting the hired help. From this point of view they were also held responsible for their child's death. This hostile response, which was particularly aimed at Matthew's mother, Deborah Eappen, was recorded on placards raised outside the courthouse. One banner read "One Less Baby, One More Volvo" (ibid.).

In this instance Woodward became a cipher for all that was going wrong with American civil society at the end of the twentieth century. The case and the response to it marked a backlash against feminism that saw working mothers as one of the prime movers in the breakdown of family values. According to Barnett and Rivers' account[5] there is no evidence to suggest that the children of working parents suffer as a result of their parents' life and career choices. On the contrary, they argue that their data supports the idea that families who retain a more conventional home life (father at work, mother at home) are more likely to be poorer, less happy, and more prone to the kind of familial crisis that overspills the boundaries of the private sphere (juvenile crime, teenage pregnancy etc). Barnett and Rivers state that their study supports the actuality of the continued and successful emancipation of women. However, I want to argue that this evidence is premised on a study that upholds the exclusionary boundaries that continue to support capitalist ideology. At the beginning of their book the authors state that: 'the couples in our study were *typical Americans, not some exotic breed.* They were largely white and middle or working class; this book is not a picture of the urban poor or the underclass' (1996: 4 – my emphasis). By making this statement of intent, Barnett and Rivers underwrite an ideological imperative that seeks to hide social or cultural exclusion with academic evidence. They go on to argue that the modern marriage now consists of 'collaborative couples' rather than

---

[5] This evidence was based on a Barnett and Rivers four-year study of three hundred dual-income couples in full-time employment, spanning the working and middle classes and funded by the National Institute of Mental Health in the USA.

hierarchical relationships, asking: 'Can women have it all? Yes, if "all" is defined as having a good job and a reasonable family life. The authors of this book have just that' (ibid: 243). Forwarding claims of liberal equality for some (as long as the benefactors maintain strict family and economic structures), the authors secure a position of success for some and at the same time condemn others to a life of low-wage exploitation. In other words, by claiming that there is less stress on a family when both parents are able to work (because they are economically better off), the authors unquestioningly support the capitalist ideological imperative that necessarily relies on the exploitation of low-wage home-workers such as Woodward. However, through their reflections upon such research many writers in the American news media became worried about the anti-working mother sentiment expressed in the public response to the Woodward case. They rallied to the defence of working mothers. The consequence of this counter-response was the vilification of home-workers:

> Trying to blame mom is beneath contempt. The words may sound extreme, but as killer nanny Louise Woodward heads for prison, the anti-mom sentiment is widespread and alarming. These are the facts: A grown woman has been found guilty of murder – the violent shaking of a defenceless baby too young to even call out in pain. Common sense would dictate locking the killer nanny in jail, then doing everything possible to help other parents avoid entrusting their children to unstable strangers with smiling faces. But we live in a time when sense is anything but common. A time when criminals call public-relations spin doctors before dialling their lawyers. And victims of violent crimes are routinely tarred as villains who simply got what they deserved (Peyser, *New York Post*, 1 November 1997).

Such media intervention, which aimed to tip the balance back in the favour of working mothers, would be admirable if it did not coincide with the denigration of those already in a degraded social and economic position. However, Brian Robertson (2000) does not blame the media for advancing this position, but criticizes the authors and researchers for allowing such a skewed vision of family life to enter the debate about social relations as a truth claim. Arguing that the science of sociology should remain detached from any ideological agenda, he maintains that the politics of individualistic fulfilment in late modern society has filtered into socio-cultural consciousness to the detriment of the family. Robertson argues that feminism is symmetrical with the business world because capitalism could only benefit from the feminist programme that sought to push women out of the private sphere and into the public world of work. He explains:

> From child care to marriage law, the common thread running through the policy prescriptions of the new feminists and their allies in the business world – no matter what the rhetoric has emphasized – has been the transfer of women's loyalties from family to career. This has entailed weakening the bonds of the traditional family, particularly those that provide the economic and legal security necessary for married mothers to raise children in the home. It has also meant constructing a system of incentives to encourage and reward the workforce

participation of married mothers and to make the choice of nonparental childcare more feasible (Robertson, 2000: 143).

This passage shows how capitalism fractures the organization of the traditional family by creating a situation whereby mothers are too heavily reliant on wage labour to care for their own children. In this regard Robertson suggests that the economy infects the institution of the family by pushing mothers into wage labour and creating a secondary economy of low-wage domestic workers who stand in for absent mothers. However, although Robertson's examination of the debate highlights the problem of the economic condition informing contemporary home life, his thesis seems to fall back on a similarly contentious axiom of family values. In other words, Robertson's position rests on an acceptance of the idea that the ideology of capital corrupts family life by encouraging women to work. Clearly the problem with the debate between Barnett and Rivers and Robertson is that neither proposition recognizes that both positions advance an equally conservative ideology. Each pole of the argument is contained within the bounds of a wider socio-political context. Both the drive to get everybody working and the will to maintain the traditional family structure are part of an ideology that sustains itself through the dialogue which these two paradoxical positions sustain.

Within the context of this debate it is possible to examine Louise Woodward as the scapegoat created by media reporters keen to articulate a moral commentary on family structures in late modern America. However, before the reader can understand Woodward from this position there must first be an examination of those represented in the case as part of a greater narrative that describes the socio-political conditions occurring at the time of the trial's exposure. To this end I want to refer to the notion of the mediated public sphere as a site for the working through of such articulations. I see this space as a screen where narratives unfold to reveal a dominant discursive order that binds its subjects to a specific view of the world rather than involve them in any form of democratic free speech.[6] It is against this framework that I will be able to read the Woodward/Eappen case by looking at the organization of the modern nuclear family, taking particular notice of the power politics at work inside its structures.

The coverage of the Woodward/Eappen case exposed a fear about the breakdown of contemporary western family values. The move away from traditional heterosexual gender roles is overturned when the public and private spheres merge: women are allowed to 'have it all' until the family appears to fail, at which point they become responsible for its breakdown. Moreover, this also shows that the traditional model of the family – where a woman's role is that of wife and mother, a position that finds her firmly embedded in the private sphere of

---

[6] For a discussion of this idea we can refer to the work of Jürgen Habermas (1989). Habermas argues that the public sphere provides an ideal space for democratic communication, despite the fact that its technologies currently support strategies of corporate manipulation and distortion. Similarly, Peter Dahlgren (1995) argues that the mass media provides a simulated arena for public debate, but remains tied to ideological discursive orders.

the home, and the man maintains his role from within the public sphere of work – is always the standard against which other forms of family life are measured. In other words beyond the ideology of gender equality, the traditional model of family structure acts like a kind of patriarchal safety net. The discussion of the extracts from *The Boston Globe* and *New York Post* reveals how this debate surged in the popular press in the USA as the lifestyle of millions of middle-class Americans was put under the moral microscope. Cases such as this provided an uncomfortable reminder about the costs of the individualism of capitalist ideology. However, although media institutions continue to criticize the contemporary family for its failure to live up to the ideology of conservative family values, they also provide an arena that promotes individualistic economic aspirations. Commentaries on the dominant social order maintain a dim recognition that the end of (or crisis of) family unity is fatally linked to the ideology of possessive individualism that infects all areas of life with an 'everybody for themselves' economic imperative. On the one hand the moral rhetoricians condemn single-parent families and working mothers for provoking increasing crime rates, spiralling numbers of teenage pregnancy, and extensive drug and alcohol abuse amongst the youth of western nations. On the other hand, the same authors continue to promote the kind of economic excess that drives the family apart. As such parents are now encouraged to both raise a family and continue their own individualistic desires. This 'lifestyle choice' is justified by the understanding that capital individualism will provide a comfortable economic upbringing for the products of their family unit: their children (Beck and Beck-Gernsheim, 1995).

Judith Stacey (1996) criticizes the politics and rhetoric of the moral majority for continuing to emphasize women as the engineers behind the collapse of 'decent' society. Looking at how the family has changed in late twentieth-century America to include single-parent, gay, and post-divorce re-structured households, Stacey articulates the need for a more liberal attitude to the diverse family structures that make up the majority of communities in many contemporary western societies. With this in mind, she argues that the conservative stance takes a backward step by providing a rhetoric that undermines a woman's right to work; the logical conclusion of which, she states, would be to reinforce man's economic and ideological dominance in the home. Again this reminds us of the inherent contradiction between the conservative ideology of economic individualism and its own right-wing agenda that warns the community of the dangers of familial collapse. Stacey argues that whatever issue wider society is concerned to evade – be it rising crime rates or lack of educational achievement – the family provides a convenient discursive container for accepting the rest of the collective order's share of responsibility. In terms of Stacey's argument the Woodward/Eappen case provided an opportune focus for re-visiting debates about family values for a liberal democracy that wanted to leave many of its problems in the care of one institution. Here, Stacey maintains that the recent return to moral discursive practices is 'Less a revival than a creative remodel job,' where 'the 1990s media blitz on family values signals the considerable success of a distinctively new political phenomenon' (1996: 53).

Recognising that the family values debate comes from an old conservative agenda, Stacey asks: how did America, under Clinton's progressive Democrats, renew the moral campaign without resorting to right-wing stereotypes? To answer this she claims that many mainstream social scientists, who have gained policy-making roles under the Clinton administration, have helped restore this interest in family life as a rebuttal against the past few decades of feminist scholarship which has done so much to undo the patriarchal rhetoric of family values. Stating that 'revisionists argue that the presence or absence of two married, biological parents in the household is the central determinant of a child's welfare, and thereby of our society's welfare' (ibid: 56), Stacey asserts that their polemic is yet another way of reinforcing the supremacy of middle-class ideology. Supporting this idea, the news reporting of the Woodward/Eappen affair entered an already structured discursive arena that established the childcare crisis at the top of its agenda. Following Stacey (who views conservative morality as an attempt to support the place of the middle class) the popular news media sought to locate childcare within a framework of class antagonism. The following extracts from *The Sun*, *The Guardian* and *The Boston Globe* highlight this mood. They also reveal the developing ideological conflict between two nations:

> Debbie and Sunil Eappen treated Louise Woodward like a slave – making her do hours of work for a paltry wage. Little Matthew's parents also imposed a rigid set of rules on Louise, 19, just five days before the boy lapsed into a coma. They covered almost every aspect of Louise's life, and reveal she was being treated more like a house servant than an au pair (*The Sun*, 31 October 1997).

Furthermore, in the following extract from *The Guardian* can be seen to embellish the class structure outlined by *The Sun* with a nationalistic perspective that views American capital as more oppressive than its British counterpart:

> It is a far cry from Britain, where under government regulations au pairs are allowed to work only 25 hours a weeks, with two clear days. Their stated purpose is to learn English and their duties are light chores and a bit of childminding. But in the US, the deal is 45 hours a week – a full-time job, which can be hard and lonely, with no network of friends or colleagues to talk to (Boseley, *The Guardian*, 11 February 1997).

However, from the American perspective *The Boston Globe* was able to recognize that the anti-American viewpoint of the British papers, which saw capitalism as an indirect cause of infant mortality, was related to a deeply conservative attempt to reverse the gains of feminism:

> OK, welfare mommies are monsters, but what about entrepreneurial MD mommies? What about women who delayed childbearing to finish school, had babies in their 30's and 40's and work part-time? Well, now we learn that they are also monsters. Why? Because they don't stay home full time. Apparently all mommies are monsters – the indignant and highly educated both deserve to watch their babies die (Jong, *The Boston Globe*, 11 December 1997).

Erica Jong's criticism of the British news media's position highlights the problem of those reports where the degradation of family values is the main concern. The American extract allows us to see how the Woodward affair could be used to snatch back the gains of feminism by seeing its achievements as detrimental to the well-being of the conventional nuclear family. Thus, in the USA the Woodward/Eappen case became an opportunity not only for right-wing campaigners to highlight the debate about family values, but also for liberal spokespersons to enter the discursive arena. By contrast in Britain the Woodward case was about regaining the moral high-ground, after the revelation of several highly publicized miscarriages of justice, by demonising American capitalism and its disintegrating family structure.[7] However, I would argue that because the majority of reports in American tabloid papers provided not so much a pro-Eappen stance as an anti-Woodward narrative (that condemned the hired help for not being up to her job, rather than the parents for not doing theirs), they were able to endorse the middle-class lifestyle that allows for economic exploitation within the domestic sphere.

Against this narrative critical of working women, when men work they are considered economically independent, and therefore not necessarily tied to a familial role. Yet women are generally still understood in terms of their family relationships, either as a daughter, wife, or mother. Women maintain a closer association to home life, whether or not they are financially dependent. This is why Christine Delphy and Diana Leonard argue that instead of seeing the family simply in terms of the economic market one should look at it in terms of a hierarchically structured domestic group where there exist 'relations of production' between family members (1992: 1). They argue that in contrast to recent feminist articulations that there can exist some kind of harmonious balance between the sexes, gender inequality is so deeply ingrained within social relationships that it informs every part of life, particularly in the domestic sphere. This argument is highlighted by the statistical evidence provided by Linda Grant et al (1990) in their article about the working life of physicians. They show that there is a notable discrepancy between paid work and domestic work for women with families, but attribute this to the possibility that working women physicians are choosing to reduce their time in practice in order to spend more time at home. They take this factor to suggest that women are actually more content with their work to home-life ratio than their male counterparts.[8] The authors' argument centres on the understanding that many physicians are overworked, but that female practitioners

---

[7] For example the *Daily Mirror* displayed a front page picture of the Statue of Liberty accompanied by a headline that urged 'If this statue means anything to America, Louise Woodward will today be given back her LIBERTY' (4 November 1997) and *The Express* demanded that America 'HAVE MERCY ON LOUISE' (4 November 1997).

[8] Grant et al's (1990) study shows that on average male doctors (with or without children) work 52.9 hours per week compared to 49.8 hours for childless female doctors and 37.8 hours for female doctors with children. This study is an indication of the discrepancy between attitudes to male and female employment with regard to family responsibility.

with children are able to attain a more satisfactory balance between home and work because they reduce their hours in order to undertake domestic duties.

For Delphy and Leonard this type of evidence, which suggests that equality exists within the family, ignores an important point about who can afford these 'lifestyle choices'. Their analysis shows how the family remains a sexist institution, suggesting that scholars such as Barnett and Rivers (1996) and Grant et al (who allow 'choice' to become part of their equation) fail to see how family life is underwritten by the economic dictates which are ultimately enforced by a patriarchal ideology. Instead, they state that we must ask ourselves what choice there is for women who are socially and psychologically suppressed by a dominant patriarchal ideology that sees women as lacking in relation to men. Akin to Frantz Fanon's (1986) contention that the colonized subject is degraded by having the language and culture of the colonizer imposed upon them, thus rendering them empty of agency, women's lives too are constructed from within a patriarchal order that places more importance on exchange and exploitation than on the *apparently* feminine traits of compassion and nurturing. According to Delphy and Leonard this point is evident in the way that so-called women's work is constructed as natural labour:

> The devaluation of what women do, and the belief that what men do is what particularly counts in society, is to us not the cause of women's oppression, but rather part of the mechanism by which the appropriation of our labour is continued. That is to say, we believe that women's work is used by men, and that the low value set on women, the self-denial and masochism we are encouraged to develop, and each woman's identification with 'her man', etc., exist because our labour is appropriated by men (Delphy and Leonard, 1992: 16-17).

With regard to this passage, one can see how Delphy and Leonard can discern the difference between middle-class and working-class families as one that is determined by their position in the economic system of social stratification. In other words, patriarchy bears more heavily on those at the bottom of the economic order, whilst women who attain a level of relative independence from patriarchal constraint may be seen to inhabit the higher echelons of the economic hierarchy, while nevertheless remaining conceptually tied to the domestic sphere. According to this point, in the Eappen household Deborah Eappen maintained a relatively autonomous position of class and economic authority until the exposure of the fault (the death of Matthew Eappen) that allowed the rhetoric of family values to seize hold. *The Observer* provided an example of this process in its review of the trial proceedings, by stating that 'the implication of the cross-examination was that [Deborah] Eappen wasn't the perfect mother':

> Even before appearing in court, Eappen had been the target of hate mail. Callers to radio shows said her baby's death was her own fault, that she should have stayed at home with the children instead of pursuing her medical career. One letter accused her of 'greed and poor judgment' for leaving her child at home with a nanny 'for the sake of your lifestyle' (Vulliamy and Tran, *The Observer*, 19 October 1997).

Although providing a more balanced representation of Deborah Eappen and working mothers overall, the American news media highlighted her role above that of Sunil Eappen. The inference of this prioritization was that she was *more* responsible for the care of their children than he was:

> Eappen's composure in the witness stand rankled many observers, who were expecting tears. They found it hard to see a villain in the fresh-faced English girl, who said on the stand, "I love kids." And many found it galling that Eappen, the mother of another son whose husband also is a doctor, would opt to pursue her career – even part-time (Siemaszko, *New York Daily News*, 31 October 1997).

Such commentaries are based on an understanding that women are responsible for the home and family. In her articulation of the way that women still inhabit a confused position within the dominant cultural order of western societies, feminist economist Nancy Folbre (1994) expands on the above point when she argues that the economy of the family rests upon a principle of exploitation. Folbre argues that the nuclear family structure may be seen as a cipher for understanding the mechanics of wider global capitalism. That is, in much the same way that the family is reliant on unwaged labour (i.e. domestic work), western capitalism demands the existence of a low-wage periphery which is tied to localized forms of community. In the present case the relative autonomy of Deborah Eappen (supported by her role in the public sphere of medicalized knowledge) was dependent on the presence of the low-wage domestic help, Louise Woodward. Here one can begin to see how the American ideology and its vision of individual independence are complicated by a perspective that introduces a structural analysis. In other words, the success of one person is reliant on the failure of another. Consequently, Folbre describes the existence of interlocking structures of constraint that bind individual choice. These systems of scarcity may be based on such apparently fluid identity positions as gender, sexuality, race and class.

After the first wave of the feminist theoretical movement highlighted the subordination of women by patriarchal ideological mechanisms, black feminist scholars began to question their own position within this critical model. In doing so, writers such as bell hooks and Patricia Hill Collins introduced the idea of a stratified hierarchy of feminisms that maintained the class and racial oppression of patriarchal society by allowing a system of subordination to continue to exist at the level of critical discourse. They argued that in much the same way that previous deconstructions of the male/female dialectic exposed the ideological belief that women were inferior to men, the new wave of black feminist scholarship understood the existence of a 'matrix of domination' (Collins, 1990) that describes a social system where one can be simultaneously the oppressed and the oppressor. In other words, the concept of a matrix of domination showed that rather than there simply being a dialectical relationship between men and women, patriarchal oppression could include much more complex equations that generalized the notion of a social economy based on exploitation. This included such variables as race and sexual orientation, traits which may complicate the traditional feminist male/ female binary. A related effect of this thesis, which develops a more complex form for understanding structural oppression, is that one can begin to see how an individual's position within the social structure may be more important than his or her own identity attributes. Instead, the capital individual can be regarded as a collection of identity features that are translated into an amalgamation of structural effects, which assign the individual its precise place within the social order, rather than a person who is entirely free from social, political, cultural, and economic determinism. In this regard the idea of the matrix of domination allows us to understand oppression in terms of the kind of fine calculations that go beyond binary distinctions.

Domestic Work

Under American ideology, which states that individual freedom should be absolute, meritocratic structures should allow you to be whoever you want to be. However, rather than reinforcing the reality of this ideological discourse, cases such as the trial of Louise Woodward identify the American notion of absolute social mobility as a mythology that maintains social oppression by providing the dream of success, personal fulfilment, and wealth: the American dream. I believe that Woodward is the exceptional case which over-codes the limit of the American ideology, because at the point where her structural position required that she would be found guilty of Matthew Eappen's murder (i.e. her low-wage racialized role) her own identity attributes (that of a white woman, and as such outside boundaries of the traditional racialized domestic workforce) intervened to prevent her incarceration. Thus, what is important in the Woodward/Eappen case is the coincidence of the disjunctive elements of the white woman occupying the structural position of the ethnic worker.

Within the mediated debate prompted by the Woodward trial there was a general understanding that the low-paid economy in which Woodward was situated did not fit with her identity position. One might argue that it was precisely because of this lack of fit that the debate emerged into the public sphere. For example, an examination of the way that Woodward was presented in the American media reveals a narrative that understood her in terms of her failure to fit the structural requirements of her role as nanny. Detective Sergeant Byrne's comments about Woodward's photogenic appearance betray a recognition that she could not be dealt with as 'easily' as if she had been in her structurally correct position. Similarly Andrea Peyser, writing in the *New York Post*, identifies the contradictions of Woodward's position when she says that:

> As we learned during the trial, Woodward yearned for the America she saw on TV, but was crushed to find the path to pleasure littered with dirty diapers; her nightly escape from domestic drudgery blocked by a midnight curfew and early morning chores. But if you watched the nanny trial from Great Britain, chances are you would have seen an entirely different case. "She was like an indentured servant," a friend just back from England reported on the consensus at the local pubs. "They only paid her $115 a week, when they could have afforded a lot

more," she added – omitting that the Eappens also provided room and board
(Peyser, *New York Post*, 4 November 1997).

Peyser's article goes on to explain this mismatch in terms of class antagonism. She
argues that, as a working-class person, Woodward resented the Eappens because of
their middle-class goal-driven life. However, contrasting this position one can also
speculate that Woodward could not deal with the 'domestic drudgery' of her role
precisely because she was so similar to the Eappens. This suggests that rather than
difference causing problems, Woodward resented the Eappens because she
understood herself as an equal who was being treated unfairly. Writing about the
economy of domestic labour in America, Mary Romero (1992) argues that the very
structure of home work underpins gender, racial, and class domination. She
suggests that this unequal economy is supported by a set of cultural values that
debases the idealized notion of social equality. For Woodward, her debased
structural position in the domestic sphere was one of choice rather than economic
necessity. She wanted to see another country between school and university and so
elected to work abroad in her gap year. Because of this motivation she (as a white,
educated western woman) maintained more 'structural capital' than if she had
occupied what is now understood as the more conventional racialized structural
economy of the contemporary domestic worker.[9]

The 'double day' experienced by most women includes both paid work and
unpaid work. The structural position of domestic workers often leaves them subject
to personal constraints which, for much of the time, engineer a double-shift of
debased household duties. In other words, because many domestic workers are
socially stratified into the underprivileged echelons of the community in terms of
both economics and race, they end up doing the same job at work and at home. The
repressed truth of home work is contained within the western conception of
domestic labour, i.e. one that encodes the worker into a naturalized role within the
family unit. As domestic work is seen as 'common sense' or 'women's work', it is
difficult to identify it *as* work. The domestic employee, therefore, becomes trapped
within an ideological understanding of what it is to be a woman working in the
home. Because women who stay at home do not get paid for the household chores
they perform, the work they do is not considered a job. Thus, those who take on
domestic work for pay fall into a grey area between the two roles of worker and
family member/interloper (Romero, 1992).

What I suggest, however, is that in the case of Woodward, whose stratified
position was one of employee, her whiteness over-coded the structural elements of

---

[9] Although there are no reliable figures to detail the trade in domestic labour in the USA, a
study into domestic migration by Heyzer et al (1994) shows that the 'export' of domestic
workers from countries such as the Philippines, Bangladesh, Sri Lanka, and Indonesia lies
somewhere between 477,567 and 705,584 people per year to receiving countries. However,
the receiving countries they surveyed estimated that between 979,397 and 981,397 domestic
workers entered countries such as Saudi Arabia, Hong Kong and Bahrain. The authors argue
that the discrepancy in these figures indicates the unofficial nature of the trade in people,
and that the figures are probably much higher.

her status just enough for both her and the Eappens to misrecognize the determinism of their situations. In other words, Woodward misrecognized her place in the domestic labour economy because she did not conform to the racial category normally associated with low-wage nanny work in America, while the Eappens failed to understand the determinism of the same economic system by misunderstanding how Woodward's whiteness could not permit her to be reduced to the status of racialized other. This contradiction, which led the Eappens to employ Woodward as a high-status white British nanny but at the same time expect to enforce accepted low-wage (racially peripheral) labour conditions upon her role, led Woodward to exceed her position. According to Deborah Eappen's trial testimony, Woodward transgressed her role to such an extent that she caused the death of their youngest son. The Eappens expressed their dissatisfaction at her ability to do the job of nanny properly saying that 'she would be on the computer doing e-mail, on the phone for long periods and taking showers when she was supposed to be watching the children' (Deborah Eappen quoted in Tran and Patton, *The Guardian*, 16 October 1997). However, critics of the au pair system suggest that it is unfair to expect young, inexperienced women, primarily treating the experience as a holiday, to be burdened with the absolute responsibility of parenthood.

Romero argues that the exploitation of domestic workers (both economically and socially) goes beyond the structural elements of generalized work hierarchies. Working within the private sphere, she observes that the employer/employee relationship adopts a more flexible criterion, but one that nevertheless maintains a strong dialectical relationship. In this space there are few codes of conduct other than those contrived by the concerned parties. Therefore, according to Romero, 'as domestic workers developed strategies and practices to open up new areas of freedom, employers developed new forms of control' (1992: 16). In terms of Louise Woodward and Deborah and Sunil Eappen's relationship this process of negotiation meant that tensions developed in line with Woodward's transgressive social position. Thus, when we read that she made long telephone calls and stayed out late at night, we also read about the Eappens' list of conditions and imposed curfew. The nanny's excesses are counterpoised by the prohibitions of her employers.

According to this scheme my theory rests on the existence of two nanny positions. Woodward illustrates the idea of the au pair, a position that is based on an individual's choice to work abroad as a means of travelling and broadening personal horizons. The western au pair as domestic worker is primarily about gaining a cultural education rather than professional training or experience in a career they wish to pursue. The other nanny position indicates the childminder as a low-paid peripheral worker. In this instance the worker is often contained within a racialized and debased economic position that determines their job as one of necessity rather than choice. In the first scenario, the domestic worker generally remains outside economic concerns. Coming from a rich western country herself, she maintains enough relative autonomy to be able to either make demands or leave poor living and working conditions behind. For this worker the job has little to do with money. For the second kind of nanny, however, money is the absolute goal.

The Eappens might serve to expose the problematic nature of the middle-class suburban family trying to live the American dream. To do so they had to maintain a dual-income and get outside help with domestic duties. However, as suggested by some of the newspaper articles, not only does hiring childcare in the United States (as elsewhere in the world) hold many risks, it also reflects who you are: the choice of domestic labour is, in this respect, little more than conspicuous consumption. For the Eappens, Woodward represented the prestige of a British nanny. The related effect of this choice was a liberal statement that sought to distance the Eappens from the hiring practices prescribed by the racialized domestic economy, i.e. the use of an underprivileged and/or migrant workforce that is exploited by low pay and poor working conditions. In light of such statements one might argue that the Eappens wanted the low-wage child-minder *and* the liberal acceptability that accompanied the British nanny. However, the use of an au pair can only debase this strategy as a viable option because she is under no obligation of economic necessity to stay with the family. Because Woodward was situated in an undertrained workforce she could not command financial accrual. Nor did she want to pursue the accumulation of high wages. In this regard, Woodward might have appeared suitable for the Eappens vacancy. Professional childcare is a financial strain for parents. In order to maintain both position and economic security, they must hire low-wage domestic workers: to be financially viable for both parents to work, domestic labour must be cheap. However, the Eappens' bargain-hunting (valuable worker for low wages) fell apart because Woodward did not need their money. She was unwilling to accept tough labour regulations. With regard to these issues, many news reports criticized the childcare system in America for exploiting young people who go to the country for a cultural experience. The suggestion was that au pairs are subject to poor working conditions like America's own racialized migrant workforce. These reports also sought to criticize parents who attempt to exploit this system by extending the exploitative low wage economy to au pair workers. The following quote from *The Observer* suggests that Woodward was a victim of middle-class American angst about balancing motherhood and work. The added bonus is the belief that childcare should be cheap:

> At the top end of the market they do little training of their own; there is no US equivalent of our National Nursery Examination Board courses, which is how some British nannies are able to go there and clean up. But American parents as a whole do not yearn for the top end. They have had years of being allowed to believe that cheap child care is an inalienable right and years when they received precisely that from illegal immigrants (Sarler, *The Observer*, 2 November 1997).

This example, from *The Sun*, is illustrative of many of the British press responses to the Eappens over the duration of the case:

> Who was really on trial in the Massachusetts courtroom? Was it 19-year-old nanny Louise Woodward – or middle class parents who rummage through the

bargain basement when looking for childcare? Either way, it is clear Louise has been used as a scapegoat to help relieve the guilt of the latter (Moore, *The Sun*, 1 November 1997).

These articles from *The Observer* and *The Sun* represent the unease at being forced to face the reality of class, race, and gender stratification in the domestic setting. Middle-class parents are condemned for exploiting cheap labour from both a migrant workforce and untrained travellers seeking a cultural experience. According to this ethos Woodward is a debased worker because she is not trying to be a professional nanny: the main objective for her was a cultural education. Against this idea ethnic domestic workers are debased because of their social position and their race. Without professional training the childcare worker (either western au pair or peripheral ethnic worker) is seen as little more than a housewife. This reinforces the idea that domestic work is seen as 'common sense'. Romero explains that housework has become fused with the idea of being a 'good wife and mother' (1992: 21). In terms of domestic labour the worker is considered unskilled and as such outside the sphere of paid employment. Like many au pairs Woodward was paid £71 a week (she did not have to pay for food and board). In return for this wage she had sole responsibility for two small children and the home of her employers. She was also on call for much of the day. From this that one can suggest that 'housework', including childcare, is seen as a non-professional and non-structural job. However, even though both Woodward and ethnic domestic workers occupy the same non-professional category, the ethnic worker does not transgress the boundary of the low-wage economy, because the ethnic worker is excluded from the category of desirable professional worker due to her ethnic status. In contrast, Woodward was unconcerned about the professional sphere, for her the role of nanny was not determined by economic concerns, but rather by cultural education.

With regard to this difference between Woodward and ethnic domestic workers, who are economically and culturally distinct regardless of occupying the same peripheral wage-labour category, Collins argues that the employment of ethnic domestic workers continues to contribute to the discrimination of certain sections of American society. In an exposition of her previous writing on the subordination of race and class within a gendered economy, she states that this condition occupies a paradoxical relationship to the notion of individual rights afforded to American citizens in the Constitution. She asserts that the rhetoric of the family 'normalizes and naturalizes' (2001: 5) familial hierarchies into everyday social settings. Using fictional monologues presented in the work of African American writer Alice Childress to express this idea, Collins shows her readers how this rhetoric underscores an American ideology that preserves a picture of a national 'family' and obscures the discriminatory micro-politics experienced by many of its citizens. Drawing from a story where 'Mildred' is an African American domestic worker whose white employer 'Mrs. C' is telling a friend about her relationship with her 'servant', Collins illustrates how the racialized domestic workforce characterizes an idea of equality that ultimately maintains a social hierarchy based on a principle of exclusion:

Mrs. C's perception that she treated Mildred 'like' she was one of her family mirrors widespread beliefs among white Americans that African Americans, Native Americans, Chicanos, Puerto Ricans and other historically oppressed racial/ethnic groups are treated *equally enough* [my emphasis] within US society. Marked with the status of subordinated workers, such groups are tolerated as long as they remain in their proscribed places. This is not a politics of exclusion, but one of containment. American non-whites are *like us*, they are *connected* to us, but they are *not* us, such views suggest (Collins, 2001: 5).

Related to this idea of liberal tolerance, Melvyn Dubofsky notes how the racialized economy is primarily dictated by fiscal factors, i.e. the ebb and flow of migration, or the cost of living. Discussing the socio-historical relevance of the female domestic workforce, he points out that unlike other wage-labour relationships, 'What truly separated domestic service from other forms of wage labor was the absence of capitalism's fundamental economic calculus – the creation of surplus value and hence profit for the employer of labor' (1980: 89). Dubofsky's idea that domestic work refers to an anachronistic employer/employee relationship relates to Collins' assertion that domestic labour is based on the model of a familial relationship. The site of the family might then be seen as a screen for obscuring the effects of market forces upon home work. Its role is to hide the way that domestic work is embedded in inequalities which allow for the exploitation of the underprivileged labour market. For this reason Dubofsky argues that home workers have the least labour rights. The role of the family has allowed for the conditions of the current domestic economy, whereby only the most marginalized members of a community are employed in such jobs because of their degraded economic status.

However, this phenomenon does not only relate to divisions between racial groups, i.e. black/white, it is also maintained by the exploitation of ethnic subgroups based on an economic stratification within the aforementioned 'matrix of domination'. Collins argues that those people of whatever ethnic origin who embrace the dominant culture and ideology of the society they inhabit, maintain greater autonomy over those who fail to fit into the standardized system. As Fanon shows, there are two kinds of racial alienation. The first kind may be represented by the ethnic who adopts the knowledge of the dominant culture at the expense of their indigenous compatriot, who is simultaneously relegated to the status of debased other. The second kind of racial other (who fails to adopt the norms of the dominant culture) is, therefore, lower down the scale of social stratification than their conformist counterpart, but also more dangerous to the dominant order: the second kind of racial other holds onto their revolutionary status. Moreover, this division within ethnic identity, between insider and outsider alien subgroups, is replicated within the wider economic system, whereby those people of ethnic origin who are seen to embrace the dominant culture attain higher status. Thus, according to Collins, 'internal racisms occur when powerful racial groups subordinate less powerful racial groups within one society, typically because they need such groups to maintain their standard of living' (2001: 6).

Stranger Danger

Reading Woodward's structural position in the Eappen household against the ideas put forward by Collins, Dubofsky and Fanon, one can understand that she is *too much* 'like one of the family' to be able to maintain the necessary distance required by exploitative economic relationships. As such, Woodward not only over-codes the composition of the generalized racially stratified domestic workforce, but also exerts more structural capital than her employer (Sunil Eappen). In contrast to Woodward's situation, the arrest and conviction in San Diego, California of Asian childminder Manjit Basuta, herself a 44-year old mother, provides an alternative perspective. This example will emphasize the inequalities at play within America's socio-cultural values and allow us to understand how these differences are reflected by the judicial system. Basuta was also accused of shaking a child in her care to such a violent extent that it caused his death from a brain haemorrhage. In October 1999 Basuta was imprisoned for the minimum sentence of 25 years. After her conviction (which hinged upon the conflicting statements of her Guatemalan assistant) Basuta's case was picked up by the broadsheet press in the UK. Here, the news media understood Basuta's conviction as a reflexive example of the way the media reacts to such stories, and sought to contrast Basuta with the publicity that surrounded the Woodward trial.

The similarities of the two 'shaken baby' murder cases are striking; the one major disparity being that Woodward was an unqualified white au pair and Basuta was a qualified nurse whose debased status was grounded by the fact that she was Asian. Of course the case of Basuta also hinged upon such variables as evidence and witness testimony. However, these factors seem to have been insignificant in determining the case's eventual outcome. To explain this point one can look to how the trial Judge, William Kennedy, apparently keen to avoid the contention caused by Judge Zobel's controversial decision to overturn the jury's decision in the Woodward trial, commented on the damaging effects of media amplification in the earlier case. Under Californian law anyone found guilty of killing a child under the age of eight is liable to face a mandatory minimum sentence of 25 years, the only alternative being probation. Before passing this sentence, however, Judge Kennedy asked the prosecution and defence attorneys to come up with arguments for and against the sentence respectively. This undertaking can be seen as an attempt to avoid a damaging media spectacle. In an article in *The Independent*, Andrew Gumbel (7 August 1999) commends the trial judge in the Basuta case for ignoring public and media pressure to opt for a more dramatic decision, i.e. one that displaced the public perception of acceptable courtroom practice. Gumbel states that it is an example of the judicial system becoming more reflexive in the face of sensationalistic media coverage. In other words, it no longer bends to media pressure to provide the most pleasing outcome precisely because it is so aware of the presence of outside viewers.

Against this idea of rational debate, prejudice is exposed. Basuta's eventual conviction reminds us that ultimately she inhabited the position of alien other. Despite her qualifications to do the job required of her, Basuta could not escape her debased racialized position. Furthermore, she fitted into a pre-written discourse that saw her quickly return to the colonial vision of otherness, i.e. that of being strange and devious. Although Basuta's friends and relatives in Britain campaigned on her behalf much like Woodward's supporters had done previously, they did not have the same high profile effect as the Woodward campaigners in her home town Elton. Basuta's friends and family occupied the same racially debased status as Basuta herself, and as a result failed to rally public support. On trial Basuta was portrayed as having lost her temper with Oliver Smith, shaking him to death in a violent rage. She was then accused of forcing her alien assistant, who was living illegally in America and had little grasp of English, to back up a claim that the child had fallen, or else face deportation. The evidence in the case, therefore, hinged upon the assistant's conflicting and legally unreliable statements: first, that the child had fallen; second, that Basuta had shaken him to death. One might conclude that although Basuta was an employer who ran her own childcare service, and as such appeared to occupy a dominant structural position, ultimately she found herself being expelled due to her subordinate racial and gender position (Anthias and Yuval-Davis, 1992).

Woodward, on the other hand, was too much like the western public sphere she occupied to be considered a stranger. Basuta did not need media rehabilitation to turn her into other – she already occupied that position, something that the lack of publicity surrounding her case and her conviction illustrated. Commenting on the harshness of the sentence, Basuta's legal advisor John Cooper stated that 'if this sort of sentence was passed in a so-called lesser developed country, the whole world would be up in arms' (Gregoriadis and Campbell, *The Guardian*, 2 October 1999). In America, however, it was all too easy to perceive her as evil, as capable of committing the crime knowingly and malevolently. Unlike cases where white westerners have been convicted abroad and given long-term prison sentences, it was also easy to accept the American justice system as fair and just, and Basuta as deserving of her condemnation.

In contrast to Basuta's debased structural position, which led to her imprisonment, Woodward had to be constructed as evil in order to expel her from the family picture. This representational move was engineered in order to protect the familial institution from ideological harm. As a stranger in the home, Woodward's position was one of instability. What eventually stabilized her position was her inclusive white, western status. As such, Woodward constituted a hidden threat, one that had to be made a scapegoat in order to protect the middle-class ideology that she threatened to jeopardize. In other words, Woodward had to be turned into a metaphor for danger *symbolically* before she could be temporarily expelled from normal moral society. Her initial conviction for second-degree murder, a verdict that carried a mandatory minimum sentence of fifteen years imprisonment, provided such a disciplinary measure.

With regard to this point, Anne Lloyd (1995) argues that historically women have been biologically categorized in terms of their reproductive status in order to subjugate them in an overwhelmingly patriarchal society. Lloyd uses the example of pre-menstrual syndrome (PMS) in order to describe how violent women are attributed with overly unstable hormonal characteristics that govern their mental state in order to ideologically construct them as deviant. This also has the effect of characterising women in terms of a debased physical and mental make-up that degrades their ability to make rational decisions. Unlike male criminals, who are more often perceived as rational and capable of judgement, women who commit crimes are repeatedly seen as somehow irrational:

> When women commit violent crimes they are seen to have breached two laws: the law of the land, which forbids violence, and the much more fundamental 'natural' law, which says women are passive carers, not active aggressors, and by nature morally better than the male of the species. Such a woman is doubly deviant. Not only is she being tried for her crime, but how she measures up to the idea of proper womanhood is also being judged (Lloyd, 1995: 36).

One can draw parallels with Lloyd's argument when considering the way that both Louise Woodward and Deborah Eappen were portrayed in the mass media's analysis of the trial. According to Lloyd's description of stereotypical ideals of womanhood, where one is either a 'proper' woman or a 'fallen' woman, Woodward and Deborah Eappen both find themselves negotiating these roles throughout the duration of the trial. One of the main features in the media coverage of the trial was the representation of the two central female characters. It was argued in the American press that not only was Woodward on trial for the killing of Matthew Eappen, but so too was Deborah Eappen, for not protecting her child from harm: 'It was as if Eappen had shaken Matthew to death, not the nanny' (Siemaszko, *New York Daily News*, 31 October 1997).

In the courtroom Woodward was seen to giggle or, alternatively, sit calmly and silently. Her actions were interpreted by media commentators as insolent and an obvious sign of her lack of compassion: 'Is Woodward, as she has been portrayed in much of the American media, a cold, unfeeling young woman who came to America on a "visa to party"?' (Goodwin and Wark, *The Sunday Times*, 26 October 1997). Accordingly, her outward behaviour seemed to prove that she had little respect for the seriousness of the situation. Certainly this appearance was reflected in the American media's reporting of the case. Moreover, the watching mass media extended the rationale for her conduct, to an apparent lack of respect for American morals and perhaps more importantly their judicial system: 'Our courts are being slammed as unfair to defendants. Even our hard-won notion of a free press is coming under attack' (Peyser, *New York Post*, 4 November 1997). Therefore, Woodward's actions allowed her to be portrayed as callous, unfeeling, and disrespectful of the law – attributes that positioned her within the parameters of 'fallen woman'.

Contrary to the idea that Deborah Eappen should then occupy the role of 'proper woman', she was also renounced for allowing such an abhorrent act to occur. As wife and mother it was her job to guard the domestic sphere against danger. However, because she had already cast off her position in the private sphere by entering the public arena of medicalized knowledge and following a career path, she had to be restored to her 'natural' role before the symbolic sacrifice of Woodward could take place. As such, Deborah Eappen had to be discursively re-ordered as 'good mother' against Woodward's 'evil monster'.

Stating how Deborah Eappen was 'Pale and barely choking back her emotion', and describing her appearance in court as 'Wearing a high-necked, knee-length floral cotton dress, with simple pearl earrings' (Varadarajan, *The Times*, 16 October 1997), the news media acted to unite the image of mother and the concept of the sympathetic victim.

One can argue that the rise of feminist discourse has helped to disrupt the manner in which women are constructed as subordinate to men. However, Carol Smart (1977) notes that before this time female criminality was generally understood in terms of pathologies created in order to label female offenders in terms of their peculiar socio-cultural conditions. Looking at early studies of female criminality, Smart shows how the work of Lombroso and Ferrero, and Thomas and Pollack exerted great influence over both academic study and public perception of female deviance. These positions argued for an 'innate character' (nature) of womanhood, in other words, a biologically determinist approach to the study of women and femininity. As such the above thinkers can be seen to corroborate the accepted scientific and medical ideas of the day, where women were studied as a degraded part of man. Smart argues that this perception mirrored the eugenics movement at the turn of the century whereby people considered deviant or criminal by middle-class society were categorized in terms of their dominant physical features. Here, the shape of a criminal's head or eyes became proof of an innate disposition to delinquency. Much like Foucault's (1978/1990) genealogy of sexuality, which shows how the categorization of sex and sexuality has been historically used as a form of social regulation, or his study of the disciplinary effects of medical knowledge, Smart's examination of contemporary perceptions of female criminality exposes the way that modern society continues to dictate the prescriptions of what it means to be a 'real woman'.

Smart's formula reveals that the need to criminalize women (for example the construction of prostitution as a criminal act) stems from the requirement to maintain moral authority over the means for reproduction. By this I mean that a woman's status as a sexual being is the main characteristic by which she is judged. Because women have been attributed with cultural traits that picture them as mothers, wives, and nurturers (in other words as *good*), anything that appears to transgress this image sees them as being presented as more than just criminal, but debased, *evil*. Smart argues that 'the assumption that women are evil and malicious and gentle and caring is part of our cultural heritage' (1977: 30). In this respect a female criminal is deemed to be *more* deviant than her male counterpart. Much worse than a man's violent attributes, she is 'cunning', 'spiteful', and 'deceitful' (ibid: 33). These tendencies can be seen as contrasts to the 'normal' (i.e. male) criminal qualities.

A woman who kills without the excuse of PMS or temporary insanity therefore risks harsher condemnation than if she had accepted her hormonal destiny. Louise Woodward failed to fulfil her nurturing capabilities and the ultimate defence proof of this was founded upon her unwomanly status. Articles in *The Sun* in particular, portrayed Woodward as 'young and vulnerable, really just a child' (Moore, *The Sun*, 1 November 1997), whilst news reports in the USA interpreted her behaviour as an aggressive response to her incapacity to fulfil her feminine role. This judgement in turn engendered her a deviant woman. Unable to perform her domestic role successfully, she became a scapegoat in the name of reforming family unity. Here, Woodward was coded as 'unnatural' because of her intrinsic inability to manage her feminine role. Relating this idea back to my analysis of domestic labour, one might consider the demonization of Woodward (as aberrant woman) as a categorization that turned upon the idea that a woman need not be qualified to do domestic duties because it forms part of her innate character. Hence, because of her failure as a surrogate mother, Woodward was sacrificed in order to maintain the ideology of femininity and the family. This strategy, together with the representation of Deborah Eappen's desertion from the domestic sphere in order to fulfil her own individualistic objectives, contributed to an undermined image of the emancipation of women, which in turn demanded a return to 'family values'.

Outside the domestic economy Sunil Eappen remained absent from representational blame. The trial, both in the courtroom and in the media, centred on Woodward and Deborah Eappen as women that lack. Although he was like Manjit Basuta (ethnic other), Sunil Eappen's role as male doctor allowed him to escape her fate. He was able to maintain his adopted position of relative dominance through his role as arbiter of the discursive arena of medicalized knowledge. This double-status, as both father and ethnic other, encoded Sunil Eappen on a symbolic level that allowed him to be used as a metaphor for both failure and success. Although considered successful because of his professional status, his failure as a protector and provider was exposed when his son died at the hands of a stranger in the home. Had Deborah Eappen not needed to work outside of the home, in order to maintain the middle-class suburban lifestyle to which they aspired, Woodward would not have been brought in to shore up the gap left by her absence, and the exposure of an unstable family system would not have occurred. In this regard Sunil Eappen's success was necessarily related to failure. By working long hours at a professional job he neglected his family role. Moreover, because of the organization of the economy this failure was doubled. Even though he worked long hours he was unable to fully maintain the family in an economic sense. For this reason his wife, who should have acted as primary care-giver, was also required to work. Here, the father's absence caused absence on the part of the mother also.

Media reporting of the Woodward/Eappen case revealed an obsession with the fate of the postmodern family. By painting a picture of familial breakdown, public sphere debate suggested the failure of contemporary structures that demanded attention and action. That the whole affair played out in the symbolic arenas of the media and judiciary directs this discussion toward a further consideration of the ideological functions of the story. Consequently, the following chapter will consider the socio-historical context in which the case unfolded and attempt to draw comparisons with other notable media stories.

Chapter Two

Symbolic Transformations

Building upon the discussion of socio-political narratives in chapter one, this chapter seeks to develop an argument about the way the dominant social order is re-established through media representation. Against the exposure of faults in the family institution, I want to propose that the symbols provided by the media representations of the Woodward case over-coded reality in order to secure the image of familial integrity. In particular I mean to show how Judge Zobel's decision to overturn the jury's verdict (which found that Woodward was guilty of second-degree murder) and instead return his own ruling for the lesser charge of manslaughter (together with a sentence of time served) was a pivotal action that both disciplined the family and recoded Woodward in terms of her inclusive, white, western status.

Before reaching this conclusion, however, I must first consider the socio-historical context within which the drama was played out. At the time of Louise Woodward's trial, Britain had undergone two critical changes that I will argue altered our reaction to her case. Tony Walter (1999) has argued that Britain was in a time of exaggerated mourning for Diana Princess of Wales, who had been killed in a car crash on the 31 August 1997. Public grief sustained by an extreme sense of English nationalism, itself buoyed by the virulent media coverage of events surrounding Diana's death, allowed the same kind of unrestrained support for another English rose – Louise Woodward, the innocent abroad. This reaction, together with the election of New Labour to Parliament in May 1997 after an eighteen-year stretch of Conservative rule, led Britain into a pre-millennial state of flux that saw it negotiating the caring and compassionate ideal symbolized by Princess Diana with the concept of a 'rebranded Britain' that forced it to reassert a patriotic duty to nation (O'Neill, 1998).

Like Britain, America was also reeling from the aftershock of several major specular events.[1] I want to suggest that these events provided a mass-mediated understanding of the Woodward case. Against a backdrop of political scandals centred on President Bill Clinton's extra-marital sexual liaisons, O.J. Simpson (the African-American football star turned actor who was accused of murdering Nicole Simpson and Ronald L. Goldman) provided the USA with a media spectacle that was seen to undermine their criminal justice system and question a media that were

---

[1] For an understanding of specular capital we can refer to Debord who argued that: 'The SPECTACLE is *capital* accumulated to the point where it becomes image' (1994: 24) suggesting that the mass media reduces the 'real world' to an image that is emptied of meaning.

turning criminal proceedings into a showcase. At the same time as Simpson was on trial, Timothy McVeigh exploded the Oklahoma City bomb. Paul Thayler (1997) argues that the second event was subsumed by the first: the Oklahoma City bombing by Gulf War veteran McVeigh was dominated by the massive media impact of the Simpson case. To account for this separation in media coverage Thayler explains that the difference between the treatments of the two cases resulted from the refusal to allow television cameras into the courtroom during the McVeigh proceedings. In this regard America could not deal with the arguably more 'real' horror of the death of 168 people that struck at the heart of its ideological system. Indeed, one may argue that it found the almost soap-like alternative of a celebrity court case more acceptable.

By reading these events in relation to Woodward's trial, in this chapter I propose to develop a thesis which links the powerful institution of the mass media to Girard's model of mimetic desire that will be discussed in greater detail in chapter three. Here, however, I want to focus on the role that specular capital plays in formulating ideological discourse. My aim is to show how media institutions act as agents for the scapegoat mechanism in their role as distributors of knowledge. As such, I want to show how media institutions step in when normal disciplinary systems breakdown, i.e. the police, judicial system and state authority. Akin to both Foucault's (1977/1991) ideas about social regulation, and Louis Althusser's (1970/1993) notion of ideological state apparatus, I want to show how cases such as Woodward's interrupt normal regulatory practices because of their socio-legal ambiguity, and provide a forum for public sphere debate devoted to reinforcing social norms.

Crashing into the New Millennium

With the death of Diana Princess of Wales a fresh memory in the collective memory of the British public, the trial of Louise Woodward in the USA appeared at a time when the press in Britain were still in turmoil about the loss of the 'People's Princess' (Walter, 1999). The tabloid press in particular had recently portrayed the French nation as depriving 'us' of the 'Queen of Hearts', and now they cried aghast as it watched America publicly crucify an innocent abroad for the heinous crime of child killing. Princess Diana's fatal car crash on a Parisian underpass, after a high speed chase with the paparazzi in pursuit of the car in which she and Dodi Al Fayed were passengers, was followed by a media spectacle subsumed by rhetoric of xenophobia and extreme English nationalism. The images of public grief that followed Diana's death, and the allegations of a royalist plot against her, engaged the British tabloid press in a way that had rarely been seen before.

In *The Abolition of Britain*, conservative social commentator Peter Hitchens argues that the Americanization of British culture, most importantly attitudes toward sex, adultery, and divorce, has 'fanned out across this country like an infectious disease' (2000, xxxiii).[2] Pointing to the election of the spin-doctored New Labour as the culminative moment of a nation infatuated with style over substance, Hitchens senses a decline in the traditional *essence* of Britain as a place that once 'ruled the waves'. For Hitchens the death of the Princess of Wales became a defining moment in a new model Britain that had been heading to this point for some time. At once it was perceived that the 'stuffy' old-style monarchy had driven this iconic woman – style icon, young mother, compassionate champion of humanitarian causes – toward this one instant that with hindsight was the inevitable consequence of speed and violence at the height of modernity (Featherstone, 2000).[3]

To explain this point one can refer to Diana, like Woodward, as the accident victim: who is the scapegoat sacrificed in order to reconstitute the moral order. The crash itself signified the collision of old and new, the archaic monarchy set against the new-style royal, more national celebrity than national institution. To this end Diana's life became a cipher for staging a transition between old and new (modern and postmodern) and it was through the mediums of television and newspapers that her death washed away the dominance of old. Such an idea, of course, mirrors Baudrillard's (1983) idea of the hyperreal, where reality has been subsumed by its representation. To the public Diana was an icon, a mediated representation of her real self, but this was the persona with which they identified. To all intents and purposes the spectacle became reality. Indicating the Weberian position on religious order as his primary thesis, Harris argues that Diana's status as ousted royal represented a tension between sacred and celebrity:

> Diana personified the end of monarchy, the end of the sacred, of things set apart and forbidden. Her fascination depended crucially, however, on her being *royal*, on the contradiction between her formal status and the interpretation of her role, a contradiction which depended on the existence of a traditional Royal Family of which she was, so signally, through the revelation of her vulnerable humanity, not a part (Harris, 1999: 103).

It was precisely this tension between self and other (sacred and celebrity) that allowed Diana to be sacrificed. Outside of the ideal type, she became vulnerable to the irrational gaze of the public sphere, which in turn was made scapegoat for her death. Unrestrained by the bonds of the sovereign organization, Diana represented a threat to the idea of a stable and ongoing monarchy and in turn an unchanging Britain. But not only this, she also signalled a threat to what it meant to be a

---

[2] Hitchens' work is an example of the literature arising from the election of New Labour and the close of the twentieth century. He indicates disdain for pop culture and the politics of liberalism, against what he sees as the decline of tradition, morals and conservatism.

[3] Paul Virilio (1999) suggests that the collapse of time in global communications has led to the end of the distinction between reality and its representation. He argues that the exposure of the accident is an inevitable consequence of social construction, simulation, or, what he calls, tele-presence. Virilio sees destruction or failure as being tied to technological invention and development. In the case of Diana this would mean that her public lifestyle was already shadowed by the spectacular nature of her death.

woman. Diana's capabilities as a mother and carer were mythologized and sanctified, but as a wife she was seen to falter. In other words, she failed to fulfil her role supporting the traditional authority of her husband (Holt, 1998). It is with regard to this feature – Diana's (secular) specular rehabilitation – that she can be understood from the context of Weber's (1992) study of the ideological force of religion. Weber argues that it is within the power of an extraordinary individual to incur social change in order to combat ideological stasis. This revolutionary mechanism occurs in Christian societies because there is a constant struggle against sin, and also because of the idea that the perpetrator of sin can be rescued from damnation by the grace of God. As such, a tension is generated that leads to the kind of dynamism which can challenge the existing power structures. Diana's presence as an imperfect version of herself, a martyr, challenged the dominant order's position of authority. This in turn led to an excessive mobilization of media scrutiny, which perhaps ultimately led to her death, or sacrifice.

Following this reading of Princess Diana, Woodward too was understood in terms of the irrational gaze of the media. She was represented as a flawed but nevertheless symbolic version of womanhood, and in the aftermath of the death of the Princess of Wales her reinvention by the British media marked a critical moment in late-modern Britain. To contextualize what was happening in Britain at the time of the Woodward case, we must see 1997 as a time of crisis. The Conservative government (which had been in power for the previous eighteen years, arguably providing a sign of stability) lost the general election; not to Neil Kinnock, a signifier of old Labour (trade unionism and high taxes), but to a *new* Labour. The new Prime Minister Tony Blair was a 'new man', his party had a new moderate image, they employed spin doctors versed in media manipulation, and it was all these things combined that were going to move a Labour-led Britain into the new millennium (Jones, 1997; 1999). By noticing how the changing climate was moving away from the political in British society, the Blair government cleverly associated themselves with all things specular. They were championed by the elite of the celebrity Brit-pack: the image was 'Cool Britannia'. Along with this revision of politics, Diana could also be reinvented in death to stand for something new, something virtuous: a mythologized version of the Princess replaced her previously tarnished image.

Together with these particular incidents followed other 'crashes' in British culture. For example the building of the Millennium Dome signalled the transition from old to new in terms of both politics – conservatism to neo-socialism – and the passage of time. But instead of an acceptance of change, such symbolism invoked mass resistance. In this instance, as in many others, the British media led the way in condemning the building of the Dome. As such, it became a metaphor for the growing pains of a new stage in specular capital where image is dominant over reality (O'Neill, 1998). This idea undermines the idea that the public sphere acts as a forum for rational debate (Habermas, 1989). Just as the discussion surrounding Woodward hinged upon the spectacle maintained by *Court TV* encapsulated by sound-bite interviews with prosecution and defence lawyers, together with the Internet judgement, so too the death of Diana triggered a media response that saw her emptied of real meaning and replaced with symbolic meaning. For example, as a result of a public outcry wholly manufactured by the press, the Royal family was forced to change custom and lower the flag on Buckingham Palace to half-mast in mourning for her death. This act symbolized the way the public seemed to feel about Diana, but more importantly made a statement about our conditional relationship with the monarchy in contemporary Britain.

Nevertheless, in specular terms the UK lags behind the USA. Arguably Britain has maintained an amount of the real through its links with the past, providing a heritage of unmediated reality. Writing in the 1960s Umberto Eco (1967/1986) states that late-modern America's fascination with spectacle stems from its lack of history. It is his contention that because America is in the unique position of being a manufactured country that it fails to maintain any relationship between representation and represented. To explain this idea Eco gives the example of the Museum/Theme Parks where reproductions of international works of art, life-size models of historical objects, and places of interest have been sanitized and displayed for public consumption. Building upon Walter Benjamin's (1986a) original analysis of artistic reproduction, one can see how these works are sanitized because they have been taken out of context. However, Eco's idea expands Benjamin's point by showing how postmodern culture goes further than re-contextualization. These works have not just been removed; they have also been reconstructed to iron out their apparent flaws. The aim of this re-making is to show the audience a bigger, better, shinier, and newer version of the real object. Citing examples that vary between a three-dimensional statue that seamlessly represents a seventeenth-century portrait of Peter Stuyvesant, to the technologically up-to-date version of a nineteenth-century Mississippi paddle-steamer, Eco describes how the gap between representation and reality has been minimized to the extent that the representation has overtaken the original material. In other words, the new object is *better* than reality because the real one was flawed:

> This is the reason for this journey into hyperreality, in search of instances where the American imagination demands the real thing and, to attain it, must fabricate the absolute fake; where the boundaries between game and illusion are blurred, the art museum is contaminated by the freak show, and falsehood is enjoyed in a situation of "fullness," of *horror vacui* (Eco, 1967/1986: 8).

Improving on reality negates the need to deal with fault or doubt. We would understand that the point of the imperfection is that it has been written into the object historically and culturally, thus providing a link to the past. Accordingly Eco argues that it is because America has no history of its own that it cannot understand the flaw. It is because of this lack of historicity that America tries to correct the errors. This of course looks absurd within a historical sense that knows the value of reality. But to the reconstructionist's vision the representation surpasses reality – reality pales by comparison. Here the argument feeds back into the excessiveness of the scandal. In the same way that America aims to correct artistic flaws, its political sensibility is governed by a hypersensitivity to any fault or indiscretion. Thayler argues this point in relation to the media manipulation of the O.J. Simpson case when he states that the narrative took on epic proportions because of the absolute need to develop an *end* to the story. Here, Thayler insists that, 'in the final analysis, the media did not just report the Simpson case but were instrumental in creating it' (1997: xv).

To this end the argument offered by Hitchens, when he states that the England of old was a better place to live, reminds us that the heritage he talks about is one that has inevitably been re-packaged under the banner of 'Olde England'. In this sense there is little difference between Hitchens' mythologized Britain and the hyperreality of Eco's America. In contrast to this point, I argue that Hitchens' idealization of the past is to all intents and purposes founded on the same premise as Blairite rhetoric. The reality to which Hitchens points is similar to the correction of reality found in the American art galleries and theme parks that both he and Eco critique as constitutive of the abandonment of history and culture. However, what separates Eco from Hitchens is that while Eco is well aware of the formal properties of this process, Hitchens seems to imagine that the effects of hyperreality only work on obvious American examples. He fails to see how his own argument rests on a mediated version of the past because it looks British and he is unable to see how this is determined by the same image-making technologies as the artistic representations Eco refers to in the American context.

While Hitchens understands the idealization of the past in the heritage industry, he repeats this formation through his own construction of the past as an English ideal. Where Hitchens differs from the English imaginary, as it is represented by television programmes such as *Heartbeat*, is that his image of Britain asserts an elite position and excludes popular culture. It does this precisely because the parameters of his argument require a return to a traditional society where women, ethnic minorities, and children know their place: outside of culture:[4]

> In everything from children's magazines to advertisements, a message of hedonism and impatience is spread. The soap operas promote and bring into the mainstream such things as incest and transsexualism, and because so many of us no longer have real neighbours or neighbourhoods, we come to believe that the world around is full of such things, and to tell ourselves that we must accept a new morality because it is pointless to resist change (Hitchens, 2000: 346).

Herein lays the precise difference between Hitchens' traditional conservatism and the postmodern media spectacle used in Blairite politics. That is to say that Blairite politics seeks to advance its dominant class claims by engineering the consent of the popular classes through media channels, as opposed to Hitchens, who would seem to advise a form of authority based on naked class, race, and gender domination. In other words, Blairite politics differs in that it appears inclusive. Nevertheless, my critique of Blairite ideology does not seek a return to some traditional form of social organization, but rather sees such a position as itself mediated, albeit in a way which does not understand the media mechanics which

---

[4] This recalls the views of writers such as Richard Hoggart (1958) who was critical of the Americanization of culture that was infecting what he thought of as 'authentic' working class culture, i.e. pubs and going to the dogs.

operate in the construction of its own position. In contrast my argument seeks to privilege those who are excluded from both the Blairite ideology, with its friendly face, and Hitchens' more overt conservatism with its more oppressive ideological stance.

Accordingly I would propose that the historical perspective found in both the Girardian analytical framework and Habermasian notions of public sphere debate provide a more communicative forum for democratic discussion because they allow for conversation, reflexivity, and judgement. This perspective is against both Hitchens' argument for a return to old conservative values that are not repackaged for the media age and the Blairite media ideology, which obliterates historical reality with a timeless media spectacle that overwrites the contingencies of reality with an antiseptic version of the socio-political life-world. Following Althusserian Marxism one can see how the latter perspective sees the media as an appendage to the judicial system – upholding at the level of spectacle what the law fails to secure at the level of traditional, modern, legal discourse.

Inside America

The O.J. Simpson murder trial and subsequent civil lawsuit took place during 1994 to 1997, while the Oklahoma City bombing occurred during the Simpson trial on 19th April 1995, and came to federal court just a few months before Woodward's case began being tried in Massachusetts. In America both of these events occurred against the backdrop of political scandal, which saw the president of the United States impeached. By examining how Bill Clinton's administration had been blighted by accusations of sexual harassment, infidelity, and financial infraction since he first ran for presidency in 1992, we can begin to see how the media treat scandalous cases in terms of re-ordering and legitimating dominant authority. The first scandal to befall the Clinton administration was the Whitewater affair, and then came an accusation of a ten-year affair by Gennifer Flowers, a sexual harassment claim against Clinton by Paula Jones, and then most famously statements about sexual infidelity with White House intern Monica Lewinsky. All of these scandals led to the Kenneth Starr inquiry ('Monicagate') into Clinton's character and integrity to act as president (Gronbeck, 1997).

According to Bruce E. Gronbeck (1997), the Clinton administration was subject to mass-mediated interpretations that blurred the line between politics and celebrity. He argues that the very thing that allowed Clinton to be exposed as a sexual actor after the Jones and Flowers accusations, also afforded him celebrity status that lifted him out of the realm of the political. This had the effect of negating the importance of Clinton's misdemeanours. In other words, much like Princess Diana in Britain, he could get away with his moral transgressions because the debate became one of media ethics rather than personal culpability. Moreover, Gronbeck argues that the media in this case confused the public's perception of Clinton's real character (political morality) with his celebrity image (popularity, likeability) by focussing on certain characteristics above others. In terms of spectacle, the media heightening of Clinton's moral transgressions made him appear more humanly vulnerable, a sympathetic character whose personal life was being unfairly exposed. Suddenly it was the media being questioned for criticising a popular figure, rather a political figure under scrutiny for sexual transgressions. Once the work of making Clinton appear a more human leader was done, the media's attack on his sexual exploits was recast as a monstrous witch-hunt aimed at gaining political advantage for the government's Republican opponents.

In terms of Foucault's and Althusser's theories of social regulation, this mechanism illustrates how the media acts as an ideological apparatus when it steps in to shore up any glitch in the application of regulation. These glitches or fault-lines occur when common moral or repressive authority seems to break down. Accordingly, because the absolute figure of authority in America, President Clinton, transgressed his role of supremacy, becoming more celebrity figure than leader of the free world, the media had to intervene to act as moral governors. By questioning Clinton's individual ability to lead Americans, they restored America's ideological dominance. However, because the media's authority is transient (it legitimates state command but lacks any real power to produce discipline) it too must be re-coded in terms of its debased regulatory position. That is to say that once the emergency had subsided (in fact, in order to help it subside), the influence and ethics of the media were criticized in order to restore legitimate authority to state control.

This way of seeing the media as both the response to social problems as well as the cause of them is discussed by Ericson, Baranek and Chan, who argue that the individualization and personalization of events provides a dramatic means to allocate responsibility whilst at the same time removing its political significance. They state that 'by individualizing problems on a case-by-case basis, the news and law rule out systematic and structural accounts that might question the authority of cultural values, the state, and legal institutions themselves' (1991: 9). In terms of Clinton's impeachment, his individual culpability allowed him to be temporarily sacrificed in order to reconstitute moral authority as a government preserve. Similarly, the criminal justice system requires legitimation by cultural institutions in order to work effectively. Thus, spectacular criminal actions, such as the Simpson murders and the Oklahoma bombing, work to legitimate wider social norms of what is acceptable behaviour without interfering with political process.

The horror of the McVeigh bombing for America resided in the fact that McVeigh presented an image of the American ideal gone bad. For this reason it was difficult for Americans to understand his crime as soap opera without confronting their own potential for un-American actions (i.e. he was an American hero, everything they wanted their sons to be). By contrast, Simpson was far less dangerous to the American ideology. While his actor/L.A. lifestyle made him a convenient subject for *Court TV*, his blackness meant that he could always be seen as other despite the fact that he too was an all-American hero. Thus, Simpson was only acceptable as an insider – allowed to be screened on television – because he was cast an outsider: black. This idea, which shows how Simpson could become a real-life soap-star because he would not offend the centre of American life, also relates to the outcome of his murder trial. He could be pronounced innocent – thus an insider – only by virtue of later becoming an outsider. This refers to the fact that

Simpson was indicted in a civil lawsuit brought against him by the families of Nicole Simpson and Ronald Goldman. Found guilty of the wrongful deaths of his wife and her friend, he was ordered to pay punitive damages of $33.5 million. Not only did this leave Simpson bankrupt, but it also coincided with the declining interest of the mass media. At this end-point of the televisual narrative Simpson was non-threatening, the castrated other.

Against this Timothy McVeigh presented America with the ultimate consequence of their strong-held belief in freedom and individualism. As a patriotic white Middle American and Gulf War veteran he exercised extreme individualism as an expression of protest against a government he felt was un-American. The outcome of his actions reveal McVeigh as the insider gone bad. However, one can also argue that his murderous actions exposed an inherent contradiction or paradox within the American ideology: that one can only be an individual within the collective frame of reference. In the Woodward case this fact is made apparent by the tension between family and capital. In other words, for Deborah Eappen to attain her individualism outside the familial institution, she had to sacrifice her role within the family unit while fulfilling her individual desire to work. This drive for capital individualism works to sustain market competition (the collective order) under the more acceptable guise of the ideology of democratic free will (Althusser, 1970/1993).

Akin to Eappen's role, which shows how individualism remains caught within the dictates of political ideology, McVeigh's situation also allows one to understand how the paradoxical relationship between individual and collective plays itself out in contemporary society. In order to explain how this double-bind functions one might refer to the difference between a dialectical and a transgressive philosophy of the subject's place in the wider society. According to transgressive philosophies, such as that expressed by Jacques Derrida (1994), McVeigh can be seen to provide a true example of transgression, as an individual who corrupts the work of the social order and paves the way for the invention of a totally open asocial freedom. Against an individualistic point of view, which retains the bias of capital ideologies of the individual, a collective understanding of the person's role in society allows us to see that such transgressive acts are actually functional for capitalism because they help to renew its violent cycle of production/consumption. This theory, which has been expressed by philosophers such as Hegel, political theorists such as Marx, and later literary critics such as Girard, shows how the transgressive person appears to disrupt the violent social system only from the point of view of the individual. On the contrary, these dialectical thinkers suggest that the adoption of a wider social perspective allow us to see how the outsider is absolutely necessary for the continual renewal of any insider/outsider social order (Derrida, 1994). Therefore, the difference between the ideas of the 'dangerous individual' (Foucault, 1988) as either disruptive or functional resides in the perspective of the viewer: they either have an individual or social viewpoint.

In McVeigh's case the ideology of individualism is taken to its logical extreme. He was disillusioned with a nation that seemed to fall short of its own ideology, so he acted against America and for the ideology of America. In other words, he took the ideology literally. Much like soldiers from the Vietnam conflict who felt they were fighting an unjust war, McVeigh could not reconcile his own idealistic patriotism for a mythologized America with what he saw as the cynicism of absolute destruction for the sake of votes. To kill for one's country a soldier must believe that he is on the right side: fighting against evil, and fighting for freedom. But in the Gulf McVeigh discovered the cynicism of postmodern war, whereby the image of (related effect) became more important than real events (immediate effects). This idea suggests that the war was not fought for war's sake, but for the sake of public relations, because President George Bush believed that a successful campaign in the Gulf might help him secure re-election. In line with McVeigh's disillusionment with this form of cynicism that seemed to determine American foreign policy, Baudrillard discusses the Gulf War in terms of hyperreality. In *The Gulf War Did Not Take Place* he proposes that the sheer force of America's intervention in the Gulf negated any chance of real warfare. Instead, he argues that the mediated effect of the war replaced its bloody reality:

> Since this war was won in advance, we will never know what it would have been like had it existed. We will never know what an Iraqi taking part with a chance of fighting would have been like. We will never know what an American taking part with a chance of being beaten would have been like (Baudrillard, 1995: 61).

As Baudrillard explains, the Gulf War appeared on television screens immediately. Like the separation of real effects and by-products (the images), which determined the war itself, the battles in the Gulf were divided between the real events and the media images of these events. Thus, real events became artificially processed through news reporters, media sound-bites, and cameras riding on missiles that filmed the destruction of their Iraqi targets as it happened. But for McVeigh and other soldiers who were trained to fight a 'real war', the fact that there was no real contest, that technology was fighting the war for them, undermined their purpose, and as such undermined the very ideology that took them there in the first place:

> Fake war, deceptive war, not even the illusion but the disillusion of war, linked not only to defensive calculation, which translates into the monstrous prophlaxis of this military machine, but also to the mental disillusion of the combatants themselves, and to the global disillusion of everyone else by means of information (Baudrillard, 1995: 68).

Back on American soil, however, McVeigh's individual actions of terrorism were deemed transgressive. His failure to accept the cynicism of the postmodern ideology – whereby war was fought for the sake of its by-products – led to his expulsion from the social order. McVeigh, although actually culpable, was also made a scapegoat for the dominant social order because he was unable to accept the gap between the ideology and its aims: that the individual should be cynical enough to adopt the image of the ideology whilst avoiding its actual implications. However, while McVeigh's actions meant that he remained transgressive at an individualistic level, he was never transgressive enough to de-stabilize the dominant American order. On the contrary, McVeigh's function was to help sustain America. In essence this is because its ideology is too dynamic. An individual cannot undermine ideology because although his/her actions seem to threaten its sustainability, its cynical approach leads to his/her interpellation as an enemy of the state – an alien that America must organize against if it is to remain a dominant world power.

In much the same way that Baudrillard argued that there was never a real Gulf War, just a series of reality effects put together by the media (which was detected by McVeigh); we can see that McVeigh was never a real threat to the stability of the American social order. However, while Baudrillard was able to understand the cynicism of postmodern ideology, McVeigh could not accept the gap between what the ideology said and what it actually aimed to achieve. For this reason he continued to take the American ideology of individualism literally. He became disillusioned with the system that appeared to betray its own notions of freedom, justice, and democracy, the very ideals he was concerned to follow, and so he began to fight for the American ideology and against America gone bad. It is precisely this paradox that makes McVeigh both ultimate American hero (self-made man) and an American monster, the ultimate anti-American. According to this situation it is clear why McVeigh can be seen to epitomize an American myth, the renegade that fights for justice against a corrupt system he hopes to destabilize. Akin to the traditions of the Wild West, where outlaw figures become romantic heroes, McVeigh's mythology could only begin to emerge after his execution. That is to say that while McVeigh was alive he remained a threat to the cynicism of the socio-political order. Only upon his death was he able to become an ideal symbol for the virtual ideology that exists only to remain apart from practical application: for the American ideology we are always failures, we can never live up to its goals.

In this regard McVeigh's stay on death row, which can be seen to symbolize a period where the prisoner is at once alive and dead, should be understood as the entry point to the realm of ideological signification. Death row was the place where McVeigh's actual pursuit of the American ideology was blocked and where he was prepared for his transformation into a virtual symbol of ideological achievement. On death row the prisoner is actually alive but virtually dead. This condition allows for the emergence of death row celebrity as a precursor to the organization of the outlaw as post-mortem symbol of ideological idealization. Within the cynical ideology, which attempts to uphold the ideals of American individualism only insofar as any attempts to follow such extreme ideas are punishable by expulsion, McVeigh's *image* might become a support for the dominant ideas of American society. From this point of view we can see how the cynicism of the American ideology revolves around its laundering of McVeigh. The process which pushed the former Gulf War hero through death row, and the culmination of his metamorphosis, execution, saw the consumption of the body and the recreation of McVeigh as symbolic American outlaw. In this way his actions, which resulted in his transgression of the law and subsequent execution, can be seen to re-assert the idealism of America once his real body was expelled and he was turned into an image. Like the Gulf War example, where the importance of the image took precedence over the real event, McVeigh's elevation to the status of an image displays the cynicism of the American ideology.

Finally, much like the Marxist theory of capitalism, whereby the organization of the system leads it to produce ever more commodities for consumption, McVeigh displays the mechanics of a form of capitalist order that has moved onto the level of image production/consumption. This is postmodern capitalism, where the production and consumption of images, as well as things, re-states the value of the dominant order. Asserting this point Douglas Kellner notes that 'signs and modes of representation come to constitute "reality", and signs gain autonomy and, in interaction with other signs, come to constitute a new type of social order in which it is signs and codes that constitute "the real"' (1989: 63). This perspective illustrates how the social system produces such figures with the very expectation of consuming their images. This occurs because people's disillusionment, which leads to their transgressive acts and thus their re-configuration as imaginary commodities, is a product of the system's cynicism. Fatally, this is the very same cynicism transgressive people go onto feed. Such people become disillusioned with a system that fails to live up to its own ideals of freedom: in McVeigh's case the government itself (symbolized by the federal building in Oklahoma) represented the system. This is the way the production/consumption of capitalism works: the idea of 'America' (the land of the free), followed by the consumption of the individual who believes the dream but goes on to expose the faults, and finally the re-statement of the ideology through the image of the transgressor. In other words, the real villain (McVeigh) is re-made as a heroic image; one that we can see supports the (cynical) American ideology that he tried to undermine with his terrorist action. This reveals the scapegoat as both villain and hero. Accordingly, the consumption of McVeigh represents a sacrifice (like Matthew Eappen or Louise Woodward) to the imaginary capital which allows the American ideology to be reconstituted. This happens in much the same way that the nuclear family was re-ordered in the Woodward scenario.

Specular Re-organization

By reading the above conditions in relation to the Louise Woodward trial, we can begin to see how the mass media's treatment of issues of social disorder have, in this case, provided a link between Britain and America in terms of spectacle, but a divergence in terms of national ideology. In the Simpson case television and media coverage became a part of the judicial system. The same can be said for the Woodward court proceedings. This mechanism showed up the functional relationship between political and cultural institutions whereby both the legal profession and media discourses performed the same purpose: to re-order transgressive individuals in terms of the dominant social order. Even in the extreme case of Timothy McVeigh, the media treatment acted to recode him in terms of an ideology that sees the outlaw as an integral part of American culture. Notwithstanding Britain's lack of some of the more sensationalistic aspects of the American mass media (for example television cameras in court), the British press still acted to protect the dominant social order. *The Sun*'s partisan treatment of

Louise Woodward in particular illustrates how the British tabloid press attempted to appropriate the story from the American media. The aim of this re-organizational effort was to manipulate the story so as to discipline America as monstrous other and recode Woodward as innocent victim (only to later regulate her[5]).

Again Baudrillard (1998) enables a reading of the process whereby the consumption of mediated images becomes the principle by which all things are measured. Baudrillard understands how reality is reducible to the codes of its representation: its culturally signified meaning. According to this thesis the fundamental differences between the two nation's (UK and USA) media coverage of the Woodward case became void in order to assert an overarching rhetoric of social order. In other words, the guilt or innocence of Woodward became an inconsequential aside to the more (ideologically) important matter of gender discipline and family regulation.

It is with regard to this last point that I want to focus on the way that the media presented a picture of moral family life in the Woodward case. Indeed, we might see the outcome of symbolic reordering as the creation of the image of moral family unity. My specific interest in this point concerns the way that social norms are organized around the transgressive or supplemental element of criminality. For example Young argues that we need to consider how mainstream society and crime are written by media sources. She suggests that because of such mediatization and representation 'it is the aestheticization of everyday life – and the place of crime in it – that needs to be addressed' (1996: 22), meaning that the way we look at crime is as important as the crime itself. Young's argument is that individuals agree with and adhere to personal regulation in order to protect their own interests. This understanding of both written and unwritten social norms provides a powerful social contract between state and subject that is negotiated by cultural institutions set up to speak to and on behalf of 'the people'. The result of this contract is a society based on a tense relationship between binary oppositions (good/bad, inside/outside), against which we are able to understand our own role. Under these circumstances the role of the media is one that presents spectacles of disorder as markers for sustaining order by showing people the terrible consequences of a totally free, unregulated society.

Media scandals or the over-reporting of high profile criminal cases, are not recent phenomena. Earlier instances of notable criminality, such as Leopold and Loeb in the 1920s,[6] prompted similar sensationalistic responses to those of O.J. Simpson or Woodward in the 1990s. Janice Scheutz (1994) states that this factor points to the need to reorder different aspects of society at different times. Issues that cause concern at one time may be seen as insignificant at a later date. This

---

[5] This refers to the way that Woodward was received upon her return to the UK. Again the tabloids led the way, but this time to condemn her for her interview on *Panorama* where, they argued, she tried to emulate Princess Diana's appearance on the programme.

[6] In 1924 Nathan Leopold and Richard Loeb were convicted for the premeditated murder of 14-year-old Robert Franks. The story gripped the USA, which was shocked at how two wealthy and educated young men could murder to see 'if they could get away with it'.

may be the case because different responses to instances of criminality can reflect the changing values of the collective order. Nevertheless, the enormous frequency with which criminal cases have been reported has increased over the course of the late twentieth century and upon entering the twenty-first century. One explanation for this is that in global society images of disorder are transmitted faster and amplified to a greater extent because of the speed with which new technology allows disparate communities to interact. But this does not mean that national boundaries have been dismantled. The war of words that waged between the British and American press during the course of the Woodward case exposed a form of localized allegiance that would seem to belie the dominance of a global cultural economy. John Tomlinson (1997) argues that this kind of local reaction to globally mediated events uncovers a moral code that remains culturally distinct from country to country or even from community to community. Put another way, what would appear to be an important facet of a criminal case or political scandal in one country would perhaps be insignificant to another national group depending on its particular moral codes. The point of a scandal is, therefore, to unite a community by means of moral reflections which are, in turn, based on their own cultural codes of regulation. Tomlinson asserts that many news stories lose power as they move across national boundaries because of the lack of immediacy and cultural recognition. In other words we, as individuals, or in our relationships with friends and family, are not really all that interested in the fate of O.J. While we may balk in horror at the spectacle of the Oklahoma bombing or ethnic cleansing in Bosnia, we cannot really identify with the situation because it lacks the immediacy and personalization required to gain culturally specific legitimacy.[7]

However, the appearance of globally reported criminal cases, such as O.J. Simpson and Woodward, together with the global Internet coverage that they generated, would suggest that there is something about certain cases that overwrites the apathetic response to many news items. Suggestive of the Weberian position discussed earlier, Tomlinson claims that this facet lies in the subject's 'extraordinary ordinariness' (1997: 78). While Princess Diana was outside our experience in terms of social hierarchy, she was presented as 'one of us' in terms of her marital problems, her trouble with the in-laws, and her eating disorder. Of course the 'extraordinary ordinary individual' must also have something uncommon about them. Being royal was Diana's facet, while having her own teeth and not having tattoos was Louise Woodward's. In this regard Weber's thesis, which suggests that it is the extraordinary individual who has the power to combat ideological stasis because of their ability to appear both self and other, relates to contemporary celebrity. However, this potential is representative of only half the story. Celebrity must be regulated in order to restate dominant authority. Accordingly the same function that promotes the celebrity's extraordinariness also disciplines them in terms of any attempts to be outside group control. Paradoxically, it is eventually the 'extraordinary ordinary' individual's very ordinariness (sameness) rather than their difference (otherness) that eventually

---

[7] For a discussion of this point see Renata Salecl's book *Spoils of Freedom* (1994).

excludes them: they become too much like us and therefore not celebrities at all, or too central, and thus dangerous, to remain within the social order.[8]

The mass media's part in presenting the human-interest angle of the extraordinary ordinary individual is important insofar as they provide the mass circulation required to dispense political and legal discourse to a wide audience. Lull and Hinerman (1997) explain that for a spectacle to function effectively demands some kind of invasive visual apparatus. In America this comes with the presence of cameras in the courtroom, and the twenty-four hour news culture provided by multi-channel television. Britain, however, cannot contend with the USA in terms of mass-mediated spectacles because for one thing it does not allow the televization of trials. This would suggest that it was the media in America that played the strongest part not only in recounting the facts of the Woodward case, but also as a key player in the social structure that enforces the regulatory mechanism. Then again, the British tabloid press performed the same disciplinary function when confronted with the aggressive treatment of a British national abroad. I would suggest two key facets in this trans-Atlantic process of discipline and counter-discipline. One is America's lack of a unified national media because newspapers are localized state by state and many television networks require consumer subscription. I believe that because of this 'distance' it was difficult for the media to effectively communicate an overarching narrative against Woodward. One can contrast this with Britain's own national press, who were successfully able to mount a campaign on behalf of Woodward. The second point takes into account the colonial past of Britain and America, whereby the USA legal system is seen as a debased form of British law. Considering this point, the media in Britain were able to sustain the rhetoric of legitimate authority based on the conviction of a nation that has historically dominated other countries. Furthermore, the British tabloid press were able to make a martyr of Woodward in order to expose America's monstrousness.[9]

One thing that could be seen to over-ride this division in terms of national boundaries is of course the emergence of the Internet. In her ethnographic study examining Internet sites dedicated to the Woodward case, Christine Hine (2000) states that the number of sites that proliferated would seem to suggest that an arena for democratic discussion had emerged apart from the ideologically constrained treatment by traditional forms of mass media. However, Hine goes on to say that Internet discourse is very much enacted from within limitations already set out in conventional forms of media communications. Technological structures of the Internet may *ideally* be seen to form a democratic system. However, as Raymond

---

[8] In the event of this case we can see that Woodward got too close to the role of mother (over-coding her domestic worker role), thus necessitating her expulsion (literally and discursively) from the family institution. This refers back to the discussion of Princess Diana who became *too* ordinary to maintain her celebrity position.

[9] In particular *The Sun*'s 'Justice for Louise Campaign' (1 November 1997), which asked readers to 'wear a ribbon for Louise' and showed popular UK celebrities such as Jimmy Tarbuck pledging their support, whilst condemning the American justice system for what it perceived to be a miscarriage of justice.

Williams (1981) argued in relation to the development of large-scale print press, this democratic potential is restricted by access to the means of socio-cultural production and consumption. Hine's key point shows us that technological systems of communication are always embedded in the social system in which they exist. Such systems are therefore subject to the interpretative practices of the people who understand their potential through the ideological structures of that society. Regarding this point, Hine refers to Manuel Castells, whose idea of the 'temporal collage' suggests that the Internet has disrupted our perception of time and space, thus perhaps allowing a more free-flowing understanding of events. However, arguing against this idea, Hine states that it 'overlooks the interpretative work which participants do to make sense of conflicting temporal orders and the cultural competencies which they draw to do so' (2000: 103). Accordingly, when discussing Woodward, the Internet acted like an extension of existing media discourses rather than a radical alternative. Bound by partisan narratives already set out in the press and on television, the Internet provided a further space for discussing the pros and cons of a debate that ultimately centred on the question of whether or not women should sacrifice their children for the sake of their own independence. The following comments represent some popular opinions that were left on the message boards of *Court TV* and *BBC News Online*:

> There has to be something that we as citizens can do to get this verdict overthrown. I will not say that she is innocent, only that I firmly believe that she is not guilty of murder.

> Why is everyone second-guessing this jury? Isn't this a classic instance of our judicial system at work? Is anyone saying Louise Woodward did not receive a fair trial? For the critics in Britain, did anyone ever stop to think this girl may be guilty?

> The parents of this baby are doctors – how on earth could they miss a broken arm? That makes them for me not just incapable parents, but also incapable doctors.

> The issue is: did she cause Matthew's death? Everyone who judged this case said strongly YES. Is 279 days a suitable punishment for taking someone's life? I submit that it is a farce, and the trial judge should be ashamed of himself for desecrating Matthew's life that way.

> Why is nothing being made of the fact that these parents deliberately left their child in the hands of someone whom they knew to be young and inexperienced? Is it not the case that they acted negligently and without due care for their child?

Behind this allusion to a democratic arena for debate one can discern the dominance of traditional forms of media and their portrayal of legal institutions. After the realization that crime shows (fact or fiction) multiply viewing figures, competition between television networks in the USA has been a deciding factor behind the increasing coverage of judicial proceedings. This has also been a consideration in the broader development of factual programming along entertainment lines (Surette, 1998; Thayler, 1994). The Woodward trial was aired live in its entirety on *Court TV*, arguably giving it the appearance of an ongoing soap opera rather than criminal proceedings. The audience were able to tune in at regular intervals, there were Internet tie-ins that gave character profiles of the participants which enabled viewers to build a picture of the key players, and after the trial finished we were able to buy highlights of the court proceedings on video.

Together with these features, defence and prosecution lawyers, as well as Eappen family members, gave 'sound-bite' interviews to the awaiting press outside the courtroom at the end of each court session. To heighten the sense of drama being played out in the media spotlight even further, the Woodward defence team was led by Barry Scheck, O.J. Simpson's trial attorney. This last point can be referred back to Daniel Boorstin (1961/1987), who argued that the upward spiral of the media representation turns factual news into a 'pseudo-event', something that takes place only because the media are involved. An example would be the fame of someone associated with the celebrity circuit, i.e. 'famous for being famous' rather than for any personal talent they might possess. However, in Boorstin's account crime and the judiciary are, together with sports, the last remaining 'non-pseudo-events'. He argues that audiences crave these events because of the lack of authenticity found in other forms of media:

> One example is the American passion for news about crime and sports. This is not simply an effect of the degradation of public tastes to the trivial and the unserious. More significantly, it is the expression of our desperate hunger for the spontaneous, for the non-pseudo-event (Boorstin, 1961/1987: 254).

Forty years after Boorstin mourned the demise of authentic events against the escalation of trivia, even the actions he described as being non-pseudo-events – crime and sport – have befallen a similar fate. In the Woodward trial not only was the case reported on a global scale, but it was also subject to the entertainment treatment through its coverage on *Court TV*, together with late-night interviews with talk-show personalities.[10] Through such media representations the trial became a kind of technological theatre, which was able to stage the re-organization of Woodward (as renegade element of society) through a postmodern version of classical tragedy. This comparison of the Woodward trial with tragic theatre, whereby we see a dramatization of the fall of the rebel hero, also relates to the larger-than-life quality of many of the trial's other main players (Hariman, 1990). In this regard, Woodward's celebrity defence lawyer, Barry Scheck, became a kind of flamboyant leading man. However, while the invention of figures such as Scheck was originally seen as advantageous for their clients, due to the media's increased reflexivity popular opinion has begun to turn against such celebrity lawyers as symbols of the cynicism of a postmodern star system that values spectacle over truth. Inside this complex, where figures such as Scheck seemed to be more concerned with their own image rather than legal truth, Aucoin writing in

---

[10] This refers to Deborah and Sunil Eappen's interview with the popular American chat show host Larry King.

The Boston Globe has speculated that Woodward might have lost popular support because the public perceived her defence as being about creating the *appearance* of innocence as opposed to proving the reality of her freedom from guilt:

> The tactics employed by some of the defence lawyers...aroused public distaste...which parallels the changing view of lawyers on TV. "Perry Mason was a good guy in the old-fashioned sense," notes Thompson. "But he gave way to the antihero type personified by Arnie Becker in 'L.A. Law', who showed an ability to operate in the sleazy world of the 90s" (Aucoin, *The Boston Globe,* 14 November 1997).

This comparison of Woodward's defence team with a fictional character from USA television drama *L.A. Law,* shows how Scheck's manipulation of media reality, for the purposes of portraying his client in the best possible light, fed into the stereotypical image of the corruptible lawyer. Indeed the prosecutors, who relied on images of the grief-stricken Eappens, were concerned to off-set the cool set-plays of the Scheck team with the harsh reality of a child's death. According to this strategy Thomas Reilly, Martha Coakley, and Gerald Leone Jr. sought to cut through the presentations of the defence. As Aucoin continues:

> But for those who believed Woodward guilty of killing Matthew Eappen, there was the corresponding passion and conviction of the prosecutors...who never let the public forget the child whose life was cut short (Aucoin, *The Boston Globe*, 14 November 1997).

The parameters of the Woodward case thus revolved around the believability of Scheck's defence team. While they attempted to construct the image of innocence, which due to the specular nature of any legal trial is more important than actual innocence or guilt, the prosecution tried to develop a case that could under-cut these appearances through repeated reference to the dead child (Reik, 1961).[11] Within this debate the final status of guilt or innocence was dependent upon how well the presentations of each side sat with the watching audience. In the first instance, the idea of the watching audience relates to the judge and jury, while, due to the doubling effects of media coverage, the concept of the audience also refers to the wider newspaper, TV and Internet consumers. In the case of the second layer of the audience, whereby an idea of guilt or innocence is determined by popular judgement, Aucoin reveals how it is understood that beyond the legal verdict's traditional authority there exists a far greater social arbiter. In the age of mass media re-presentations legal authority merges with politics:

---

[11] In his book *The Compulsion to Confess* (1961), Reik explains how the *appearance* of guilt or innocence is often more important than *actual* guilt or innocence. Through his use of psychoanalysis he criticises this misrecognition by suggesting that judge and jury are often influenced by their unconscious belief in the theory of the 'omnipotence of thoughts' whereby the idea that somebody has thought about murder (i.e. the death wish) is confused with the physical act of murder.

"We debate our political issues through these cultural events," said Stark. "People don't debate race anymore in politics; they debate it through the O.J. trial. Clinton had a child-care initiative last week: Did you hear anybody discussing it? But they'll debate the same thing through the Woodward trial" (Aucoin, *The Boston Globe*, 14 November 1997).

This idea of the specularization of politics that Boorstin understood as total (apart from the spheres of crime and sport) thus appears in an expanded format. While the Woodward trial shows how decisions about criminal events are no longer made outside the concerns of specularization, the figure of O.J. Simpson appears as a conflation of the spheres of crime, sport, and race. Like Scheck, the legal representative of both Woodward and Simpson who aroused such suspicion because of his amalgamation of the ideas of legal truth and media appearance, the multi-talents of O.J. Simpson also illustrate how the worlds of sport and celebrity converge to support an entertainment format rather than uphold the integrity of either profession. Additionally, the mediated connection, or inter-textuality, of the Simpson and Woodward trials – whereby, not only were they both represented by the same attorney, but Simpson also put forward his own views on the Woodward case and expressed his sympathy and support for Louise via *Court TV* – was encapsulated by the very media technologies that represented them both.

To explain why the media magnification of factual events occurs in some criminal cases and not in others, one should refer back to the ideas investigated by Cohen (1972) and Hall et al (1978) showing how certain acts of deviance are amplified in order to sustain the moral dominance of the social order. Using this thesis to explain the fact that most criminal and legal events do not get reported to the same extent as certain super-trials, the Woodward case can be understood in terms of the moral climate dictated by state authorities and family-values campaigners. However, state or moral crusaders could not sustain a significant debate in the public sphere on their own. It is also questionable as to whether media institutions could act independently in order to influence public opinion one way or another. The answer, then, lies somewhere in between.

The conspicuous presence of *Court TV* and its function as primary facilitator of information about the Woodward case betrays both the theatrical as well as the regulatory relationship that the law has with its audience. This would support the idea that the media, through its fascination with the law, acts as a point of moral mediation between the state and public. The courtroom is meant to be an objective arena, a panoptic space that maintains its 'natural' moral values. From this perspective comes the idea that the law is somehow organic. However, Foucault's (1977/1991) suggestion is that the visual nature of the law (e.g. public executions) arose in order to contain the disordered violence that followed chaotic legal processes. In this regard, the law is part of a larger regulatory mechanism that transmits norms and values, together with the social, cultural, economic, and political structures which such legal prescriptions contained through presupposition. In turn the discourses generated by these structures develop in order to naturalize the word of the law. According to Foucault the panoptic technologies promoted by utilitarian philosopher Jeremy Bentham's existed to regulate those under its gaze. The prisoners of Bentham's machine had to internalize its presence. They were subsequently disciplined through their knowledge of the omniscience of the regulatory ideal:

> Hence the major effect of the Panopticon: to induce in the inmate a state of conscious and permanent visibility that assures the automatic functioning of power. So to arrange things that the surveillance is permanent in its effects, even if it is discontinuous in its action; ... that this architectural apparatus should be a machine for creating and sustaining a power relation independent of the person who exercises it; in short, that the inmates should be caught up in a power situation of which they are themselves the bearers (Foucault, 1977/1991: 201).

However, this mechanism does not take place without problems. If problems did not occur, the media would not need to take over as a regulatory mechanism when the actual structures of law and discipline fail. According to Foucault it is only when these fissures appear in structural authority that other institutions have to intervene directly in order to shore up the gap left by visible problems occurring in the law. Miscarriages of justice, for example, seem to be uncovered in clusters at times when there is a slide in public confidence in the ability of police and legal institutions to do their jobs properly (Reik, 1961). In the case of Louise Woodward, the authority of the legal institution had been damaged by the outcome of the Simpson criminal trial subsequently 'proven' wrong by the guilty verdict of the civil lawsuit, itself a reaction to self-reflexive criticism by the media and its liability in the outcome of the first case.[12] However, difficulty occurs in this set-up because the disciplinary function of the media is intended as a transient intervention and as such it is not equipped to deal with the specific intent of the law. Thus, the momentum that is carried with the representations of crime and justice, i.e. the exaggerating affect of spectacle rather than the more ordered method of legal due course, demanded a guilty verdict for Louise Woodward (regardless of her guilt or innocence) in order to re-establish the dominance of the law over the cultural institution that stepped in to ensure that order was sustained at a time when the law was seen to falter.

Consequently, the cultural intervention was overturned by Judge Zobel, who represented the re-establishment of judiciary power when he ordered that the jury's decision to convict Woodward for second-degree murder be thrown out, and instead instigated his own verdict of guilty of manslaughter with time served. The effect of this action was four-fold. First, it had the effect of disciplining the media in terms of its debased moral authority. Second, the law had to be seen to discipline Woodward for her gender failure. Thus, the fact of her guilt was not contradicted, only the degree to which she was liable for her own actions. Third, the Eappens (the visibly dysfunctional family) were regulated in order to secure familial

---

[12] Against this idea we can see that O.J. Simpson was initially subject to sympathetic rehabilitation by the media and legal institutions as a reaction to the Rodney King incident, where it was argued that King was subject to racist treatment by the judicial process.

integrity. And, lastly, Zobel's judicial action functioned to re-order Woodward in terms of her inclusive white, western status.

From the above process one can discern that one of the reasons that the Woodward case magnified into a media spectacle above other cases was the need to re-form and stabilize the family in the public imagination. Following the arguments put forward by Smart (1977) and Lloyd (1995), Deborah Eappen had to be publicly chastised for neglecting her role as a 'proper woman' (wife and mother) and Woodward had to be exposed for failing to make the successful transition from girl to woman, and, thus able to perform her 'natural' function of caretaker. Evaluating the divergence between the language that newspapers use to describe men and women respectively, West, Lazar and Kramarae state that 'language does not merely reflect a pre-existing sexist world; instead it actively constructs gender asymmetries within specific sociohistorical contexts' (1997: 120). The implications of this for Louise Woodward and Deborah Eappen are contained within the media representations that branded them in terms of their relationship to the home, their gender, and their respective maturity/immaturity. For example in Britain, *The Sun* supported Woodward, but only in the context of her being a 'girl', infantilized to show her vulnerability and innocence. Woodward was written and bound as an object rather than a subject, and therefore was regarded to be unaccountable for her own actions.

Schuetz (1994) supports this idea in her examination of women on trial. She shows how women have been subject to similar kinds of legal and cultural interpretation that have focused on their gender. From accusations of witchcraft to crimes of passion, Schuetz illustrates how a woman's motive for enacting a crime is overwritten by a discourse that sees her in relation to a constructed role as woman. Thus, against Woodward's vulnerability, Deborah Eappen is then perversely written in terms of her relationship to the home, or rather her desertion of it. Regardless of the fact that the Eappens were mourning the death of their son, the key facet latched onto by the watching media was that of Deborah Eappen's role as a working mother. According to this interpretation of the media's representation of Deborah Eappen, as with many representations of womanhood, she was understood against the norms of a society that generally writes woman as victim. This image of the fragile female – which allocates women the subjective role that the media capitalizes on in order to legitimate dominant patriarchal hierarchies – did not fit Eappen's role as a working person. As such, she was criticized for her transgressions of the role of traditional mother. Thus, to re-order the integrity of the familial institution it was Deborah Eappen that had to be disciplined and re-coded in line with the dictates of the dominant ideology, e.g. during the court proceedings it was explained how she only worked three days a week and fed her new baby with breast milk.

Woodward was also reconstituted into the dominant sphere by Judge Zobel, who excused her behaviour as childish and immature, rather than malicious or murderous: 'I am permitted to believe that the circumstances in which Defendant acted were characterized by confusion, inexperience, frustration, immaturity and some anger, but not malice (in the legal sense) supporting a conviction for second-degree-murder' (Commonwealth v Woodward). After the media had stepped in to reassert the dominance of the social system's central ideological beliefs (i.e. those of its middle-class audience) by condemning Woodward against the model for the ideal middle-class family (the Eappens), the law had to intervene so as not to leave the situation unresolved. The law could not convict a white, western subject and thus disrupt the ideological centrality of that category of subjectivity. According to this logic Woodward was representative of an unstable scapegoat. Her white subjectivity meant that she evaded the status of safe sacrifice. For this reason she had to be sacrificed symbolically, rather than actually. This is a contrast to the status of Manjit Basuta who, because of her racial subjectivity, could be safely sacrificed at the level of actuality: she was imprisoned. Arguably, beneath this ideological complex the forgotten element of the discourse of patriarchal social organization became that of child abuse. This aspect of violence, which often remains hidden, is far easier to expose when a stranger is the perpetrator. This is because the notion of the abuser as alien evades the issue of violence within the family. Against the idea of stranger danger, the exposure of a case of family abuse is a threat that may undermine the family-values lobby and its picture of the perfect American middle-class dream.

However, this issue of abuse, which revolves around ideas of strangers and family members, is context specific. Therefore, while Woodward remained an alien to the model of the American family, she was very much an insider who was being prosecuted by an alien power to the British media. This debate, which turns off Woodward's shifting position (America/outsider, Britain/insider) within a matrix of international relations, might have been conditioned by America's history as a colony of Britain. In other words, the response of the British press to Woodward's plight might have been determined by its attitude to American justice as a pale imitation of the British legal system as law of the motherland. In light of this one can perhaps now understand why Woodward's situation changed once she arrived back in Britain. At this point, her role as a cipher for a critique of American justice was spent and she reverted to the imaginary position reserved for criminals and outlaws. In part this alteration was dramatized by the response to Woodward's *Panorama* interview. Against the image of the innocent child in America, the *Panorama* interview displayed Woodward as a produced image, an independent woman. Upon her return to Britain, therefore, Woodward became representative of woman, a change that was re-coded in terms of the idea of the calculating criminal. Press coverage criticized her attempts to manage both her televisual image and media questions as evidence of her calculating nature, and exposed her parents' apparent mismanagement of the 'Free Louise Woodward Campaign' funds. In this event the interpretation of justice is determined by structural issues that go beyond the ideas of legal objectivity, i.e. guilt or innocence.

Chapter Three

The Scapegoat Mechanism

By examining the ideological implications of the media spectacle in the previous chapter, I have gone some way to explaining the intersection between reality on the one hand, and its re-ordered representation on the other. In order to further understand how fact, speculation, sensation and opinion merge and mutate to form a mythical event that reinforces dominant structural formations, I now want to address the theoretical perspectives advanced by Freud and Girard. Using these two thinkers I will argue that the death of Matthew Eappen was the *originary event* that triggered the hostile response to both Louise Woodward and Deborah Eappen, and resulted in the media's disregard for Sunil Eappen. In the last two chapters I uncovered narratives of familial fragmentation and domestic labour, and discussed the mass media's contribution toward shaping public sphere knowledge in terms of dominant patriarchal ideology. Here I want to link these two explanations by introducing Girard's (1996) model of mimetic desire and Freud's version of the scapegoat myth advanced in *Totem and Taboo* (1950/1994). Through a discussion of these two perspectives the figure of the father as emblematic of the law of patriarchal society will be explored.

In this chapter, then, I argue that it was a political and social climate hostile toward, and anxious about, the collapse of family values that allowed such a sensationalistic response to develop in the public sphere. In her *Panorama* interview Woodward called herself a scapegoat, landed with a murder charge because circumstances dictated that someone must be to blame for a child's unexplained death. Beyond Girard's general theory of crowd law, I believe that a dim recognition of the scapegoat mechanism also occurs when individuals come up against the power of mass media attention and the mythical re-ordering of events that this process entails. Girard's (1986) model of the skandalon (or scapegoating process) states that an innocent victim must always suffer the consequences of collective violence to redeem a society of its ills. By creating a sacrificial figure to absorb the hostility of the collective (against the perceived threat of the moment), the dominant social order is able to diffuse mob violence that would otherwise inevitably become redirected toward authority.

Similarly, the argument provided in *Totem and Taboo*, where Freud explains that in the originary scene the father-leader is killed by his sons in an act of jealousy and resentment of his absolute position, offers an understanding of the law based on a model of sacrifice. Freud's Oedipal interpretation of the scapegoat myth as law or taboo sees the brothers fighting in unity against their father in order to secure a share of power against the overarching domination of the father-leader. Based on the idea of the primal scene, Freud's psycho-sexual theory (the Oedipus complex) shows how in much the same way that the brothers kill the father to secure possession of his harem, the male child always desires his mother against the law of the father. In his theory of the Oedipus complex Freud explains how the father prohibits the son access to the mother. In this regard the mother becomes taboo while the father becomes the totemic figure of the law. As Lacan (1977) shows, the master signifier, the paternal 'No!', becomes the symbol that founds the legal system, or the 'Name-of-the-Father' (Boothby, 1991). From *Totem and Taboo* one can, therefore, see how the death of the father becomes the foundation for new law. Girard understands this originary murder as the obscenity of sacrificial violence that is encrypted at the law's very foundation. In this version of the originary, or primal scene, the sons/brothers are representative of a society that has recognized the oppression of total dominance. For this reason incest is banned and intra-group conflict is resolved. However, the brothers also realize that the act of murdering their father was a violent expression of hatred that founds their new law on oppression and murder. Their guilt leads to the persistence of the father as totemic figure of the law. The law's suggestion is that this (murder) can never happen again.

In order to further overcome the appearance of their unjust actions, the sons/brothers also invent a story (the scapegoat myth) to attempt to justify their parricide. In the story the brothers tell to themselves, the father was killed by a lone hero rather than a mob. The effect of this foundational myth is to lessen the violence of the social system by projecting its aggression onto a singular saviour. The creation of the hero leads to both the ideology of individualism and the creation of a scapegoat, which can stand in for social ills when required. When Girard reads Freud he argues that the hero and the scapegoat are two sides of one character. The scapegoat, Freud's father, is initially a villain. However, post-mortem, the patriarch's ghost founds the law. Similarly, the hero starts out as rebel who over-turns the tyranny of the father, only to become murderer after the foundation of the legal system. In this regard, Girard's figure of the scapegoat, who is both villain (as evil contaminant) and hero (body that founds new social order), embodies Freud's father/rebel couple in one person.

Following Freud's thesis one can argue that the death of the father was a prehistoric miscarriage of justice. The popularity of the ideology of individualism in capitalism provides evidence that scapegoat mythology, which began with the primal scene, still sits at the heart of the contemporary legal system (Žižek, 1998). This can be seen by the way society still blames individuals for structural events. The individual becomes the murderous exception, as described by the idea of Woodward as a child-killer. For this reason one can argue that contemporary society is still concerned to accept the brothers' version of events whereby the evil father was killed by a lone hero rather than a murderous mob. While this thesis may appear to be purely speculative, Freud argues that the reality of this originary miscarriage of justice still exists in the contemporary unconscious. The concept of the unconscious, the seat of humanity's destructive impulses, allows us to understand why sacrifice is required. To bind society together, to live as social beings, humans must project and focus their anti-social desires on a single victim or sacrifice. The scapegoat dies so that everybody might live as social beings.

However, the institutional hypocrisy of sacrifice resides in the fact that the social order also understands that sacrifice is, and must remain, illegal and unjust according to the myth of the lawful society that we continue to believe. In light of this, we can now understand why the excavation of any miscarriage of justice threatens to uncover the necessary violence of the law/society as dramatized by Freud's analysis of prehistoric murder. Following both Freud and Girard, the psychoanalytic criminologist Renata Salecl (1993) identifies the primordial murder as the event that organizes social morality:

> This myth offers a way for the individual to imagine his relation to law and the ultimate congruence between the authority of the law and the authority of symbolic order. Each criminal act undermines the founding prohibition of the law and thereby questions the very principle of legality (Salecl, 1993: 8).

For Freud, the legal system is built upon the repressed knowledge of the violence of the primal scene. As such, the law contains an element of lawlessness. As I have discussed in previous chapters, this lawlessness is hidden by a particular form of mythology that seeks to hide the violence that sits at the foundation of the law. Moreover this image of the law projects a perfect version of justice. It is this imaginary construction that the idea of a miscarriage of justice threatens to undermine. Therefore, where Girard uses examples from historical literature and myth, such as the crucifixion of Christ and the massacre of Jews during the plague, to account for this scapegoat mechanism, Freud discusses regulation from a psychoanalytic anthropological perspective. In an attempt to extend these two positions, I will interpret the idea of the scapegoat mechanism through a reading of media representations. That is to say that I understand the views of the media as a modern-day indicator of social and moral unity (and conversely perversion). In other words, I believe that the media acts as a technology that creates the idea of the hero/villain and preserves the *concept* of a lawful society.

In order to clarify the relationship between Freud and Girard one can refer to the way in which each approaches the object of desire in the triangular model between mother, father and son. In both of these models the mother is the object of desire and the source of conflict between father and son. According to Freud's interpretation of the Oedipal drama from *Totem and Taboo* (Figure 3.1), the son must kill the father in order to possess the mother. The father is the stumbling block that stands between desire and possession. Girard, on the other hand, believes that Freud was mistaken to abandon his 'mimetic intuition' (1996: 227) in favour of a model that refers to sexual desire over social identification. In other words, although Freud identifies the presence and importance of recognition in his case studies – a boy takes his father as ego-ideal – his thesis remains structured around the desire to gain possession of the mother.[1] Conversely, Girard states that although the mother is presented as the object of desire, and the reason for conflict between father and son, her true role is to justify the intra-familial conflict. Girard

---

[1] Girard uses Freud's *Group Psychology and the Analysis of the Ego* (1953-66) to discuss this point.

believes that the mother is not the actual source of antagonism or sexual want. Instead he argues that the true source of conflict lies in the mimetic relationship between father and son (Figure 3.2). In other words, the son does not actually desire the mother, or want to possess her, but rather wants to be his father – to have the power that the father possesses. The mother is, therefore, transcendental, an empty signifier of what it is to *be* 'Father' (the mother is other to father's self). Whereas for Freud the object (mother) is the cause for desire, for Girard the model indicates a more complex articulation of conflictual social relations whereby the object is only ever of secondary importance (Girard, 1996).

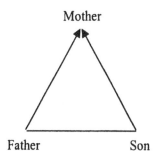

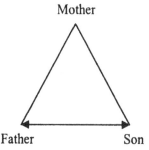

Figure 3.1 Freud's model of the Oedipus complex

Figure 3.2 Girard's model of mimetic desire

In his model of mimetic rivalry, Girard explains the function of deviance by deconstructing historical events in the context of the social climate in which they were articulated. Through these descriptions he shows how the scapegoat (the hero/villain) is made the other, sacrificed for the benefit of the greater community. Once the sacrifice has been made the community, whose cohesion was at stake, can form a collective identity that ex-communicates the person, who now becomes deviant because their presence reminds society about the violent foundation of the law. Later, the sacrifice is rehabilitated as saviour of society and the historical image of the society of the past is condemned for its failure to achieve the moral security of the society of the present. However, this process serves a more powerful function than merely easing the collective conscience of the community. It must also reflect the moral ambiguities that have allowed the disjuncture to occur, and therefore act as a warning sign to others. Here the scapegoat mechanism serves a dual function. First, it creates an arena of individual persecution that exonerates the wider community from blame by stopping the spread of further moral panic or social disruption. This represents the argument for individual agency over social breakdown. Second it also exposes a wider problem related to the situation. As I will argue later, exposing children to murderous outsiders (in this case the au pair) allows a patriarchal system to put in question a society that allows mothers to work outside the home and risk the breakdown of the family institution. In this respect scapegoating targets an individual who becomes a cipher for the expression of social problems.

Mimetic Desire in the Familial Structure

Reading both Freud's and Girard's models of individual and social conflict against the case of the Eappen family and Louise Woodward, it becomes easier to understand how an actual or perceived act of violence serves to unite society around an unethical foundation of sacrifice and scapegoating. Considering the mass media as the mechanism by which events become subject to reinterpretation in terms of the function of the skandalon (scapegoat mechanism as scandal), I have shown how theories of communication suggest that the media distorts reality in a way that renders its content less important than its form. In other words, watching the trial on the television, or reading about it in the newspapers, does not mean that people are engaging in socio-political discourse according to their own specific fragmented identity – an idea put forward by postmodern theorists such as Lyotard. Instead, this process imposes a structure upon events, which organizes the reader's or viewer's perception of events. According to both Freud's and Girard's models of desire/rivalry, the media form turned Matthew Eappen into the primary object. The adoption of the role of primary object locates the child as empty signifier in order to justify Woodward's (as hero/villain) specular treatment by the media and thus obscure the underlying, structural, politics of violence. Interpreting this case through Girard's ethical reading of the scapegoat (scapegoat as victim of social violence, rather than as perpetrator of social ills), reveals how the media process unravels against a history of violence toward the other – the other being the person sacrificed so that the status quo can be maintained without undue damage to the institutions that replicate the symbolic social order. Of course the actual events of the case can be interpreted in many alternative ways. The purpose of imposing the model to the unfortunate circumstances is to reveal the mythologyzing function that the contemporary mass media plays in stories of deviance. As Girard shows through his own reinterpretation of historical stories, the model could indeed illustrate any contemporary tale of scandal or intrigue.

To examine what happened in the Woodward episode through Girard's theory of the scapegoat, involves an understanding of how his idea of the mimetic triangle works in relation to the chain of events of the case. Mimetic means to imitate but, as I have already discussed, Girard uses the term to reflect the conflictual aspect of desire/rivalry. He states that mimetic desire/rivalry enacts itself in all cases of persecution, the culmination of which must be either the actual or symbolic death of the victim. We already know that the victim is a surrogate for the actual source of conflict: 'Mimetism is a source of continual conflict. By making one man's desire into a replica of another man's desire, it invariably leads to rivalry; and rivalry in turn transforms desire into violence' (Girard, 1979: 169). By adapting abstract theory to a contemporary scapegoat story, Figure 3.3 shows that the rival in the Woodward case is Matthew's mother, Deborah Eappen, who has been usurped by the 'child-woman' who steps into her nurturing role in the family. In terms of his role as patriarch, Matthew's father, Sunil Eappen, is made uncomfortable by this situation because his wife, the person who should hold the nurturing role, no longer represents the maternal figure. The violation of the patriarchal role castrates the father. In effect he becomes superfluous, an appendage to the mother (as father), nanny (as surrogate mother) and son (as transcendental object of desire) triangular relationship. In this way the case highlights a situation whereby the patriarchal figure is made impotent by the mimetic desire/rivalry between surrogate mother, mother and child. As contaminant of the proper nuclear family, Woodward's presence reminds the mother, as well as the exiled father, of her proper role. It is this tension, I argue, that invites conflict/revenge.

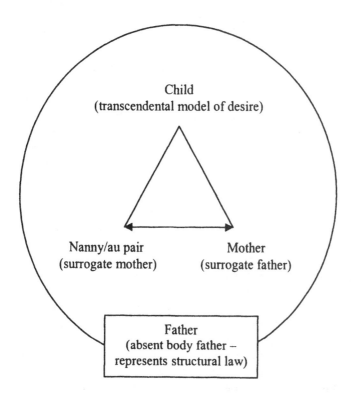

Figure 3.3 Mimetic desire/rivalry in the postmodern family

To explain how mimetic theory unravels, one can clarify the positions of all the players in terms of Girard's scapegoat mechanism. In the first instance, we can identify the mimetic rivals, Nanny and Mother, who are the hero and villain of the piece. These two are in a relationship of mimetic desire; they desire each other's roles. Their roles are interchangeable because, according to the triangular model, the nanny, or surrogate mother, wants to be the mother/wife proper. Conflict arises because Deborah Eappen, or the surrogate father, also wants to maintain her proper role, as the mother/wife, despite her patriarchal move. Contrary to Freud's interpretation of the model of desire, the role and *not* the person, is the key to the rivalous relationship. From Freud's point of view, Matthew Eappen would become the object of desire and consequently the basis for rivalry between the two women.

However, the death of Matthew exposes the true nature of the mimetic relationship between Deborah Eappen and Louise Woodward, which is premised solely upon their rivalry over the familial position of the other. It is important to note that, in this scenario, Deborah Eappen sustains more power than Woodward because she is a double rival: rival to Woodward, who has taken over her job as mother, and rival to Sunil Eappen, because she makes his role as father-leader superfluous. The implementation of the scapegoat mechanism resolves both these positions. By sacrificing Woodward, society is able to supply a suitable scapegoat for the foundational murder and provide an effective critique of working mothers. The sacrifice pushes Woodward out of the picture and opens the way for a discourse aimed at shifting Deborah and Sunil Eappen back towards their proper mother/father roles.

Because Matthew Eappen represents the transcendental object of desire for both rivals (he deflects their true desire), he provides the mediation that sustains the integrity of the relationship in the mimetic triangle. Here, the true mother/wife equals the hero, and the nanny equals the villain. However, this position remains fixed only until the scapegoat mechanism takes over and the roles collapse to reveal their interchangeability.[2] Woodward is transformed into a figure of abject scrutiny. All the elements required for sacrifice are present: Woodward becomes the 'pseudo-individual' who is at once the same as everyone else, but different, elevated above the rest of us. This function exaggerates her evil-doing by turning her into the monstrous other (Boorstin, 1961/1987). However, Girard's theory shows that the scapgoat is both guilty and innocent. True to this perspective, Woodward can be seen as both the reason for death and rebirth.[3] She is the catalyst that renews family unity (re-binding the structurally correct family) by striking at its heart. This explains how the transcendental object of desire, 'little Matthew', acts as a catalyst for the desiring relationship between the two rivals (Louise and Deborah). He shows each woman what they want to (what they must) be, namely a loving caretaker. It is Matthew's death, therefore, that throws the situation into chaos and undermines the law of the family.

Girard's model of the mimetic relationship between the scapegoat, rival, and transcendental model of desire, might now be expanded to reveal how the absent patriarch is fed back into the familial triangle. This necessity is, of course, the actual trigger for violent breakdown and media exposure. Transformed into a remainder (that is, an appendage to the necessary family structure) Sunil Eappen had to be restored to the family system to ensure the reproduction of symbolic authority in the home. In this respect, the death of the child creates the catalyst needed in order to accuse the inferior mother/wife rival of murder in terms of mimetic theory. The key function of this event is its re-stabilization of Sunil Eappen's position as patriarch.

---

[2] To explain this point we can refer to the way that the media articulated dual positions for both Woodward and Eappen. They were presented at the same time as both good and evil: Woodward as child killer/victim of middle-class exploitation – Eappen as bad mother/wronged mother.

[3] This point refers to the birth of the Eappen's third child a year after the death of Matthew.

In order to explain this mechanism, Kelly Oliver (1997) says that the power of the father is based on an idea of the father as a leader/authority figure prescribed by nature. Against the father, the mother is understood as an anti-social body. According to psychoanalytic theory, the idea of primary identification and separation insists that the child's relationship with its mother must be broken off because it is anti-social, and replaced with an acceptable form of social identification: the law of the father. Referring back to Freud's notion of the Oedipal conflict, the child's problematic relationship with its mother forms the basis for the incest taboo. In other words, the child's pre-Oedipal love for its mother must be interrupted in order to re-locate its desire in terms of social acceptability. The first form of censure is the father's 'No!'. Dad disciplines (castrates) the child in terms of structural authority/law. When the father says 'No!', the child is forced to find external social replacements for the mother. In other words, the child has to find a surrogate for the desired mother-love. It is precisely because the incest taboo forbids intra-familial desire that mother-love must be reconstituted through another person: object choice. Once socialized by the threat of the father's 'No!', the child repeats the process instigated by the father. In the world of the symbolic order, the subject finds an object that recalls the mother, reproduces the child, and censures the new child's access to mother. It is clear how this process reinforces existing family structure as image of law. As an example of this link between family and law, Oliver states that family values campaigns seek to restate the law of the father in the face of changing patterns of postmodern fragmentation signposted by such factors as women's employment and single-parent families.

The flaw in the structural formation of society is uncovered by the understanding that the father's power is dependant on its promise. When fear fails ('wait 'til you father gets home'), the execution of power proves its impotence. There are of course many instances of literal violence by the father/law, but these extreme incidents only illustrate the impotence of the authority figure. When violence becomes necessary to uphold the law, the legitimacy of the ruling order is over. Oliver shows how this situation presents a paradoxical position that exposes the inadequacy of paternal authority. She explains that 'even when he is present in the lives of his children, the father is present as an abstraction; his body is merely the representative of abstract authority or law' (1997: 5). The father's 'natural' leadership qualities (his powerful body) are understood to be the foundation of his dominance. However, when the physical threat of the father's body is replaced by legal abstraction, the father becomes symbolic authority. In other words, law becomes language. At this point the father's power is conceptual. And because it is conceptual it is of utmost importance that people believe in it. If/when people stop believing in the threat of violence, the father's power has gone, the law crumbles, and society becomes state of nature. When the police or army become involved the state disciplines through coercion, rather than abstract right. At this point, might is right and legal legitimacy holds no water.

Consequently, media myths on (paternal) authority are bound up with asking people to believe in the natural order of the law in the face of fragmenting social relations. This is how the media rehabilitates the father. That is to say that spectacles surrounding events such as the Woodward case assert the idea of the father's (i.e. the father as representative of structural authority) power by scandalising the delinquent role of the mother. Here, the Woodward case provides an example of maternal threat to structural authority. Against this problem, the working mother becomes the sign that must be sacrificed and re-ordered in terms of dominant ideology in order to re-establish the father as the authority figure. Furthermore, this process allows the father to return to his role as absent, but powerful patriarch (this process is demonstrated in Table 3.1, which shows how scapegoat theory unravels in terms of key events in the case).

Table 3.1 Relationship between Woodward case and model of mimetic desire

Chronology of Events	Relationship to Mimetic Desire
4 February 1997 Louise Woodward makes a call to the emergency services saying that 8½-month-old Matthew Eappen is having difficulty breathing and is unresponsive.	*Exposure* The breakdown of the nuclear family is revealed. The surrogate mother's failure to fit into the structure allows patriarchal order to be re-established.
9 February 1997 Matthew Eappen dies in hospital from a brain haemorrhage. "Shaken Baby Syndrome" is immediately suspected to have caused his injuries.	*Absent child* Matthew Eappen becomes the transcendental model of desire when he is removed from the mimetic triangle. His death reveals the breakdown in the familial structure.
In the following days Louise Woodward is questioned by police and admits to lightly shaking Matthew in order to resuscitate him. She is arrested and charged with murder.	*Scapegoating* The failure of the western middle-class family must be limited. A scapegoat is found to take the blame. The media, as mythmaker, creates the tension required for the condition of persecution.
6 October 1997 Woodward pleaded not guilty to the murder of Matthew Eappen at the pre-trial hearing in March and bail was denied. Trial by jury now begins with her already having spent 279 days in prison.	*Persecution* Woodward's time in prison adds to the idea of the corrupt system. This function permits the media to be seen as a just forum for debate.
15 October 1997 Deborah Eappen testifies. She tells the court about Woodward's late nights and unreliable behaviour.	*True mother disciplined* Her failure revealed, Deborah Eappen is re-ordered as the structurally correct wife/mother.

16 October 1997 Sunil Eappen testifies. He states that Woodward "hated" them for being so strict with her and thought that their children were "spoilt brats".

True father re-established Exposed as a remainder to the mimetic triangle, Sunil Eappen returns upon the expulsion of the intruder who has corrupted the family structure.

23 October 1997 Louise Woodward testifies. She states that she may have been "a little rough" with Matthew in an attempt to get him to respond to her.

Confession The trial provides the forum for Woodward to confess. It also re-presents her as corrupt, i.e. as an inferior wife/mother substitute.

30 October 1997 The jury finds Woodward guilty of second-degree-murder. She breaks down in court proclaiming her innocence, crying, "I didn't do anything... Why did they do that to me?" The verdict carries a life sentence of 15 to 20 years.

Sacrifice As a woman and as a foreigner, Woodward provides the perfect sacrifice in a tragedy that reveals the breakdown of family values in contemporary western societies.

10 November 1997 Judge Hiller B. Zobel overturns the guilty verdict reducing it to involuntary manslaughter and the sentence to time served. He states that her actions did not amount to the "rage or malice" required to secure a murder conviction, rather the evidence pointed to "confusion, fright, and bad judgement".

Atonement Now re-ordered by a disciplinary mechanism, Woodward is freed the abject/object of a just society. Her ordeal serves as a reminder about the dangers inherent in the corruption of the correct family structure.

Against such a reading, it is clear that when Louise Woodward entered the Eappen family home and adopted the duties of mother/wife, she had already entered a structure of instability created by the wider social condition of women leaving the family home to go to work. However, her ability to be all things (mother and provider) gave Deborah Eappen greater agency within the familial structure than Sunil Eappen who, as absent father, was pushed out of the system. Woodward's presence, therefore, did not threaten him directly, but sparked off the process that led to his redundancy. This domino effect created a situation whereby the nanny and mother were rivals for the child. They became undifferentiated and anxious about their roles. It is this instability that helped to produce the monstrous event of the child's death. It was only at this point that the father could re-enter the structure to reconstitute the public family. As a consequence, Woodward was made a scapegoat for Matthew Eappen's death. Thus, we should see the foundational murder as both the death of the child and the symbolic death (sacrifice) of Woodward. The death of Matthew offered the media a smokescreen, or an imaginary projection, for what was really happening – the expulsion of the surrogate mother from the familial triangle. Later, Matthew was reinvented as the transcendental model of desire because his role in the equation was only ever of secondary importance against the mimetic mother/nanny rivalry.

Of course the violent expenditure of the child is not endemic to the familial situation. In the case of families that employ a traditional home-worker (in other words women who occupy a low position in the racialized, gendered socio-economic system) the need to re-order the family structure is never demanded. It is only because Woodward over-coded the care-taker role that a violent resolution was required in the first place. This process was illustrated by the media's reaction to Woodward when the case first appeared. She was portrayed as the 'British Nanny' rather than au pair (the role she was actually employed to carry out). Woodward's white western status elevated her low-paid position beyond that of the traditional Filipina or South American home-worker, not only in the reality of the situation, but also in the perception of the public who were to take part in the ensuing persecution. Woodward's increased status (to nanny) provided the media and its audience with the opportunity to consider her equal to the Eappens and equal to the job that, as an au pair, she was under-trained to perform. Because of the perception of her equal status to the Eappens, Woodward could be considered to provide the replacement mother-love required by Oedipal law. This was particularly the case for the older son. However, entering the family home as surrogate mother to a pre-Oedipal child, meant that to all intents and purposes Woodward was his actual mother. For Deborah Eappen this meant that she was a rival for his desire, or rather what his desire symbolized, to be a good mother. But the death of Matthew exposed both Woodward's alien position inside the family, and her inadequacy as a true-mother replacement. As a consequence, her doubly debased mother status made her an obvious sacrifice. Woodward was expended in order to allow Deborah Eappen back into her true-mother role.

From this reading we can see that Woodward's role as mimetic rival posed a problem for the patriarchal family. Although the rivalry is resolved by the death of the male child, the event disrupts the dominant social order. For instance, as Engels (1987) shows, capital is passed via the male heir. Consequently, Woodward's crime equals more than just murder. Because she over-steps the primary order, her crime is also about the disruption of the capitalist system of father/son transference. This theory, which allows us to understand the capitalist structure in terms of the Freudian law of the father, shows that patriarchal society demands that the roles of men are prioritized over those of women. For example, today many employers still maintain unequal pay structures assuming that men are the main breadwinners of the family, or that women will be unable to commit to long-term company life because of an innate desire to have a family (Folbre, 1994). According to this, sexual discrimination is based upon the patriarchal authority that governs all areas of society. From this point of view the Woodward case highlights the reorganization of an apparently liberal family around the oppression of patriarchal authority. In addition to this the process of familial reorganization was underscored by the public sphere response that called for a sacrificial offering in exchange for the death of a child.

The Function of the Scapegoat in Democratic Systems

Read through a model of mimetic desire, it can be understood that the Eappens' youngest son is the sacrifice that underwrites the public mechanism of its media representation. Matthew was the secondary scapegoat expended to allow Woodward to be consumed and the family to be re-ordered. The death of Matthew Eappen supplemented the media in its function as a family myth-maker and became the catalyst for the unfurling symbol of familial breakdown. In other words, once a serious family misadventure forced itself into the public gaze, its excess was mopped up by outside forces in order to limit the damage done to the mythic image of the family. Girard explains that such expenditure is required whenever it looks as though societal breakdown might result in moral panic. The crisis, however, is not only imaginary:

> We are aware of the imaginary element, but it is the very specific imagination of people who crave violence. As a result, among the textual representations there is a mutual confirmation. This correspondence can only be explained by one hypothesis. The text we are reading has its roots in a real persecution described from the perspective of the persecutors. The perspective is inevitably deceptive since the persecutors are convinced that their violence is justified, they consider themselves judges, and therefore they must have guilty victims, yet their perspective is to some degree reliable, for the certainty of being right encourages them to hide nothing of their massacres (Girard, 1986: 6).

In the Woodward/Eappen case, the persecution and sacrifice of both the Eappens' son and Louise Woodward feeds upon a real and ongoing fear about the breakdown of the nuclear family. The Eappens were publicly articulated as bad parents for exposing their children to danger and their private identity was sacrificed to stop it happening again. Furthermore, Woodward was sacrificed by a disciplinary mechanism that needed to remove the remainder to the family structure. The postmodern condition of the fragmented family structure created a tension that had to be broken. The end result was produced through the 'collective appetite for violence' (Girard, 1996: 126). In Girard's terms a myth is cultivated in order to drive a wedge between 'them' and 'us'. This antagonism serves a society determined to maintain order. In other words, a social problem must seem to be an anomaly that ought to be eliminated to avoid anarchy: the ends justify the means. People are anxious about social problems that appear to stem from the breakdown of family values and the failing moral unity cultivated through the myth of the American nuclear family. Divorce, single-parent families, step-families, and child abuse are seen as the *cause* of greater social ills such as poor mental health, poverty, criminality, and violence.

It is here that the scapegoat mechanism comes into action. In order to legitimate the irrationality of people's fears, which in turn legitimates the law/authority, a scapegoat is needed to function as villain: a fictional device to feed the unfettered broadcast of conjecture and prejudice. The necessity here is to regulate the outcome of any such reporting – an object of guilt must be found. In this case Louise Woodward provided the perfect sacrifice because of her role as outsider – both as foreigner and woman. The historical and political theory which relates to this situation explains that violence toward woman has indicated her status as other whenever she transgresses her prescribed role in the dominant order. She is always inferior to man. Therefore, the function of the scapegoating process becomes one that finds woman the abject object of social discipline. Here, her deviance represents her transgressive nature within a patriarchal society. Nature becomes a symbol with which to degrade femininity. Young explains that it is easy to see women as hysterical, even murderous, against the male norm of objectivity. She argues that women are discursively bound by the symbolic order because 'the belief in the natural origins of the inferiority of Woman is one of the columns which supports the masculine economy of signification' (1996: 33).

Problematizing this position, however, Cynthia Willett (1995) explains that in the past influential theoretical perspectives have supported the idea that woman lacks against man because her social relationships may be determined by her body relation with her child. The dominance of man, on the other hand, is sustained by the myth of the 'man from nowhere'. This theory has been idealized by writers such as Nietzsche (1961) to show how man functions independently in the world. In political terms this abstract man is the perfect capitalist individual because he seems to come from nowhere. The man from nowhere has no ties that bind him to any particular time or place. From the feminist perspective, the meaning of this mythology is to deny women the power of generation. By asserting that once man gains independence from the mother-child relationship (i.e. he has been castrated by his father and thus socialized in terms of culture), he becomes both creator and performer of his own destiny. This is against woman, whose biological tie with her child (symbolized by the umbilical cord) provokes an impression of dependence. Regarding this point, Oliver (1997) notes that the medical gaze (outlined in Foucault's *The Birth of the Clinic* [1973/1993]) acts to reduce the importance of the maternal body in relation to its reproductive qualities. Oliver argues that this gaze constructs women as passive containers 'that exists for the sake of the "unborn child"' who is seen as the 'active subject of its own gestation and birth' (1997:13). However, while the unborn child is understood through reference to its own subjectivity, the maternal body that harbours it is subject to social and biological regulation.[4] The effect of this belief is to sustain the dominance of patriarchal ideology.

From my reading of the Woodward case it is clear that the paternal model of society is violated when Deborah Eappen leaves the domestic sphere in order to enter the individualistic arena of paid work. Here, the woman who gave birth cuts ties with the child herself. Capitalism then asks her to become a virtual man. From Oliver's perspective, one can argue that although this move into paid employment appears to refer to Hegel's master/slave narrative (where the master is crippled by

---

[4] We can understand this point in terms of how an unborn child's development is medically monitored continually throughout a woman's pregnancy, with the woman's health assessed as a means to the child's good progress. Medical advice is backed up by social indicators that discourage women from drinking and smoking whilst pregnant.

the fact that he already occupies the best possible position, while the slave can still strive to attain the master's position), the male/female dialectic cannot be said to constitute female emancipation. This is because the master/slave narrative finds both actors performing within culture; in other words, the patriarchal sphere. Typically, woman's work is already defined outside this economy; therefore, she cannot enter the public sphere on an equal footing to men.[5] Oliver points out that 'whereas the slave triumphs through his work and preserves the mastery of the master, woman's work leaves her nowhere' (ibid: 38). Instead, she argues that women are defined by their place in the unconscious (the body, emotions), against the masculine conscious (language), and that their being outside culture 'threatens to destroy man and the community' (ibid: 39). This is because they are un-familiar or, to use Freud's term, uncanny. To overcome this problem, Oliver explains that women have been tied to culture through the social structure of the family. Thus, the function of the family is to bind woman to paternal law.

Consequently, when Deborah Eappen left the private sphere in search of economic independence she was bound to replace the maternal role with a surrogate nurturer. Woodward entered the domestic sphere to perform the role of caregiver, but because she had no primal relation to the children the care she gave was also tied to the economy. Like Deborah Eappen, she too entered the social system as a virtual man. But in order to avoid fracturing the paternal model of society both women had to be made different from men in some way. This is where the myth of the hysterical woman came into play. For Foucault the gaze on the body has the effect of writing the other in terms of abnormality. The myths created about the other always relate to body differences. For example, when a woman is angry or upset she becomes hysterical. Her hysteria is then blamed on bodily influences that are contained by medical discourse. Examples of this process include tags such as PMS. Arguably such discursive constructions are used as an excuse to demonstrate that women are unstable and unreliable. They are used as a reason to subjugate women (Young, 1996).

Capitalism is paradoxical in this respect. It demands more labour power and does not care who performs it. However, social order requires some form of patriarchal, racial, or class stratification. The demands of capitalism threaten the social order by disrupting systems of power stratification. In this regard the job of the social order becomes about holding back the revolutionary nature of capitalism (Deleuze and Guattari, 1984). I have already considered the way myths (particularly those articulated through the contemporary mass media) create this unequal stratification through ideology. By this I mean to show how media technologies might act to re-order society against the dynamic mechanisms of capitalism. Dominant ideology can now be understood in terms of the paternal model of subjugation (the father's 'No!') through which we are all raised to maturity. In other words, the social order, which attempts to control the disruptive forces of capitalism, becomes an extension of the father's prohibitive speech act

---

[5] When a woman enters the public sphere of work she transgresses her 'feminine' role. In other words she is required to lose the attributes that bind her to womanhood and become a virtual man in order to successfully compete.

against the child's desire to return to its mother, an imperative we might identify with the pure drives of capitalist production/consumption (Deleuze and Guattari, 1984).

Contrary to this position, which would see the child's primal desire for the mother as anti-social, Willett (1995) maintains that the mother-child relationship is the primary social relationship. Against the Hegelian model of recognition, which instructs that the mother-child bond should be broken in order for the child to become a proper social being, Willett argues that the 'maternal turn' provides an ethical alternative to the trap of the self/other dialectic. Explaining that this model is exclusionary because it predicates the rational/social over the emotional/body, Willet finds Hegel's version of rationality phallocentric. The maternal ethic, on the other hand, suggests that a social system based on body relations (i.e. nurturing) would be more inclusive. It would be able to resist the phallocentric order because it would revolve around the figure of woman as mother. However, the key problem with Willett's attempt to reassert maternal sociability is that she fails to consider the Oedipus complex which underpins Lacan's idea of the symbolic order. She ignores Freud's notion of the mother as site of un-differentiation to argue instead that she has a social relationship with her child based on primary recognition. Reading this mechanism through Julia Kristeva's discussion of the pre-Oedipal stage, Willett attempts to locate the infant's primary sociability in the pre-linguistic space of movement, or as she describes it 'music and dance'. For both Oliver and Willett the mother's body is the principal site for infant development because it is the foundation for the child's recognition that the whole body is a container of both good and bad parts: the primary model for society. Oliver explains:

> ...culture and language are not instituted through the father's castration threats...but through the introjection of the good and bad mother and father. The mother is not associated with anti-social nature; rather, the mother-infant relationship is the prototypical social relationship (Oliver, 1997: 57).

In this attempt to locate primary social relations in the maternal body rather than the paternal symbol, both Oliver and Willett explore the possibility that the problem of negative socialization can be circumvented. Willett, for example, argues that the mirror stage, described by Lacan as the primary moment of self-alienation of the child, is actually anti-social because it always relies on reflection of the self. It is, therefore, a narcissistic basis for sociability. Against this anti-social self-reflection, she explains that the mother-child relationship is properly social because it involves two people. Although Willett's argument is founded on an ethics of pre-linguistic communication that attempts to undercut patriarchal structures of language, her argument is flawed because she assumes that Lacan understood the mirror stage as a social relationship. However, Lacan's mirror stage is always anti-social. The child's recognition of itself as other is the first step towards true sociability: the imaginary comes before the symbolic (Lacan, 1977).

Because Willet's thesis remains fixed on the pre-Oedipal stage, defined by Kristeva as a possible space for negotiating human relations based on maternal care, it fails to consider both Lacan's position and the development of the Oedipus complex that goes on to provide an explanation for sociability. Here the Oedipus complex causes a problem for her theory of maternal ethics and shows how her critical reading of Lacan fails to develop a successful alternative model for social relations. One can considers the child's relationship with its mother as exclusive of others until the father substitutes the maternal bonds with the prohibitive "No!" and the child enters the symbolic arena. In other words, the child can form relationships with others who replace its mother. The problem with the maternal ethic stems from its limited application to social communication. The failure of Willett's thesis is exposed if we ask: when would the child become unattached from the mother if it did not go through the mirror stage which encourages sociability (communication with others apart from the mother)? This shows how the father has to function as the link between primal and social. Although this involves alienation, the social order would be unable to function without this state of subjective dislocation. Whereas Willett is concerned to collapse humanity back towards the private sphere of pre-linguistic mother-child relations, the Lacanian theory of progressive alienation allows us to develop a societal ethic at the level of public relations: the ethics of a society which deals with its problems at the political level. Therefore, I believe that Willett reinforces the patriarchal vision of woman as a natural being (outside culture). The flipside of this position is that man remains insulated against political criticism because he is sealed within culture: there is no self/other communication in Willett's thesis because man/woman occupy different social orders. This situation leaves woman in a state of debased sociability: she is unable to speak to man and he has no desire to speak to her. As such, sexual difference remains irreducible. For this reason I believe that we should attempt to raise the status of people to the level of culture. Against Willett, whose argument mirrors postmodern theories that argue against culture and reason as phallocentric,[6] my theory is that these structures can be rehabilitated by making them more inclusive to people who may appear to be trapped in the private sphere. In short a more inclusive public sphere is needed (macro-politics) rather than an expanded private sphere, which turns everything into personal micro-political considerations. As O'Neill (1995) explains in his *Poverty of Postmodernism*, we must save the politics of structure in the name of those people who never entered the higher echelons of modern culture. Against postmodernism and its desire to reduce the importance of public politics, he notes:

> These ideas have not grown up among the masses defeated by the empty hopes of our kind. It is not the masses who have sickened of the injustice and exploitation that grinds their lives, weakens their families, starves their children, murders and terrorises them each hour of the day and night in every corner of the world. No, it

---

[6] Here, one can refer to authors such as Hélène Cixous and Luce Irigary who argue that woman is constructed as other within the phallocentric signifying economy. Within this linguistic turn women have no language or identity of their own other than that which has been constructed on their behalf. To overcome this they argue that women must develop feminine forms of language and culture without submitting to the masculine order (Oliver, 1994).

is not these people who have abandoned idealism, universalism, truth and justice. It is those who already enjoy these things who have denounced them on behalf of the others (O'Neill, 1995: 1).

O'Neill's critique of postmodern downsizing is comparable to Girard's theory of the scapegoat because both authors seek to emphasize the plight of those who are excluded from culture and politics. In her book *Sacrificed Lives*, Martha J. Reineke (1997) attempts to formulate a politics that might save such people from the worst excesses of social and political violence. However, whereas O'Neill argues for the primacy of the social system as a disciplinary matrix, Reineke is concerned to emphasize the free will and agency of the individual, a formula she thinks might reconcile these two positions. From the perspective of O'Neill's argument, Reineke's desire to save the individual can be seen to reproduce the mechanisms of a social structure which binds people to its organisational dictates by interpellating them as free individuals. Reineke explains her reasons for attempting to save the individualism of the scapegoat through a description of socio-political crises. One of her examples is the witch-hunts that swept Europe and America for three centuries during the Middle Ages. In this instance women were persecuted for being outside of the familial structure. Charged with practising witchcraft, they found themselves punished because of their unmarried or childless state. Reineke recognizes that Girard (1986) puts forward a thesis that would expose such violence as being connected to patriarchal anxiety about the ability to maintain control over the economy of reproduction. However, she is critical of his model of the scapegoat for following a theory that collapses difference. Her feminist critique of Girard refers to Kristeva to argue that the model of sacrifice reduces the scapegoat to the level of structural effect. Reineke suggests that this act of objectification then feeds back into a patriarchal economy where the other is emptied of power. But here the focus is once again put upon the scapegoat as the centre of his/her own demise, a premise that merely acts to feed back into the social system by alleviating the tension sustained by the scapegoat mechanism. That is to say that by attempting to critique Girard's sacrificial mechanism and reveal the subject behind the object of persecution (through reference to Kristeva's project of sexual difference[7]) Reineke actually maintains the cycle of mimetic terror. By critiquing Girard's objective – to expose the structural violence toward the other in society – she allows herself to fall back into the trap of victimhood: that the victim's subjectivity is somehow related to their situation as victim. Asserting that we must acknowledge the content of the persecuted, she instead funds a return to oppression and paranoia. Her scapegoat would be plagued by the question: what did I do put myself in this position?

In this regard one might argue that Reineke reconstructs the 'man from nowhere' through her attempts to give the scapegoat some form of agency. The

---

[7] Kristeva's project for sexual difference argues against a single female voice (feminism) in order to avoid setting up an alternative dialectical trap. Instead she attempts to evacuate the lie at the base of patriarchal authority (the Oedipus Complex) in order to extend the margins of society within which we can act out individuality (Oliver, 1994).

problem with this procedure is that it sees the scapegoat apart from the social relations that determine its demise. Like O'Neill, Girard's main objective is to remind us of the primary nature of the social system. This is of course highly suggestive of Foucault's thesis on discipline. Although again criticized for his anti-humanism, Foucault evokes Girard by emphasising that the blame lies at the feet of the persecutory system, rather than those sacrificed in order to secure the integrity of the regulatory mechanism. In *Discipline and Punish* Foucault (1977/1991) shows how judicial discipline has become the preferred system of punishment. Like Girard, who shows how torture can lead to the outbreak of mob violence, Foucault argues that discipline represents a less democratic form of punishment. For example, he argues that public hangings had to be stopped because they provoked incidents of mob violence, criminal events which suggested the outbreak of revolutionary disorder, rather than the social order that the initial hanging was designed to effect. In much the same way, contemporary societies alleviate the tension that can build up at public gatherings by tempering the event through the media lens. Indeed, the need for mass gatherings is decreased by the increasing power of communication technologies and the consequent collapse of the vectors of space and time in the postmodern world.

As Foucault's panopticon watched the criminal body, allowing total recognition, commentators on the postmodern condition such as Baudrillard (1995) show how the mass media disperses the crowd and subjects it to anaesthetized control. Here, the media performs the role of Foucault's panopticon. It watches without allowing the subject of its gaze the opportunity to engage in democratic conversation. Thus, Baudrillard shows how the media creates what Foucault called the docile body. In light of the Woodward case, the docile body refers to the mass audience that witnessed the scapegoat mechanism at work. The media not only considered the possibility of guilt, but also extended an argument for Woodward's innocence, thereby providing the crowd with all the necessary positions. In this way the media shuts down any potential unrest by refusing to allow its audience any kind of open say. In providing its audience with a list of options, it allows no choices other than those possibilities that have been presented and articulated through disciplinary channels. Armed with this list of options (rather than choices) the media audience is then kept in isolation (there is no social contact) by the media technology that feeds the ideology of the dominant social order to the populace. Akin to Foucault's argument, whereby discipline came to the fore because it allowed those in control of power to disperse elements of critique, the media is an agent of social control, rather than democratic free speech. Against authors such as Lyotard, who would suggest that the growing influence of communication technologies can lead to the dispersal of social, economic, and political power to the people, my argument explains how the function of communication technologies is to deny the social organization of the public sphere by keeping people apart from critical debate. From this point of view one can follow Habermas' explanation of rational communication and argue that media communication binds the individual to the dominant regime of power. Further to this idea, the media keeps the citizen's interpretative faculties apart from the resources of critique (i.e. social interaction and debate) by placing him/her in a one-way relationship to communication that presents the image of free debate, but actually simply feeds its viewers a series of ideological versions of reality.

Finally, the Confession

From my examination of the Woodward case it has been revealed that the scapegoat represents an expendable commodity, a symbol of transgression that must be exposed as deviant and pulled back into the regulatory system. Of course this is not to ignore the real feelings of loss and anger inspired by the death of a child that acted as catalyst for Woodward's persecution, but rather to expose the disregard that capitalism holds for its subjects. I am not trying to empty the tragic circumstances marked by the death of a child as Reineke might suggest. What I want to argue instead is that by establishing the victim, rather than the scapegoat, as the primary focus for concern, we can fund a return to ethical discourse that exposes the inequality of the social system. For example, it is easy to understand parents' paranoia about child safety when we live in a society that exposes every minute detail of disturbance and transforms it into a moral panic. But it must also be understood that the purpose of such specular organization is to underscore the necessity for regulatory modes of justice. Here one might argue how in much the same way that cases such as James Bulger's murder or the Denver schoolboy massacre exposed children as monsters – as the signature of a society at the point of collapse – the Woodward/Eappen case persecuted a young woman, not for the death of a child, but for the corruption of the family structure. In this case the media acted as a disciplinary mechanism, turning us all against the scapegoat it had created and whose destruction it called for before any trial had taken place.

Although previous writers in the media, law and order debate (e.g. Ericson, Baranek and Chan, 1991; Hall et al, 1978) show that this process of moral panic, persecution, and increased regulation is ignited at times of social unrest or unnerving change, Girard shows how the scapegoat mechanism must repeat at regular intervals in order to remind society why it needs disciplinary measures in the first place. If these events do not occur, we are in danger of forgetting about the authority of the law. Therefore, the myth constructed to represent the problem also has the equally important function of repeating dominant ideology. As discussed in the previous chapter, the globalising effect of communication technologies acts to perpetuate the frightening image of a pattern of social disorder. In other words, the global technologies of the mass media disperse chaotic images and disrupt socio-political structures on an international level. Frederic Jameson (1991) tells us that this facet of postmodern society necessitates a high level of amnesia. Put another way, because the social order needs its subjects to be regulated, it requires myths of social disorder to circulate as justification for further disciplinary political activity. But because it does not want to invoke excessive moral panic that could lead to further disorder or even revolution, the exposure of such stories must be limited in its critical discursive scope. To explain this process Jameson shows us that one feature of the globalising process is the speeding up of messages across national boundaries. This procedure facilitates the increased movement of information and the excessive revelation of crises to the extent that they might begin to look like an epidemic. To combat this viral infection, each story must be bigger and more sensational than the last. This sensationalism is necessary to counter the effect of the last story and hold the attention of an increasingly indifferent audience. The effect of the spectacularization of news echoes what Baudrillard (1988) calls 'the ecstasy of communication'. The media-produced story never really allows active public involvement, but rather promotes a detached fascination that paradoxically sanctions tighter controls over public democracy. Because we are told that a crisis exists, and that another one is just around the corner, we do not have enough time to debate in depth the pros and cons of any situation. Out of time, we must, therefore, allow a moral arbiter to do so for us. This would suggest that we do not engage in public sphere debate to any great extent, but rather allow the mass media, as agents for the social system, to provide the discursive points of contact for us. According to Jameson this is the paradox of the postmodern condition. The increasing fragmentation that was meant to provide enough discursive space for everyone to articulate their difference actually lessens the possibilities for individual agency because it is bound up with the contraction of time and space.

Nevertheless, through my examination of the Woodward case I have shown how the mass media continue to perpetuate the myth of democratic debate by engaging in national and international quarrels. Even though family structure in the UK now resembles the American family, in Britain America was vilified by the media as monstrous and unjust for imprisoning a young girl for a crime it says she did not commit. In this respect the media created an English martyr, persecuted for the crime of exposing the breakdown of family values in American society. By contrast, in the USA Woodward was presented as a monster nanny. In this way the paranoia around child abuse was related to the infiltrations of the other. Without the other abuse would be seen to derive from parents who do not/cannot look after their own child. In this regard, I understand the Zobel judgement to overturn Woodward's guilty verdict as the point of negotiation between these two conflictual perspectives. Zobel's decision can be regarded as the crux of the scapegoat mechanism because its function was to re-state order. Zobel's judgment could be seen to (1) criticize the fragmenting, postmodern, family, by arguing that mothers should return to the private sphere to care for their children, and (2) return Woodward to her rightful social position, by castrating her as a dangerous surrogate mother and extracting her from the position as place-holder for racial domestic worker that she had occupied as a low-wage au pair. In particular, one might generalize the idea that Zobel's judgement re-stated the patriarchal model of American society by showing how his decision also enacted a settlement between the disparate American and British perspectives on Woodward.

When Woodward broke down in court, Zobel was able to place her as a frightened child, thereby re-ordering American labour, and critiquing the changing nature of the American family. The related effect of this ideological judgment was to excuse Woodward the necessity of being found guilty in any actual sense. At this point Woodward was allowed to return to Britain as a virtual innocent, guilty of causing Matthew Eappen's death, without actually *intending* to commit the crime. The scene of Woodward broken contrasts her initial TV appearance. On trial for second-degree-murder, she appeared almost unconcerned about the situation – an appearance that was heightened by the contrasting expectations of every media consumer. It was only when she broke down following her guilty verdict that public opinion began to waver as to her guilt or innocence and the limited channels for democracy could be opened. Perhaps the Woodward case can now be understood in terms of the history of the public trial, conviction, and finally, confession. It is against a history of the public confession that the accused must breakdown and expose their vulnerability before sympathy can be evoked. Finally broken by the system, the scapegoat is freed, the abject object of a just society.

After American society had been re-ordered by Woodward's confession, she came back to Britain an innocent. However, apart from her function as a cipher through which Britain could augment the supremacy of its own legal system against the power of its post-colonial other, Woodward was no longer seen as an angelic heroine. Although Zobel had freed Woodward, she remained guilty of playing some part in the death of a child. Thus, because she was now free of the shackles of the American legal system, British society could understand the idea of guilt/innocence (that had previously referred to the contest between America and Britain) through Woodward's own double status: she was seen as being innocent, because she had been absolved by Zobel, but guilty because she had (it was assumed) played some part in killing Matthew Eappen. In this regard, Woodward's *Panorama* interview – where she appeared to ape the image of Princess Diana in a way that suggested a cool manipulator of media opportunity – contributed to the feeling that the nanny was no longer wholly innocent.

This interpretation shows Woodward as the central sacrificial figure around which the social system was attempting to resolve interruptions to the patriarchal order, with secondary scapegoats found in Deborah and Sunil Eappen as representatives of the structured nuclear family. A victim-centred discourse would necessarily supersede structural considerations without attempting to isolate the individual from the social, a procedure which would actually fund a return to the politics of exclusion. By examining the Woodward case through a reading of Girard and Freud, I have shown how the legitimation of structural authority through representations of perceived deviance tends to hide the real cause for concern. In other words, child abuse/the death of a child, the victimary event is hidden behind the need to uphold social structure. For the family of Matthew Eappen there was no real explanation for his death, nor did they receive justice, because ultimately they were also victims of the sacrificial mechanism. It was only the social system that triumphed when family unity and the dominant social order were restored.

In accordance with Girard, who seeks to expose the violence supported by the structural system's ability to legitimate its regulatory actions by manipulating people's desire for, and belief in, individual agency, in part two I want to argue for a model of society that exposes the tendency to scapegoat individual actors. To illustrate this point I will reveal how a singular legal intervention negotiated the boundary between public outrage and individual need.

PART II

READING RACISM

Chapter Four

Ethnic Subjectivity and Identity Reformation

When Stephen Lawrence was stabbed on an Eltham street in April 1993, there was little media interest in the story. For the police and press alike he appeared to be just another black teenager involved in street fighting who had unfortunately come off the worse for it. However, several years later there are probably few people left in Britain who remain unaware of Lawrence's name, the circumstances of his murder, and the political maelstrom that followed his parents' search for justice.

The second part of the book reads the Stephen Lawrence case in order to further explore the relationship between media politics and the politics of exclusion. Following my analysis of Louise Woodward's media treatment in part one, in which I showed how the media moved her image from monster nanny to innocent victim, part two undertakes an examination of Lawrence to provide us with the example of the re-ordered black man: the dangerous outsider rehabilitated to fit the image of multicultural Britain. A deconstruction of this specular process will show how from the outset Lawrence (as a cipher for black Britain) was reformed from dangerous black man to disciplined black man, or virtual white man: that is re-packaged for consumption by the middle-English audience. To this end, I discuss how the Lawrence event acted to re-stabilize white Britain's image of itself as tolerant, democratic, and multicultural. Against the image of race riots, which spread across the country in the early and mid 1980s, and the more recent racially charged disturbances partly influenced by British National Party election gains in Oldham and Bradford,[1] the representation of the Lawrence family during much of the 1990s offered an antidote to the idea that Britain might be a racist nation (Holohan and Poole, 2002).

Considering the events surrounding Lawrence's death from the perspective of critical race theory, I want to trace the news media discourse that sympathetically constructed the Lawrence family as the acceptable face of black Britain. I will show how the reporting of Stephen Lawrence as a hardworking student with ambitions to become an architect, together with how his parents Doreen and Neville Lawrence were written as dignified, moral and church-going people, can

---

[1] In the constituency of Oldham West and Royston, the BNP took 16% of the poll during the 2001 general election. In Oldham East and Sadleworth, they took 11% of the poll, and in Burnley they gained 11.25%. However, tension escalated in the run up to the general election due to local by-election results, where, for example in Burnley the BNP won 21% of the vote.

be interpreted through a reading of post-colonial authors such as Frantz Fanon (1952/1986) and Edward Said (1978/1995). Such an argument will reveal how the white centre attempted to overwrite the content of its black subjects with a dualistic discourse that encoded the other as either exotic and dangerous or, conversely, civilized and disciplined. From this perspective one can better understand the unwillingness of British society to admit to both the social and institutional racism of which it was accused in the Macpherson report. That is to say that the just nature of the social order is never seen to be in doubt, but governed by objective, or natural, right. Those who fail to find their place in this order are therefore understood as deviants.

The defence of the just nature of the social structure and the legal order, which institutes the social's values and principles, is represented by the succession of scapegoats that were found to take the blame at every stage of the investigation and inquiry. In each instance, the apparent failure of the legal system, and consequently of the social order, to uphold justice was transferred onto the shoulders of deviant individuals. In the first instance, the five men accused of Lawrence's murder – subsequently named and shamed by the *Daily Mail*, but never actually convicted for the crime – became the recognizable face of peripheral violence. The middle-English press[2] asserted that these men may well have been white, but they were not representative of wider social attitudes. To this end, the men were re-coded as racist 'thugs'. Furthermore, when the inquiry into Stephen Lawrence's death deemed that Britain as a whole held racist attitudes, supplementary scapegoats were found to dispute this critical notion. Additional actors in the case, such as Metropolitan Police Commissioner Sir Paul Condon (who became a singular representative of the law), were sacrificed in order to salvage the innocence of the wider collective. In other words, because it has always been the privilege of the white centre to construct its own identity and to impose meaning onto others, the accusation of intolerance and the challenge to rectify the situation seemed to prompt a 'white backlash'. This response saw the right-wing press lead an assertive defence of Britain as tolerant nation.

The necessity for Britain to insist on its tolerance stems from ideas bound up with the concept of multiculturalism. This idea has seen many different guises over the years. For example, when Britain 'opened its doors' to an ethnic population in the post-war years, racial politics talked of assimilation or integration. The idea was that a migrant to Britain should either adopt the identity and culture of the host nation, or contribute to a diverse Britain by maintaining plural cultural signifiers. In these years colonialism and the British Empire were fresh in public consciousness. White Britain could 'open its doors' precisely because it knew that the new entrants were second-class citizens brought in to fill the jobs that no one else wanted. Together with this necessity, Britain would be safe in the knowledge that generosity to its colonial cousins could not possibly backfire on its own citizens. The idea that white people were somehow naturally more intelligent and better suited to superior jobs discounted the idea that the new immigrant workforce

---

[2] This idea sees the *Daily Mail* as the self appointed voice of Middle England, the idea bound up with centre-ground politics and moral law.

would ever achieve more than their colour allowed (Anthias and Yuval-Davies, 1992).

However, the contemporary notion of multiculturalism has forgotten the imperial origins of its migrant population, and instead promotes a political rhetoric of equal opportunity for all, and intolerance to racist thugs. The 1960s and 1970s civil rights movements, and the politics of successive socialist governments, made sure that Britain would enter an era of ethnic democracy whereby the life chances of all citizens would be equal regardless of their cultural background. This drive for equal opportunities involved raising the standard of living of the ethnic population in relation to the advantages enjoyed by the white majority. In this respect the 1960s and 1970s saw the emergence of socialist ideologies, such as political correctness and positive discrimination. Such ideas sought to elevate the life chances of ethnic minorities by discriminating in their favour. Because it was assumed that discrimination was already occurring in favour of the white majority, ideas such as positive discrimination were used to attempt to organize a more equal multicultural society.

What I will go on to discuss in this chapter is the way that the ideology of social equity advanced by these principles has been eroded during the 1980s and 1990s under the auspices of multiculturalism. I want to show how successive Conservative governments have attempted to jettison the idea of social and racial inequality in favour of a market ethic, which suggests that everybody is equal in the eyes of capitalism. In this regard, the chapter will consider Stephen Lawrence as a privileged site for the battles over hegemony. Whereas the white middle-English press attempted to see Lawrence as a symbol of multicultural Britain's success – Lawrence was understood as a socially mobile black man who had advanced his position via capitalist meritocracy – a more critical perspective would suggest that the reconstruction of Lawrence's alleged murderers as thugs simply replicates the traditional racism of colonial discourse at a different level. Here, the construction of the thugs served to hide the racism of British society and its legal system behind an ideology that advanced the claims of capitalism and its rhetoric of meritocratic individualism through mass media forms. Such a discourse, which claims that inequality resides in the natural abilities or attributes of the individual, enables us to personalize narratives of antagonism, but also serves to hide one of the real causes of conflict: poverty.

With regard to such issues, in this chapter I want to situate the Lawrence case within a theoretical framework that considers articulations of race and ethnicity. I will go on to examine the competing media discourses surrounding the case more closely in chapter five through a discussion of particular media texts. In the final chapter of this section, I try to find a way to understand the Lawrence case as a discursive construction that may be unpacked to reveal the inequalities at work within modern, liberal society. Following this exercise, the final chapter will also read the Macpherson report, which followed the Lawrence inquiry, as a policy document that may suggest a new formulation of multiculturalism that takes into account the subjectivity of 'other' ethnicities.

The Politics of Multiculturalism

According to Stephen Lawrence's friend Duwayne Brooks, the pair were attacked by five or six white men while attempting to catch a bus home on the 22nd April 1993. While Brooks managed to escape from their attackers, Lawrence was caught and stabbed twice, injuries from which he died soon after. Brooks' account of the attack, and his treatment by police officers that night, has been crucial in constructing the subsequent public discourse of racism and incompetence in the Lawrence affair. Both Brooks, and Stephen's parents Doreen and Neville Lawrence, experienced suspicion and prejudice from the police (initially Brooks was treated as a suspect, whilst Doreen and Neville Lawrence's concerns were played down as the ranting of bereaved parents). This led to the sequence of events that has seen Stephen Lawrence become an icon for race relations in Britain. Due to his iconic status, one can refer to the Lawrence case to provide an unnerving reminder that racism does indeed infect all areas of society. Against the backdrop of multicultural politics now embraced by the white centre in Britain – where racism is the sole province of marginal right-wing groups – Lawrence can show how Britain is a nation still cut across by racial antagonisms.

Table 4.1 Chronology of events in the Stephen Lawrence case

Key Dates	Chronology of Events
22 April 1993	Stephen Lawrence dies in Eltham, South-East London after being attacked by 'five or six' white men.
6 May 1993	Doreen and Neville Lawrence meet Nelson Mandela.
7 May – 23 June 1993	Jamie and Neil Acourt, Gary Dobson and David Norris arrested. Neil Acourt is charged with murder. Luke Knight is arrested and charged with murder.
29 July 1993	Crown Prosecution Service drop proceedings against Neil Acourt and Luke Knight because of insufficient evidence to secure a conviction.
15 August 1993	Scotland Yard begin internal review of the investigation. The Barker Review has since been discredited for allocating blame to the Lawrences and their legal representatives.
15 April 1994	After renewed attempts to present the suspects for trial, the CPS again decline to prosecute due to insufficient evidence.

22 April – *29 August 1995*	A year after Stephen's murder, his parents begin a private prosecution. Neil Acourt and Luke Knight are again arrested. The case against Jamie Acourt and David Norris is dropped for lack of evidence. Gary Dobson is charged with murder.
11 September 1995 *– 24 April 1996*	Neil Acourt and Luke Knight are sent for trial. Dobson follows in December. Trial begins at the Old Bailey. Trial collapses after judge rules that identification evidence of Duwayne Brooks was inadmissible.
10 – 13 February *1997*	Inquest reopens headed by Sir Montague Levine. Doreen Lawrence makes a statement saying that the police and judicial system allowed racist murders to go un-solved, stereotyped Stephen as a member of a criminal gang, and lost vital evidence. The Jury returns a verdict of unlawful killing.
14 February 1997	*Daily Mail* front page headline: 'MURDERERS', printed together with pictures of the five suspects. The *Mail* defends its decision suggesting that the suspects should sue if they dare.
December 1997	Police Complaints Authority announces 'significant weaknesses' in the first murder inquiry.
24 March – *13 November 1998*	Public inquiry proceeds under the direction of Sir William Macpherson.
29 June 1998	Members of the Nation of Islam attend inquiry.
24 February 1999	The Stephen Lawrence Inquiry Report published.

Even at the time of Lawrence's murder, the politics of multiculturalism were apparent under John Major's Conservative government. The Tory Prime Minister often spoke of his working-class Brixton roots, his education that did not extend beyond 'O' levels and his belief in a culturally diverse Britain. These sentiments came after years of turbulent race relations under Margaret Thatcher's political leadership. After Thatcher, Major attempted to tie the Conservatives' individualist agenda to the recognition of difference that could advance the equality claims of the ethnic population. The previous eleven years under Thatcher had created an atmosphere of racial tension that had escalated into violence on more than one occasion. Street protests across the country in 1981, and again in 1985, were triggered by a long track record of harassment by the police (Benyon and Solomos,

1987). It was claimed by critics that police had been directing their increased stop and search powers at black communities regardless of crime figures.[3] According to writers such as John Lea and Jock Young (1984), this 'drift to military policing' created a high level of resentment in targeted communities, which rose until it reached boiling point and spilled out onto the streets. Like Hall et al's (1978) analysis of mugging, these 'riots' provided proof of criminality, which once again contributed to a discourse of the dangerous racialized other, to form a self-fulfilling prophecy that saw the victims of police and community harassment enact the violence that legitimated tighter legislative controls that, in turn, hit Britain's black citizens the hardest.

Against this backdrop of socio-political racism, writers such as Stuart Hall and Paul Gilroy wanted to privilege race as a site of political struggle. Arguing from the position that saw race not as a biological category, but as an ideology used by bigots to create and maintain difference, these writers nevertheless wanted to keep race as a discursive reminder of power structures and inequality in Britain. Hall and Jacques (1983) explain this idea in *The Politics of Thatcherism*, when they argue that the political ideology of market forces promoted by the Thatcher administration allowed racism to flourish paradoxically under the discourse of equality. Post-Keynesian Britain, under the influence of the Thatcher-led New Right, adopted an ideology of 'common sense' that sought to flatten the demands of difference under the auspices of individualistic success. In other words, the Conservative government of the 1980s wanted to promote entrepreneurialism as a capitalist ideal, and in this ideology there was no room for anyone who cried foul. In the introduction to their book, Hall and Jacques discuss the ideological erosion of the socialist notion of freedom, which states that the greatest freedom for the individual is bound up with the greatest freedom of society as a whole:

> In their place a new public philosophy has been constructed, rooted in the open affirmation of 'free market values' – the market as the measure of everything – and reactionary 'Victorian' social values – patriarchalism, racism and imperialist nostalgia. The whole shift towards a more authoritarian type of regime has been grounded in the search for 'Order' and the cry for 'Law' which arises among many ordinary people in times of crisis and upheaval – and which has been dovetailed into the imposition of authority from above. There seems little doubt that, in the absence of a credible alternative, this reactionary common sense has made significant headway (Hall and Jacques, 1983: 11).

Unlike socialist principles of freedom, the ideology of Thatcherism stated that the greatest freedom of the individual *is* the greatest freedom of the individual. Society no longer exists. It then follows that because society no longer exists, racism also ceases to matter. This is because racism, like sexism and class inequality, suggests the influence of *social* antagonism. Against these specific, thick, forms of identity, the market economy cuts out the particularities of race, gender and class difference

---

[3] Lea and Young (1984) explain that 'Swamp' 81, was a police operation 'in which over one thousand people were stopped and searched in the central part of Brixton but fewer than one hundred were charged with criminal offences' (cited in Caffrey and Munday, 1995: 266).

in favour of a legal notion of the capitalist citizen. The capitalist citizen is a thin form of empty identity, a construction that possesses rights based around the legalization of desire, but no contextual, or social, attributes (Douzinas, 2000). However, critics of this thin form of legal, or conceptual, identity, such as Douzinas, argue that social identity (i.e. the attributes which revolve around one's social situation) will always return to disrupt the coherence of the socio-political construction of the individual. In terms of those who are interested in naturalising the idea of the individual, the reappearance of social subjectivity serves as evidence that people overflow the legal concept of the citizen. The political effect of this transgression is that market objectivity, and its legal correlate, is threatened by the recognition of social subjectivity that goes beyond abstract notions of institutional justice to refer to theories of natural law. We can say, therefore, that those people who refer to social conditions subvert the institutional category of the individual without attributes. This person is the criminal simply because they disregard institutional law in favour of a wider notion of justice. They disrupt the institution of individualism by asserting their subjective situation and subverting institutional rules. From this point of view it can be argued that the street protestors of the 1980s were aberrant because they did not embrace dominant ideology and dangerous because they were seen as an irrational force of nature that contained the germ of critique against the institution of objectivity.

The riots of the 1980s were seen as an extra-legal force of nature because they relied on expressions of subjectivity, rather than the institution of objectivity. Here, against the violence of the crowd, objective critique is open to those with access to the accepted channels of communication governed by the rules and regulations that structure individualism as an objectification of subjectivity. It is clear, therefore, that Thatcher's construction of urban protest as 'riot' revolved around the necessary defence of the legal ideologies of capitalism and individualism: the market demands the equivalence of its participants, so it must be able to judge people against each other. Like money, the capitalist individual must be reduced to an objective legal (market) value. Within this ideological framework, issues such as the high levels of unemployment experienced under Thatcher's government were re-written as local, or rather individual, concerns. From this point of view, I believe that urban unrest highlights the problems associated with the reduction of the subject to an object of the rational calculations of market value. That is to say that the institutions of capitalism and individualism necessarily legalize the exclusion of those at the bottom of the social hierarchy and exert a western way of understanding the world. In this regard, western capitalism is far from objective. A more accurate description would be to suggest that the institutions of capitalism attempt to naturalize the subjective view of those in power, the dominant group.

Hall et al (1978) remind us that the shift to the right in the late 1970s was engineered by popular consent rather than imposition – the hegemonic mark of the Thatcher administration. As Gramsci (1971) shows, the function of hegemony is to naturalize the view point of the dominant class so that it functions as the world view of the society as a whole. With regard to the critical positions adopted by anti-racism, the Gramscian position is particularly relevant. The critique of the media's function as a tool for engineering social consent on issues such as race allowed authors such as Hall et al and Gilroy (1988) to suggest that the institutions of capitalism and individualism were not actually natural givens, but particular, historical formations. The value of this position was to show that market objectivity is in actuality subjective. This recognition allows us to take social unrest seriously. That is to say that the objections of those outside the capital mainstream become political protests, rather than illegal riots. The claims of poor people, women, and blacks become structural effects, rather than problems of their own making. Therefore, as a political critique of power relations that discriminated against the least advantaged in society, anti-racism provided a way to understand race relations from an alternative discursive standpoint (Mac an Ghaill, 1999).

Attempting to locate the anti-racist struggle, Philip Cohen argues that the progression of theories of racism have taken place from within the parameters of European Enlightenment thinking. As a result contemporary race relations continues to operate from a dominant discursive position in which 'the emancipation of the poor and oppressed is ... made part of a civilizing process, which is often seen to be conditional on assimilating their demands to the discourses of humanism and rationalism' (Cohen, 1992: 71). From this point of view, anti-racist struggle is locked into a double-bind: its strategies of critique are bound up with the very western discursive traditions that made them 'other' in the first place.

However, since the demise of Thatcher's monocultural society and the rise of Blair's multicultural imaginary (Kundnani, 2000), critical anti-racism seems to have been discarded in favour of theories of difference. Whereas the idea of anti-racism relies on a binary structure of argumentation that attacks racism through its opposite (anti-racism), the postmodern theory of multiculturalism seeks to move beyond the idea of self/other opposition to embrace the politics of cultural difference. For this reason the postmodern understanding of race and ethnicity put forward by authors such as Derrida (1978/1995) and Taylor (1994), can be seen to refer to policy adopted by countries such as Canada and Australia in the 1970s. In these countries anti-racism, or multiculturalism, backed the attempt to promote polyethnicity rather than assimilation (Kymlicka, 1995). In this sense multiculturalism meant that migrant settlers could, indeed should, maintain their specific cultural identity, rather than adopt the cultural signifiers of the host nation. This new socio-political agenda insisted upon an ethic that was inclusive of all, and privileged none. No one 'race' or ethnic group could be seen to benefit over another, but rather everyone would gain by merit. Embracing this (American) ideology of mass democracy, multiculturalism suggests that all cultures are equal but different. In this respect multiculturalism can be seen to individualize the traditional understanding of race politics by seeking to break down categories of mass identification. By avoiding a consideration of structural, macro power relations in favour of a consideration of difference, multiculturalism mirrors postmodern politics, such as those advanced by Derrida and Lyotard (1984).

Derrida's (1978/1995; 1998) idea of *différance* suggests that politics should move away from the conflict theories of Marxism, which saw self/other as combatants, towards a politics that replaced the slash (/) of antagonism with channels of communication based upon a mutual recognition of universal difference. As such, Derrida's theory replaces self/other with self–other in order to re-open channels of negotiation and communication. His idea is that we communicate because of our differences rather than in spite of them. Akin to Charles Taylor's (1994) politics of recognition, Derrida argues that we communicate with the other because we recognize our mutual lack of reference to any given conception of universalism. This is the meaning of Derrida's term *différance*. It signifies both simultaneous absence/presence and the eternal nature of humanity as an open mode of communication. In other words, the silent 'a' of *différance* represents the gap, or lack, that allows us to connect with the other people who are comparable, but different, in their understanding of the gap, or lack, that separates them from any totalitarian notion of universal identity. This is Derrida's definition of open communication.

One might see Derrida's politics of difference as the most influential example of postmodern theory. However, other theorists have also followed his post-structural lead by moving away from categories of mass identification towards more microscopic ways of understanding individual identity. For instance against the political landscape of critical/conflict politics of the 1970s, Gilroy's earlier work advanced a neo-Marxist theory of anti-racism. However, his later works, for example the essay 'The End of Antiracism' (1992), and *Black Atlantic* (1993), discard binary oppositions in favour of a differentialist argument that is sympathetic with the postmodern politics of mobile identity construction advanced by authors such as Derrida. Nevertheless, Gilroy continues to recognize the subject of discursive and actual violence:

> The antiracism I am criticizing trivializes the struggle against racism and isolates it from other political antagonisms – from the contradiction between capital and labour, from the battle between men and women. It suggests that racism can be eliminated on its own because it is readily extricable from everything else. Yet, in Britain, 'race' cannot be understood if it is falsely divorced from other political processes or grasped if it is reduced to the effect of these other relations (Gilroy, 1992: 150-151).

In much the same way, Mac an Ghaill (1999) explains that theories of anti-racism provided the political critique for the fight against racism upon which articulations of multiculturalism could build a vision for social futures. Multiculturalism evolved from the recognition that we are all different. This recognition became a criticism of the essentialism of the racist/anti-racist binary, which replicated the binary constructions of race itself, through an emphasis on the atomization of cultural diversity. I would argue that this position is bound up with Hall's (1992a) identification of the myths that show the idea of race as the naturalization of cultural difference. Hall's argument is that in order to successfully create the subject of the nation state, national identities must be formed around what Benedict Anderson (1983) had previously called 'imagined communities'. Here, identity is constructed around a set of shared, or collective, myths about how the nation was formed in order to illicit patriotism and allegiance to that nation. However, the Canadian political theorist Will Kymlicka explains that such shared myths, which are adopted by state institutions as discursive tools for interpellating subjects, also work to separate those that do not adhere to the current rules of nationality:

> Nation-building policies have historically been targeted not only at immigrants, but also at national minorities. National minorities have also been subject to pressures to integrate into the majority's public institutions. While subject to similar pressures, immigrants and national minorities have historically responded in quite different ways. National minorities have resisted integration and fought to maintain or rebuild their own societal culture, while immigrants have accepted the expectation that they will integrate into the dominant societal culture (Kymlicka, 2001: 156).

Against the construction of identity around national myths, which work to exclude those who pursue different cultural practices, multiculturalism puts forward an ideology that embraces difference. For Hall this can be seen in the formation of new identities, or hybridity, where the 'oscillation between Tradition and Translation' (Hall, 1992a: 310) produces new identities peculiar to the time and place in which they occur. In these communities people may remain close to their cultural roots, but also take on characteristics of the place in which they now reside. Hall imagines that this hybrid identity might take on the history and character of several different national and religious cultures that have been thrust together by post-colonial migrations. Multiculturalism thus promotes difference above national identity and its exclusionary structures. In this respect it is also, like postmodernism, against the idea of a unified nation state.

Žižek (1997) criticizes this liberal position when he argues that multiculturalism mirrors the progress of global capitalism at an ideological level. His suggestion is that in much the same way that multiculturalism transgresses national boundaries in favour of hybridity and syncretism, global capitalism breaks down national economies in favour of more cost-effective global considerations (i.e. labour in the third world may be cheaper for a western multi-national company than unionized factory workers in its own country). In this respect Žižek argues that global capitalism has become disengaged from the idea of the nation state. It appears to exist everywhere, yet nowhere. From this point of view it can be said that capitalism adheres to the multicultural ideology of difference. It is happy to treat everybody the same, despite their differences, in pursuit of maximum economic gain. Against the background of an economic system (global capitalism) and a political ideology (multiculturalism) that appear to collapse the polar opposites of difference and sameness into one point of indifference (everybody is different and thus the same: same difference), the rise of fundamentalist forms of identification (race, nation, religion, etc) can be seen as a universal attempt to organize a form of difference that matters as a principle for ordering the world (Holohan and Poole, 2002). Therefore, the rise of fundamentalisms, such as the British nationalist organizations highlighted by the visceral racism of Lawrence's alleged killers, and the visible growth in popularity of National Front politics across Europe, should be understood as attempts to assert a zero-degree notion of national identity.

Imagining the Post-Colonial Subject

Both of the above theories of race and difference have been problematized for being too extreme. Anti-racism has been criticized for standing on an essentialist platform in order to raise the debate about oppression to a political level, while multiculturalism has been seen as having a politically divisive focus on ethnic/cultural difference (Rattansi, 1992). Moreover, authors such as Cohen note that 'the question of individualism raises the issue of whether we are dealing with a 'new racism' or merely an updated version of the old 'race and empire' story' (Cohen, 1992: 93). As a way of developing an understanding of identity as discourse one must, therefore, refer back to authors such as Fanon (1952/1986), Memmi (1957/1990) and Said (1978/1995), who have discussed how the other is written in terms of its relationship to the dominant social order. The value of post-colonial thinking stems from its use as a tool for the deconstruction of the narratives of difference that undermine those people whose subjectivity overflows the parameters of dominant hegemony. In this respect, I want to now look at how post-colonial authors have discussed the construction of the black other (colonized) by the colonizer.

For Fanon the colonial subject takes on the psychology of the colonizer through a process of historicization and epidermalization. Here, the colonial condition is one that alienates the subject from their own language and culture by overwriting it with the heritage of the colonizer. This procedure is then justified through the notion of the civilizing mission, while the colonized's lack of civilization is attributed to racial characteristics that revolve around skin colour. For the indigenous child educated under colonial rule, the culture of the ruler is promoted, while indigenous ways of understanding the world are degraded. The colonial subject, therefore, internalizes a corrupt understanding of themselves which in turn legitimates the rule of the conqueror. Outlining this thesis, Fanon rejects Freud's understanding of the inferiority complex as a pathology that revolves around personal relationships. Fanon argues that Freud's thesis removes the problem of inferiority from its socio-political location and in effect excuses the colonizer/master of any wrong-doing.[4] In order to unpack the negative effects of cultural imperialism, Fanon critiques Mannoni's discussion of the African slaves' dependency complex. Situating his understanding from within western discourse, Mannoni suggests that psychology produces power relations rather than the other way around. In his view, African people have a mental disposition that leaves them open to rule, while Europeans have a more independent psychology. By contrast, Fanon argues that it is power relations that produce the psychological effects of both the dominant and the dominated, and that reproduce existing power relations.

Fanon saw slavery as a relationship that bound both colonizer and colonized to specific social roles. In other words, the master can only exist insofar as the slave supports his position. In this respect Fanon follows Hegel's master/slave narrative, which shows us how the master is reliant on the slave's internalization of his

---

[4] This argument is apparent in narratives of colonial rule. Popular Victorian authors such as Rudyard Kipling explained the civilising mission of the West as the 'white man's burden'.

inferiority to maintain his own superior social status. Of course, Hegel's point was that this inter-subjective inter-dependence also works for the slave. The slave also sees himself in terms of his relationship to the master. While the master is always reliant on the slave remaining a slave to maintain his dominant position, the slave can only aspire to serve the master. In this situation, Hegel tells us that the slave actually has more power than he thinks he has. In terms of Fanon's work, the colonized subject must somehow believe in his natural inferiority in order for this dialectical power relationship to work in the colonizer's favour. According to Fanon, slavery works precisely because the slave takes on the psychological degradation enforced by the master. He believes that his inferior position is somehow related to his specific identity, and he links social advancement to *natural* attributes. Akin to Hegel's slave, or Marx's proletarian, Fanon's colonized subject has internalized the ideology of the dominant culture. This psychology of the conquered – believing their own culture to be inferior and, therefore, their debased social position to be natural – allows the conqueror to legitimate the seizure of the colonized's ground as right over the property of their inferiors.

In *Black Skin, White Masks*, Fanon (1952/1986) explains how colonized people have a debased identity written onto their bodies. Objectified in terms of their skin colour rather than their actions, the person of colour cannot escape the epidermalization of the dominant social group (the white colonizers) without the consent of that same group. In using the term epidermalization Fanon recognizes the importance of skin colour as a marker of the visibility of difference. Following Lacan's re-interpretation of Freud, Fanon argues that the colonized person adopts a persona which is made for them by the colonizer. In this respect Fanon adapts Lacan's notion of the ego, as an imaginary figure, to show how the colonized person is unable to understand their true situation and can only *see*, and understand themselves, in terms of their imaginary identity (Seshadri-Crooks, 2000). From this point of view, the oppression of Fanon's slave is comparable to the sense of misrecognition which haunts Lacan's decentred subject (the slave, like the decentred subject, is always lacking in relation to the ego-ideal), and understand how Fanon's psycho-Marxism parallels the theory of ideology advanced by Althusser. In much the same way that Fanon's slave imagines himself as an *animal* that is naturally inferior to his master, Althusser's subject internalizes the interpellations of the state. He says: 'Ideology is a representation of the *imaginary* relationship of individuals to their real conditions of existence' (1970/1993: 36 – my emphasis).

In this formulation Althusser suggests that the theory of ideology revolves around the confusion between the way people see themselves and their real conditions of existence. For Fanon this would suggest that the colonized begin to understand themselves as worthless. The image of the colonized, given by their rulers, is that of sub-human other. Over-written by the colonizer's viewpoint, the colonized subject becomes a prisoner of his/her own epidermis – black skin – and is tempted to adopt the culture of the colonizer – white mask. The white mask that the colonized person adopts provides the appearance (imaginary) of civilization and conforms to the notion of right advanced by the western culture that has oppressed him/her in the first place. The black subject's success or failure in the new order of colonial society depends on his ability, or willingness, to disown their own culture and take on the ideas of the ruling class. Fanon suggests that the adoption of the colonizer's culture by the colonized takes the form of language. With regard to his own particular context Fanon states:

> In school the children of Martinique are taught to scorn the dialect. One avoids creolisms. Some families completely forbid the use of creole, and mothers ridicule their children for speaking it... In any group of young men in the Antilles, the one who expresses himself well, who has mastered the language, is inordinately feared; keep an eye on that one, he is almost white. In France one says, "he talks like a book." In Martinique, "he talks like a white man" (Fanon, 1952/1986: 20-21).

Following W.E.B. Du Bois' (1903/1994) notion of double-consciousness, Fanon explains that the colonial subject who has been civilized in terms of western culture (i.e. a university education in the 'mother' country) looks at their black self/heritage as debased. However, Fanon also notes that this procedure only works to the colonized's advantage as long as the colonized remain subservient to the colonizer's position of power. For Fanon, then, there is no neutral position. One is either oppressed or oppressor. When he takes on the identity formations of the dominant group, the colonized becomes part of the native elite.[5] However, as I have shown, the civilized black subject can never fully be part of the dominant group due to their skin colour. Instead double alienation takes hold: they remain outside the realm of the master and apart from their own subjugated culture. The construction of the native elite can be understood as being about divide-and-rule strategies of political domination. Following a Marxist line the master turns the slaves against each other, which in turn prevents them from fighting against colonial domination. This tribal warfare is achieved through economic oppression. Lack amongst the colonized peoples provides an antagonistic base for further tribal conflict. Fanon explains that the colonized people are usually too busy fighting each other for scraps to challenge their real enemy – the colonizer. He, therefore, questions the cultural cohesion of displaced people. In other words, if the slave has enough spirit to work for the master, they should be able to muster enough spirit for revolutionary action. Why, then, is this transformation problematic?

Following on from *Black Skin, White Masks*, in *The Wretched of the Earth* Fanon (1961/1990) notes that the disenfranchised fight each other because the real enemy is faceless. Much like the street protestors of Thatcher's Britain, who took out their combined anger on property, the colonial subject of Fanon's writings fails to target the real cause of oppression: the state. Fanon argues that the subject of oppression must escape the *idea* that he/she is inferior to the master, overturn the

---

[5] This is akin to Du Bois' (1994, 1903 and 1999, 1920) critique of African-American leader Booker T. Washington. Washington tried to gain rights for African Americans in the early twentieth century through a strategy that saw black people have to adjust their identity position to the requirements of dominant white society. Du Bois, on the other hand, called for a more oppositional movement, that would see black people demand equal rights in line with their black subjectivity.

psychological degradation of economic and epidermal oppression, and resist the lure to become part of the dominant class. Instead, Fanon's revolutionary manifesto urges colonized people to harness the force of their combined experiences of pain and suffering to form a spirit that can be used against the ruler, rather than *by* him. Hommi Bhabha (1994) explains that this state of emergency – the revolutionary spirit of the oppressed versus the desire of the colonial power to hold onto their stolen territory – is also a state of emergence. In other words, once they are able to challenge the structures of inferiority, the colonized people can begin to emerge from colonial domination and shake the foundations of empire.

Albert Memmi (1957/1990) had much the same idea as Fanon. He wanted to examine the legacy of empire in spite of decolonization in the post-war era. Memmi was particularly interested in the inter-dependence of the colonizer and the colonized as a way of understanding developing social relations. This idea of inter-dependence shows how identity relates to external power relations. Akin to Fanon, who critiques Mannoni's misrecognition of external effects on the psyche, Memmi understands human psychology as a microcosm of external social conditions. This tells us that racial neurosis (or what Fanon calls phobogenesis) undeniably experienced by the racial other, is a consequence of his debased identity being constructed in language and culture *by* the colonizer:

> ... the colonized's mother tongue, that which is sustained by his feelings, emotions and dreams, that in which his tenderness and wonder are expressed, thus that which holds the greatest emotional impact, is precisely the one which is the least valued. It has no stature in the country or in the concert of peoples. If he wants to obtain a job, make a place for himself in the world, he must first bow to the language of his masters (Memmi, 1957/1990: 173).

Memmi's theory of the construction of otherness can be linked to Said's (1978/1995) point on the conceptual nature of the other in western discourse. Said's argument is that the other's role in western discourse is not to identify the conditions of its actual existence, but rather to serve as the negative image of western supremacy. In *Orientalism*, Said discusses the way that the east is constructed in the imagination of the west. However, while discourse analysts, such as Said, argue that we possess an essential identity apart from representation, postmodern authors have tended to refer to psychoanalytic notions of subjectivity to argue that identity *is* representation. Whereas for Said representation simply conditions the way people respond to others in social settings, writers such as Derrida suggest that there is nothing beyond representation. Derrida's suggestion is that identity is absolutely dependent on language and since language is itself never neutral (i.e. it is always cut across by subjective points of view), meaning and identity are never objective constructs that coincide with the reality (or, to use Lacan's term, the real) of the body (Forrester, 1991). Thus, meaning and identity never really represent the *thing* that they aim to represent: that thing remains silent. It can never speak.

Once more this psychoanalytic theory relates to Fanon's understanding of the relationship between the colonizer and the colonized. However, unlike Derrida,

Fanon believes that there is a link between language and identity. He explains that a person's language and culture is an important marker for their past, their history, and their subjectivity. For example, local language can represent who we really are as people. As such, Fanon recognizes that the colonial situation distorts the relationship between self and society. The colonizer recognizes the value of enforcing a strange language and culture upon the colonized subject. That is to say that he attempts to attack the colonized person's identity at the level of culture, reducing it to the level of a joke. Fanon understands this process as one that removes the colonized subject from their first level of identification. They are no longer able to speak in their own language, dress in their own clothes, and they look and feel uncomfortable in their own skin. Derrida would tell us that that these splits in self (whereby the self becomes dislocated) are more about negotiating difference than about being right or wrong (Forrester, 1991). Against Fanon, who holds onto the local as the site of truth and justice, postmodern thought suggests that we can oscillate between our different identities in order to move successfully through the networks of the global society. Fanon would have understood this thesis as one that privileges dominant culture to the detriment of local modes of social organization.

In light of the above discussion, I would argue that the Lawrences were made Middle English by media coverage. Following Fanon, they were given a white mask. In contrast, the white 'thugs' were constructed as other. Here, the accused killers can be regarded as examples of unsuccessful or 'bad' citizens. While the Lawrences successfully negotiated the boundaries of difference, and jettisoned their ethnic subjectivity, the suspects were seen to be fixed within an archaic system of representation. In other words, they came to represent the past because they failed to adapt to (post)modern conceptions of flexible identity formation. Contrary to Fanon's colonial subject, the representations of the Lawrence case contain white men who were made other and turned into a joke. Their refusal to change, to take on the sensibilities of Middle England, allowed them to be subject to abject scrutiny. The culture of the working class from which they came was, therefore, subject to symbolic degradation. In other words, in order to re-code the black man as self (to support the ideology of multiculturalism) and the working-class white man as other (aberration of social system), mass media representations had to attack the subjective identity of the alleged white killers.

A Skin Condition

This examination of post-colonial writing can be used to show how racism can be understood within contemporary social systems. For example, Tzvetan Todorov (2000) explains that racism should be considered on two levels. First, we must consider Fanon's explanation. That is to say that we should see racism as being about the hatred of one ethnic group by another distinct social group. In other words, racism is bound up with the idea of 'race' as a biological category (a skin condition). However, Todorov identifies a second level of racism, which he calls racialism. He explains how racialism is about the construction of identities through culture and language, structures that attach different values to different races. In this respect, Todorov is not trying to suggest that different ethnic groups do not exist, or that all categories of ethnicity are constructed, but that the ideas which are associated with different ethnic groups are related to ideological judgements. These ideological judgements are used as a way of sorting people into a hierarchy of ethnic groups. When this structure is related back to the consideration of post-colonial texts, the hierarchy – and the racialism that stems from its ideological agenda – is always understood from the perspective of the dominant group. Moreover, such representations of ethnicity encode political ideas that are used to maintain the order of social hierarchies: they reproduce themselves through the social order:

> Having established the 'facts,' the racialist draws from them a moral judgement and a political ideal. Thus, the subordination of inferior races or even their elimination can be justified by accumulated knowledge on the subject of race. Here is where racialism rejoins racism: the theory is put into practice (Todorov, 2000: 67).

Akin to Todorov's theory of racialism (the ideology of racism), one can refer back to Said's examination of discourse. For Said, discourse is a method for constructing the other from the perspective of the west. In this argument he explains that the west has no true understanding or recognition of the east. The east (the Orient) is simply understood as a negative projection of the west (the Occident). In this respect, Said's theory tallies with the notion of a slippage, or failure, that occurs between ontological identity and its various representations. That is to say that Said's work suggests that the west's construction of the east's identity does not relate to the actual reality of the east. As such, texts such as *Orientalism* follow the Hegelian theory of inter-subjectivity and its correlative discussion of the master/slave dialectic as an episode in the progression towards absolute spirit. In the instance of inter-subjectivity, the book tells us that in much the same way that the self needs an other in order to recognize itself, one can only understand the Occident in terms of the Orient. However, Said's point is that this recognition never occurs on equal terms. His adaptation of master/slave relations explains that because the west looks at the other from a Eurocentric (egocentric) position, its image of the east is skewed by its totalitarian image of itself as natural right. For Said this modern hubris, which distorts the west's perception and leads it to degrade the other, is the slippage, or misrecognition, that can be found at the root of Orientalism.

   Said's reference to modernity as a totalitarian scheme for the exclusion of otherness is comparable to Foucault's notion of society as a disciplinary institution that controls people by developing an intricate knowledge of them. From the aphorism that knowledge equals power, Foucault (1991) tells us that the person who produces knowledge is also the one who exercises power in the disciplinary society. But this also works the other way around: the person who holds power is the one who produces knowledge in the first place. This is Foucault's theory of the circular nature of power: knowledge equals power, power equals knowledge. Like

Fanon, Foucault also suggests that this kind of knowledge/power relation works on people at a microscopic level: it works on the body through everyday forms and institutions such as education and labour. In other words, discourse is a form of knowledge that writes legal discipline onto the body. Like Kafka's (1992) famous torture machine, which writes the prisoner's crime onto his body or Fanon's slave, who is coated by the knowledge of the colonizer, Foucault's idea of discourse disciplines people at the level of bio-power. Moreover, because bio-power works on the body, it is never a cognitive discipline. In order to discipline the mind one must work on belief. The body requires discipline through action. Therefore, Foucault's idea of discourse is about discipline through movement and the organization of action:

> If one can apply the term *bio-history* to the pressures through which the movement of life and processes of history interfere with one another, one would have to speak of *bio-power* to designate what brought life and its mechanisms into the realm of explicit calculations and made knowledge-power an agent of transformation of human life (Foucault, 1978/1990: 143).

Foucault argues that discipline works in two particular ways. First, at a corporeal level, the state exerts power over the body by implementing rules of dress and action. Second, at a cognitive level, concepts that stem from the visualization of power on the body produce a second layer of disciplinary theory. For Foucault, then, it seems that corporeal discipline, or drill, comes first. Ideology, or cognitive discipline (the knowledge that we must abide by certain rules), must be supported by the performance of those particular rules: the equation is, therefore, one that places performance over cognition. The belief that supports an ideology can be sacrificed so long as the subject performs the activity. In this respect, cynicism forms the root of Foucault's conception of power. We are allowed to disagree with the law as long as we abide by its regulations. In fact from an Althusserian perspective, it is *necessary* that we disbelieve. Our lack of belief provides the image of individualism. We believe that we are individuals because we maintain a distance from ideology and continue to hold this belief while we perform the law's necessary work. This remains the case even though the subjective distance from the law is hard-wired into the law itself as guarantor of belief in individualism. For this reason cynicism pervades the individual's experience of ideology (we follow it even though we do not believe it) and the construction of ideology itself (it contains an element of individual freedom even though this maintains the ideology itself).

Further reference to another modern-day example can illuminate this over-arching logic of cynicism. In chapter three, I considered Baudrillard's (1995) idea that the images of the Gulf War were more real that the actual experience of war. He goes on to explain how people watching the *action*, screened via CNN, were given reality effects that heightened the disciplinary function of war. Viewers were shown pictures of foreign cities being bombed from the birds'-eye perspective of American fighter jets. Other pictures showed Iraqi soldiers sat on the desert floor having surrendered to American troops. Baudrillard's point is that the ideological war was won on television screens, not on battlefields. The actual victory was secondary; what mattered was the performance of the war. The way the war was packaged (as a humanitarian struggle for the integrity of Kuwait) gave Desert Storm its legitimacy. As such, Baudrillard's thesis suggests that the Gulf War was cynical because the actual war was less important than the media effects it was waged to produce. Following this recognition of all-pervasive cynicism, his thesis can be expanded to suggest that singular components of the war were also cynical; for example that the humanitarian struggle masked considerations over oil fields. According to this perspective the representations of the war packaged Desert Storm for a western audience. CNN organized the war from a western point of view. Viewers might not have believed the press, but watched anyway. As the media performed the war, we performed our duty as viewing public.

Following this point it can be said that the west experienced the performance of the war from an American perspective. Fanon understood this necessity when he argued that no matter how far one wants to divorce knowledge from its subjective base, thinking always ends up being about who we are. Looking at the Gulf War from a western perspective, audiences are more likely to identify with British and American soldiers held hostage in Iraq, than with Iraqi civilians killed in night-time bombing raids on Baghdad. Regardless of individual political belief, because discourse works at an affective, corporeal level, viewers identify with the pain of 'fellow westerners'. They are individuals; they remind us of ourselves, while the Iraqis come to represent the mass. While this idea would appear to contradict the empathy that the British public seemed to have with Stephen Lawrence above the white men accused of his murder, if a system of representation that constructs an alternative set of identity markers (i.e. the white 'thugs' as 'not like us', and the Lawrences as 'like us') is applied, one can begin to understand the ease with which the alleged killers were sacrificed in order to save dominant liberal ideology.

Although members of liberal democracies like to think they can objectively identify with the other, the feeling is always bound up with subjectivity. This is Foucault's key point: our minds can be objective, but our bodies are always subjective. When we *feel* something (which acts upon us) it is an entirely subjective experience, and there is no way to communicate the subjective truth of that feeling to an outsider. Foucault teaches us that discourse works on this subjective level. It appeals to who we are, and uses that appeal to overwrite politics. I believe that this point can be related back to my earlier discussion of urban protest under Thatcher's Conservative government. Despite the fact that protestors were enacting their subjective feelings – dissatisfaction with continued police harassment – this was filtered through a media lens that objectified their feelings of being discriminated against as illegitimate. Viewers were encouraged to side with the law which had been attacked by the mass. As such, in the same way that discourse can stimulate feelings of fear and prejudice and cause us to object to the protestors, it can also promote empathy toward the police and legal institutions.

A further analysis of the Lawrence case reveals that the newspaper coverage said one thing (public), but also encouraged the audience to make other connections (private). These private connections worked on an emotional level: they relied on fears and prejudices about mob violence. This point can be developed by looking back at Althusser (1970/1993) and Gramsci (1971). Both authors developed a neo-Marxist account of the state in order to better understand why people consent to ideological manipulation. I have already discussed Althusser's idea that the subject internalizes the ideology of the dominant culture. The key to understanding both Althusser and Gramsci, stems from their questioning of Marx's emphasis on the base (or economy) of society. Building upon Marx's distinction between the base and superstructure, Althusser argues for the existence of two forms of state Apparatus. First, there is the repressive state apparatus. This is made up of the institutions that apply regulations that control our behaviour, i.e. the law and the military. However, he adds a further dimension to repressive control, and that is ideological control, provided by the ideological state apparatus. This is the system of thought that enters our everyday lives, through education, religion, and other forms of public discourse. The important thing to remember here is that one cannot function without the other. Without ideological coercion, law would break down. Like Foucault's docile body, the interpellated subject believes that they possess a germ of free will, even though this flexibility is written into the system itself.

As I have already shown, Hall and Jacques (1983) provide a discussion of this idea in relation to Conservative politics. Referring to Gramsci's notion of hegemony, they tell us that we are bound to the state by means of coercion and consent. Akin to Althusser's two forms of state apparatus, Gramsci's concept of hegemony centres on the twin spheres of political and civil society. However, it is not as simple as saying that political society generates and enforces regulations and obtains consent from the masses by means of coercion from civil institutions. Rather, the notion of consent is worked out at a cultural level that allows us to believe that we have freedom. Moreover, this relationship is always framed by a dialogue between the dominant class and the rest of society. It is set by limits. Choice becomes about deciding between the options that are put in front of the citizen. When we step outside of the limits of capital society, we are immediately re-coded as being outside the system.

Going back to Said, who remarks that 'Orientalism depends for its strategy on this flexible *positional* superiority' (1978/1995: 7), it can be understood how notions of ethnic identity are formed from within the hegemonic structure. Said's point is that mass media institutions – newspapers, film, television – saturate our view of ethnicity. He argues that these cultural institutions produce texts which allow wider society to organize its own perceptions of ethnicity. There may, of course, be disagreement of particular representations, but this will change (as subject of negotiation) until a more acceptable representation is found within the discursive limits maintained by the dominant social order. In the case of Lawrence, Said's theory allows one to argue that the media served the needs of the hegemonic order of liberal democracy. According to this example, his argument would allow us to suggest that multicultural Britain needed to re-code black people as Middle English in order to support the liberal ideologies of equality and meritocracy. In this respect, the media's treatment of the Lawrence case allowed the black man to enter into the social, but only insofar as he was able to adopt dominant social codes of liberalism: social mobility through education, advancement through hard work, and socialization through the correct organization of the nuclear family. However, as my analysis of the Lawrence representations in the next chapter will show, the rehabilitation of the black man to produce ideological stability necessarily led to a further expulsion. That is to say that the entry of the civilized black into society necessitated the expulsion on an un-civilized other from the social. In this respect the 'white thugs' accused of Stephen's murder (who represent the failure of education, work, and family) became the others who could be demonized for the sake of the wider social order. As such, representations change to enforce the ideological hegemony of society. In the instance of the Lawrence murder, the positions of black and white man switch to support the demands of social order.

Hall (1992b) unites these propositions in his essay 'The West and The Rest: Discourse and Power'. Arguing that the west is a concept, he shows how the kinds of oppositions that I have examined in relation to the Lawrence case relate to a system of representation. Hall develops this idea following Saussure, who says that language works through oppositions. Saussure argues that words have no meaning outside the wider system that contains them. But like the societies where language is located, the symbolic system is mobile and open to change. To explain this point we can say that identity is constructed within language. As I have shown, identity is built upon an oppositional paradigm that encodes its subjects as either self or other. Hall's key point is that the west is also a concept, a world view, constructed within this model. It is not about geography, but more about understanding the world through an oppositional lens. This is precisely the function of ideology: to organize identity around these oppositions. However, in constructing our own identity through such discursive procedures we necessarily degrade that of the other. For example, Said tells us that when western explorers 'discovered' the Orient, they were struck by its lack of civilization against western standards. This of course failed to recognize different organizational structures, but nevertheless set the standard by which the west understood the east. It is this relationship of lack (the east lacks) that continues to structure representations of ethnic identity in western discourse. As the following chapter will show, the relationship between the characters in the Lawrence story revolves around their identity within, and difference from, the standard of liberal democracy: otherness is defined by the character's relation to this ideological ideal. In this regard, chapter five seeks to advance the present theoretical survey by illuminating how theories of identification and otherness relate to the specific discourse generated by Lawrence's murder.

Chapter Five

The Violence of Discourse

One could argue that the case of Stephen Lawrence, which unfolded over much of the 1990s, uncovered the early stages of a new political trend that countered the anti-black rhetoric prevalent in popular media discourse during the 1980s. Over this period it appeared to become outmoded to discuss the issue of crime in relation to the 'problem' of ethnicity. A changing political landscape marked first by the resignation of Thatcher as Conservative leader and then by the transition from Major's diluted conservatism to Blair's 'new' socialism seemed to signal a new era of racial and cultural acceptance. Under Thatcher's governance Britain's racism had remained largely unchecked. The last chapter examined how popular political discourse and subsequent legislation encouraged the view that Britain's ethnic minorities were the cause of urban trouble. According to theoretical debates that emerged in response to these conditions, such as Pearson's (1983) examination of Thatcherite policy and polemic, such an ideological viewpoint upheld the notion that Britain's white population was somehow naturally law abiding. To support these prejudicial beliefs commentators made damaging proclamations through media channels. Making clear connections between race and crime, statements such as: 'Brixton is the tip of the crisis of ethnic criminality which is not Britain's fault – except in the sense that her rulers quite unnecessarily imported it' (Peregrine Worsthorne, *The Sunday Telegraph*, 29 November 1981, cited in Pearson, 1983: 228) were common in the British press, and underscored the acceptance of an exclusionary racist ideology. Recently there appears to have been a shift in the public's acceptance of this racist rhetoric. Against the backdrop of multiculturalism, it is my assertion that British politics required a new scapegoat that could serve as the essential other to the identity of the multi-ethnic nation.

In order to locate the tension between race and place, the last chapter introduced the idea of racist discourse to show how the ethnic other is contained within a particular set of ideological representations. In this chapter I want to show how these ideas relate more specifically to examples taken from the news media's representation of Stephen Lawrence and his dialectical opponents – the five white men accused of his murder. Through an examination of the way that Lawrence was constructed by the white majority press, this chapter will show how he was re-coded to fit into an existing discursive framework, based on the colonizer/ colonized system of representation. Subsequent representational coding – of his parents, the police, the accused killers, and the legal system embodied by Sir William Macpherson – also functioned to fund a return to dominant hegemonic standards. In other words, Lawrence acted as an empty signifier upon which a reformulated idea of multicultural Britain could be written without actually disrupting any of the signifying practices of contemporary Western society. In this respect the *Daily Mail* performed a facilitating role. That is to say that in order for the white British centre to be seen as tolerant and fair, the case had to be articulated through an inverted system of representation. Here, I will examine this symbolic reversal and locate each position in light of existing discursive practices.

Blacks in the News

If it had not been for the three words, "What? What? Nigger!", shouted by his assailants just before they attacked, perhaps Stephen Lawrence would have remained an anonymous victim of the kind of violence that is seen on our streets every day. However, these words made visible the racism behind the act, which in turn triggered the very public campaign for justice by the Lawrence family, black rights groups, and perversely a newspaper at the core of right-wing media in this country: the *Daily Mail*. The reason for the *Mail*'s interest is more than likely to be found in the sympathetic characteristics of the Lawrence family. According to Cathcart (2000), most of the national press and local London radio and television broadcasters ran news of Lawrence's murder in the days following the incident; however, the story failed to pick up any momentum. From the outset Lawrence's parents, and representatives from newly formed black rights group the Anti-Racist Alliance (ARA), felt that the lack of interest, by police, public and media, was conditioned by covert racism.

The Anti-Racist Alliance[1] was contacted by a member of the Lawrence family upon hearing of Stephen's death and the racially motivated circumstances under which it had occurred. The organization was initially brought in to help deal with the police and also provide access to advice on legal rights issues. However, wise to the problems faced by ethnic families in dealings with the authorities, they instigated a campaign that would give the case maximum exposure, together with maximum sympathy. Later accused of interfering in the relationship between the Lawrences and the police, and manipulating the media in a way that jeopardized the investigation, the ARA would claim that their strategy was designed to gain justice for the victim, rather than appease the authorities. Indeed, one of the reasons that Doreen and Neville Lawrence took the unusual action of contacting the national press was because they felt aggrieved by the lack of police concern over their son's death. Mindful of the police reputation for dealing with racist attacks in the area and the general apathy, if not prejudice, toward ethnic minorities in the press, they sought to challenge the racist order in order to gain justice for their son.

Stephen Lawrence's death came at a time when police relations were strained in an area of South-East London where there had been a number of racially motivated attacks. Two years earlier, in 1991, two young black men, Rolan Adams

---

[1] This black rights umbrella group was set up in 1992. Its aim was to provide expert help by tapping into a network of black professionals who could assist people through what was regarded as a racist legal system (Cathcart, 2000).

and Orville Blair, had been murdered in two separate incidents of what were eventually to be branded racist attacks. Only a year before Stephen's death another murder took place. This time a young Asian man, Rohit Duggal, was killed after a fight between two groups of youths escalated (Cathcart, 2000). After such events, the murder of Stephen Lawrence became the focal point of a particular type of crime that appeared to be a mounting problem in the local area. However, his murder also struck upon a growing national concern about the increasingly strained relations between ethnic groups in locations throughout the country.

Antagonism between different ethnic groups has been a central concern of race relations in Britain for many years. Poverty, urban degradation, and poor employment prospects have contributed to hostility between whites and blacks; a feeling which has been seized upon and magnified by far-right groups. For fundamentalist groups such as the British National Party, ethnic minorities are seen to be the cause of tensions between culturally distinct community members simply because they inhabit the same space as white people. But in addition to the racist ideology promoted by extreme right-wing organizations, the wider populace often consents to the idea that certain social problems are the responsibility of migrant subjects. This consensus is often supported by biased news reporting channelled through sections of the national press.

In the last chapter I discussed how Gilroy (1987) tried to develop a theory of anti-racism against the hard-line politics of Thatcher's new right. However, unlike many anti-racist strategies of the time, which sought to essentialize different racial traits, Gilroy's brand of anti-racism identified a lack of recognition as the main source of antagonism between national, ethnic and religious groups. He highlights this point when he refers to how the national press depicted young black men in the 1980s. Gilroy's examination reveals a trend in the press to sustain historically stereotypical images of ethnic cultures. In stark contrast to the national culture in which they reside, the ethnic other is constructed in terms of behavioural components which make them exceptionally different from white British people. Examples can be found in the attention paid to the culture of Rastafarians. The obvious differences contained in Rastafarian culture, i.e. in visible codes such as dreadlocks, or sub-cultural codes like pot-smoking, become signifiers for *all* black people. Gilroy's example of the 1985 news story about Rastafarian Everton Samuels, who was put on trial for possessing cannabis, is indicative of the 'evidence' harnessed by the media via the law, in order to scapegoat an entire ethnic culture:

> Samuels's laziness, his drug use, his hat, his locks, his insolence and the later revelation that, two weeks earlier, he had been bound over for two years on the charge of possessing a flick knife, are articulated by his blackness. They become a powerful signifier not just of black criminality, though the folk grammar of common-sense racism would recognize them immediately as the proof of black difference, but of black culture as a whole (Gilroy, 1987: 73-74).

What is more, Gilroy explains how these discursive connections were recognized by the Judge, who told Samuels that his 'manner merely feeds the prejudice of those people who think that anybody who is coloured is automatically unfit to be a member of society' (Gilroy, 1987: 73). The Judge's notion that the figure of the black criminal serves as a synecdoche for the pathological nature of their wider ethnic group exposes the racism of society when it is set against the treatment of the white outlaw who is regarded as the exception to the rule of white legality. Against such a discursive strait-jacket, Gilroy's argument was that the anti-racist lobby needed to recognize that by adopting similar essentialist codes, they were merely repeating the racism of white society. In other words, he recognized that the same discursive mechanisms can be used for both freeing and limiting identity formation.

There is, of course, no reason to link black identity and criminality. As Gilroy asserts such a link has not always existed. Instead, disparate identity constructs have been drawn together in times of national uncertainty to create imaginary identities. For example, the moral panics surrounding black criminality, and the subsequent tightening of laws that affected black communities in the 1980s, can be linked to the anxiety felt by British society about the outbreak of the Falklands War. In this instance, Britain closed ranks against the Argentineans, who were portrayed as devious and unscrupulous in their claim upon, and invasion of, the British outpost island (Hobsbawn, 1987). Similarly, Hall et al (1978) note that Britain's moral panic about black criminality in the late 1970s was akin to America's anxiety about the 'problem' of race in the 1950s and 1960s. In the American example the panic surrounding black criminality expressed the fear generated by the Cold War stand-off with the Soviet Union. Following this logic of anxiety and its expressions, Hall et al argue that in Britain the moral panic about the new crime of mugging was a Tory response to the 'winter of discontent'. This anxious period was contributed to by trade union action, economic downturn, and rising unemployment under Callaghan's Labour government; conditions which led to the Conservatives 1979 election victory. Although Britain continued to suffer from socio-economic problems (such as high unemployment) under the new Thatcher government, Conservative rhetoric managed the situation by promoting a law and order discourse that put the blame on the most socially and economically deprived sections of the community. However, because the Tories superficially promoted an ideology of equality, sections of the community frequently differentiated by colour and class were pulled together under the shared experience of (being out of) work. Such deviant subjects were then blamed for their own lack of success as other members of society began to prosper (Benyon, 1999).

Arguably, Britain's discursive manipulation of moral values mirrored that of American politics during the McCarthy era. The main drive of this period of American history was to produce the idea of the 'enemy within' in order to create an atmosphere of paranoia among the 'silent majority' of citizens. The idea was to direct people toward suspicion of their neighbours by insisting that danger lurked behind every closed door. Outwardly this occurred in response to global instability and the threat of communist invasion after the Second World War. But America's response was actually fed by a fear of internal revolution: one that it felt would largely be led by African-Americans, who were still being openly discriminated against, particularly in southern states. The answer to this concern was to 'unite'

America against a common enemy (the communist threat), and to scapegoat any member of the community who differentiated themselves by asserting their political independence (Rogin, 1988).

The force behind this process was, of course, the rise of the American civil rights movement, championed by, on the one hand, the advocates of peaceful social change such as Martin Luther King Jr, and on the other by Malcolm X, who characterized the radical face of the black rights movement. Influenced by Islamic teachings, Malcolm X provided the antagonistic alternative to the student movement – and this was the symbol of violent revolution that the state feared. According to Ronald N. Jacobs (2000), the law and order theme carried by news coverage of the Watts uprising in 1965[2] grouped all black protagonists together (albeit differentiated by degrees of moral and social inclusion/exclusion) in order to manufacture a unifying exclusionary discourse. Although Jacobs identifies several competing discourses – some, from the (black) liberal press, showing understanding of the problems faced by ethnic minorities that led to their uprising, others, from (white) conservative publications, condemning the fighting as the actions of violent 'hoodlums' – the message implicit in every commentary on the riots drew on an exclusionary discursive binary. The following quote from the mainstream news coverage denotes the way that the white majority saw any antagonism (peaceful or otherwise) from the African-American community as a threat to dominant moral order:

It [the rioting] is very much likelier to happen so long as the nation coddles the teachings of the Mario Savios and the Martin Luther Kings, and their disciples who, seeking an honourable motivation for the exercise of their anarchic instincts, walk away from the bloodshed they have caused citing the liturgy of a black mass, which excuses on some ground or other their heinous deeds (*Los Angeles Times*, 20.08.65: B6, cited in Jacobs, 2000: 59).

Similarly, in the following extract from the African-American press, the Watts uprising remained tied to the deeds of the black community. Adopting the law and order hegemony, violence, they argued, only acted to diminish their larger political cause:

It is imperative that leaders and lieutenants of the civil rights groups of the Nation make special efforts to restrain the violence which is surging in many communities. We understand and sympathize with the pent-up frustrations which issue in demonstrations and protests, but we vigorously denounce and categorically disapprove of violent and senseless attacks upon persons and property. Lawless and irresponsible behaviour beclouds the objectives of the civil rights movement, besmirches the image created by those who have made sacrifices of liberty and even life, and surrenders to the very evils of mob rule and

---

[2] The Watts (Los Angeles) riots of 1965 were said to be sparked by a drink-drive incident after a black driver was pulled over by police officers. This relatively minor incident (there was no clear report of what happened) was eventually attributed to poor race relations in the USA (Jacobs, 2000).

injustice we all deplore (*Chicago Defender*, 14.08.65: A1, cited in Jacobs, 2000: 65).

In this regard the advocates of peaceful process were cut off from the riotous demonstrations of the violent periphery. When it is seen to challenge the power of the dominant social order, mob-rule or mass hysteria, is understood to corrupt the political cause rather than act as the frustrated voice of the excluded. This is opposed to forms of mass action that reinforce the social values demanded by the need to maintain law and order, such as those seen in moral crusades against black criminality. This point is identified by Lawrence Bobo (1997) when he talks about the way the negative representation of black people by news organizations influences not only media audiences perception of black subjectivity, but also affects policy-making decisions. For example, Bobo argues that negative stereotypes of black people, such as laziness or low moral standards, find their way into the political process with the aid of mass media forms that make the connection between 'laziness' and unemployment, or 'low moral standards' and single-parent families living on welfare. Such manufactured connections highlight the relationship of discourse to law and order and allow for public indignation to affect how real social problems are dealt with. As such, Bobo considers that political motives play upon people's fears in order to make structural issues identity-specific. He says: 'race-neutral issues and concerns ... used cynically to mobilize and polarize the mass public on the basis of race and racial prejudice' (Bobo, 1997: 8-9).

Dangerous Others

Such readings of black identity have provided the tools to detect racist discourse. This ideology continues to be played out today with the treatment of black people in the law, politics, and in the media. Linked to the media response of the Stephen Lawrence case by several news sources, such as *The Guardian* and the BBC's Black Britain documentary about Lawrence's murder, *Why Stephen?*, Rolan Adams has provided a valuable example illustrating the contrast and transition between portrayals of 'bad black' and 'good black'. Like Lawrence, fifteen-year-old Adams was a young black man living in the same area of South-East London. Also, like the initial reaction to Lawrence's murder, Adams' death was seen to be the result of what the police called a territorial dispute. In other words, the murder was linked to gang-related street fighting. In truth Adams died after twelve white men shouting 'nigger' attacked him with a knife. Nevertheless, even though Adams' killer was caught and sentenced to life imprisonment for murder,[3] and the motive for his attack was eventually accepted to be racist, Adams never received the same kind of media rehabilitation that Lawrence did. Instead he remained tied to his black (criminal) subjectivity:

---

[3] Three other men involved in the attack were charged with minor public disorder offences and given community service orders.

> When I heard that the police were treating it [Rolan Adams' murder] as a
> territorial dispute and that they were in a gang fight, I knew that justice might be a
> problem here, because I knew from a variety of people that it was definitely racist.
> The perpetrators were known in that area for doing exactly the same as they had
> done to my son (Richard Adams (Rolan Adams' father) speaking on *Why
> Stephen?*, BBC2, 16 February 1999).

One of the reasons for the disparity in treatment between these two victims of racial violence (Adams and Lawrence) lies in the way that the media depicted the cases. On surface appearance there were more similarities than differences between the two teenage victims of racial hatred. However, it was the minor differences that caused the varied media treatment of the cases. Assessment of these minor differences can help us to understand the narratives of inclusion/exclusion that these stories organized. For instance, when it looked as though Adams' killers would not be brought to justice, his father, Richard Adams, instigated a publicity campaign with the help of pressure groups sympathetic to his cause. The campaign focused on the corrupt nature of the police and the racism that was beginning to be seen as a real problem in the London borough of Greenwich. However, it failed to generate support from the mainstream press. In this case the pressure groups in question were regarded to be confrontational. Groups such as the Socialist Workers Party instigated marches to highlight the concerns of black parents in the area, and criticized poor police/race relations that seemed to be contributing to an atmosphere that made ethnic minorities feel unsafe.

For the watching media there were too few recognizable signifiers to exploit in the case of Rolan Adams. His family appeared to be distancing themselves even more from the wider (white) readership of the middle-English press when they adopted the help of black American race relations campaigner Al Sharpton. Sharpton's style was brash: for a British audience he appeared *too* confrontational, *too* accusatory. Conversely, two weeks after Stephen's death, the Lawrences met with Nelson Mandela. Like Martin Luther King, Mandela is recognized as the acceptable face of black struggle. Through his own incarceration at the hands of unjust white power in South Africa, which he was seen to take with dignity and endurance, Mandela was credited with character and stoicism in the face of *real* adversity. In contrast, race relations commentators such as Sharpton are seen to represent 'self-serving' blacks (Entman, 1990: 339), those who have not necessarily suffered physical oppression.

Discussing the portrayal of 'blacks in the news', Robert Entman (1990; 1992) suggests that the contemporary representation of black people remains tied to the same discursive codes invented in order to suppress the other in times of imperial rule. In addition to examining the usual material on white hostility toward ethnic minorities, after seeing media representations of 'black crime' on the news Entman also identifies a further component to modern racism; that of white resentment toward black politics. Arguing that exposure to images of black political leaders stimulates resistance and resentment in white audiences, his examination of news excerpts suggests that the discourse of black power emphasizes black subjectivity. In relation to this point one can see that a difference in presentation styles can influence audience perception. In an attempt to manage white hostility to black politics, Mandela, like King, wanted to work within the boundaries of the existing political system. He believed in political process, that *social justice* would win out, rather than radical black politics that alienated the white majority. In contrast black rights commentators such as Malcolm X or Al Sharpton argue against the very foundations of the existing social system, which is regarded as intrinsically racist, in the name of the black minority.

To describe how black politics is constructed around this set of limited discourses, Entman explains that media institutions are unlikely to report on black interests unless there is some sort of conflict involved. Claiming that news agencies will prioritize an act of aggression or confrontation over one that passes without incident, Entman notes that television stations and the press are prone to encourage this kind of confrontational action because it tallies with their audience's perception of how black people act. However, such representations empty the presentation of any social context by focussing on personal style over political content:

> The emphasis on politics as emotional conflict means that black politicians tend to make the news when they are engaging in conflict. The local stations' news definitions give black leaders an incentive to act confrontationally if they want to get on the air, an incentive that may parallel their image-building needs in the black community [... but] are unlikely to spur support among whites (Entman, 1990: 340-341).

This suggestion is underscored by the representations of the Nation of Islam at the inquiry into the death of Stephen Lawrence. Five years after his murder, the public inquiry chaired by Sir William Macpherson posed an opportunity to expose both the racism that led to Stephen's death, and the racism of the legal institutions involved in the subsequent investigation. However, on the day that the five men accused of his murder were due give testimonies, the Nation of Islam[4] attended the inquiry. Other than the aggressive appearance of the accused killers captured by photographers as they left the inquiry, for the media this was the most confrontational (and overtly political) statement of the inquiry. The next day the national newspapers took the opportunity to provide commentary on the Nation of Islam's presence:

> Calling itself Nation of Islam, this particular group of black supremacists is in many ways the mirror image of the white racism of the National Front, an equally repellent organization (leading article, *Daily Mail*, 30 June 1998).

Here, the *Daily Mail* identifies the fundamentalist 'militant' agenda of the Nation of Islam and draws a direct comparison to extreme right-wing organizations such as the National Front. In a second article on the same day, the *Mail* provides its

---

[4] Headed in the USA by Louis Farrakhan, The Nation of Islam is a black activist group that attributes its fundamentalist ideology to Islamic teachings.

readers with further evidence of the Nation of Islam's deviant agenda. Contrasting the 'self-serving' intentions of the group with the dignity, stoicism and peaceful protest of the Lawrences, Daniel Jeffreys and Stephen Wright give a potted history of the group. In this article readers are painted a picture of a crank organization. For example, we are told that they believe that 'black people originated from the moon and whites are the result of a botched experiment by a mad scientist who bleached their skin' (30 June 1998). Pursuing this line, the article also notes that current leader Louis Farrakhan claimed to have met founder Elijah Muhammed on board a spacecraft. Arguably such observations construct an image of black separatist politics that reduces it to an object of ridicule. This stands in contrast to the way that extreme right-wing politics is represented as an historical entity. In this respect black extremism is made illogical in a way that makes it less comprehensible than white racist groups. However, although Farrakhan and the Nation of Islam are made other through their association with conspiracy theory, their political views are similarly exposed as repellent. Jeffreys and Wright continue:

> Women members are expected to concentrate on housework and child-rearing and must dress modestly, with their heads covered. These strictures are rigidly enforced by Farrakhan, who opposes abortion, condemns welfare as 'subsidising single mothers' and loathes homosexuality (Jeffreys and Wright, *Daily Mail*, 30 June 1998).

In this passage Jeffreys and Wright adopt a typically Orientalist construction of otherness. Interestingly, however, they also accuse the Nation of Islam and its American leader Farrakhan of much the same prejudice as the *Daily Mail* has pursued over years of moral campaigning. The difference between Farrakhan's position and that of the *Daily Mail*, and indeed white extremists, revolves around the manner in which their views are presented. While Farrakhan and the Nation of Islam are referred to conspiracy theory and white extremists are tied to explicit racisms such as Nazism, the *Daily Mail*'s version of hard-line politics is bound up with the notion of 'common sense'. In this way the *Mail* seeks to appropriate the middle ground, the logical position of 'the man in the street' that is itself beyond ideology. In order to situate its own position as objective the *Daily Mail* manipulates the politics of its others. In other words, the *Daily Mail*'s argument associates *all* black politics with the Nation of Islam. Despite the fact that Farrakhan and his followers express a particular form of exclusionary politics, the Nation of Islam is made to stand for the universal category of black politics. This approach can also be seen by Jeffreys and Wright's portrayal of the other black rights groups association with the Lawrences as unwelcome:

> A few weeks after Stephen Lawrence's murder in April 1993, his parents condemned extremists, who, they said, were trying to make political capital out of his death... Their pleas for calm were ignored by radicals determined to find a new cause celebre (Jeffreys and Wright, *Daily Mail*, 30 June 1998).

Here, the authors use the Lawrences' criticism of some groups to collapse black politics into a universal signifier of otherness, regardless of the welcome assistance of by the ARA. By contrast white politics are never collapsed into a universal signifier. The extremism of the National Front, which we are told by the *Mail* is the mirror image of the Nation of Islam, remains an extreme example of politics in general. Whereas one example of black politics is used to exemplify the totalitarianism of a race, the case of the National Front is dismissed as an aberration to the rule of politics in general. This wider category, which turns off the generalization of whiteness so that it represents the marker of non-race, is defined by true universalism, i.e. it is representative of everybody regardless of class, race, or gender. The *Daily Mail*'s strategy, therefore, is to define the black norm (i.e. the extremism of the Nation of Islam equals the political agenda of the ARA) and the white pathology (the individualized extremism of the National Front) in order to situate itself in the neutral middle-ground: that of true universalism, the voice of objective democracy.

A similar process can be discerned in the Rodney King case. In 1992 King was involved in a car chase after he failed to stop on request of the Los Angeles Highway Patrol. By the time King pulled over there were twenty-five Highway Patrol and Los Angeles Police Department officers on the scene. King had already complied with their commands to lie face down on the ground when four of the officers present began to beat him unconscious. The incident was notoriously captured on video by a nearby resident who sent the tape to television stations the following day. Following the incident King was hospitalized with severe injuries to his head and torso. Numerous baton blows and kicks were said to have caused skull fractures, brain damage and kidney damage. The officers involved in the beating were prosecuted but, in the first case, were found innocent (Jacobs, 2000).[5]

Judith Butler's (1993) reading of the incident finds that the police officers' defence lawyers drew on a strategy that aimed to neutralize the law (objectivity) against King, who was re-coded as the dangerous individual. Incredibly, the defence lawyers used the same videotape that had shown the brutality of the police to suggest that it was in fact King who presented the *real* danger. Butler's suggestion is that despite the weight of video evidence, which would have led one to believe that King was endangered by police violence, the defence was able to enact a reversal of roles by mobilizing a racial lens. The existence of this racial lens can allow us to see how the roles of assailant and victim could be restructured to show white law under threat from black subjectivity. In this regard, Butler's point is that white society is paranoid about otherness. Its neurotic response to the appearance of the other is to recode them as illegal alien in order to reinforce the legality of the neutral establishment.

---

[5] This judgement sparked the 1992 Los Angeles riots in which 54 people lost their lives. In contrast to the lenient sentences received by the police, a black rioter arrested for committing a similar beating on a white man was given the maximum ten-year prison sentence. In the aftermath of the riots, a second trial found two of the four central officers guilty. They were sentenced to 30 month's imprisonment.

Butler's examination of the discursive struggle over race representation in the Rodney King affair offers a method for deconstructing British codes of ethnicity in relation to the media's construction of the dangerous black man. For Butler the inversion of danger/safety relies upon the successful reformulation of King from victim to offender. In order for this to take place, there already had to be an identifiable discursive framework. Post-colonial Authors such as Fanon and Said have shown how such a discriminatory system of representation exists. However, this formula can also be used to see how actors in the Lawrence case were subject to similar identity rehabilitation.

(Mis)recognition

Superficially the media construction of Stephen Lawrence as an undeserving victim of racial hatred (that gave his parents a voice to criticize legal process) seemed evidence of a newly-developed democratic public sphere. Certainly Ian Law (2001) suggests that the sympathetic treatment of the Lawrences reflects the new anti-racist content of the press. He explains that although the media's preoccupation with linking crime and race still exists it has now been matched by a parallel narrative of anti-racism. Law goes on to suggest that this may be evidence of a shift in media/race relations in Britain, explaining that the British media has become sensitive to racial issues in line with the national move toward cultural pluralism and structural equality.[6] However, if the details of this radical shift toward discursive anti-racism are unpacked, the inversion of Lawrence from 'bad black' to 'good black' (particularly considering the politics of the newspaper that championed this case) can be revealed more as sign of reinforcement of the dominant structural order than a critique of it.

Many involved in the case recognized this point for themselves. Speaking on *Why Stephen?*, Doreen Lawrence suggests that the media moulded her identity attributes to fit their own ideological agenda. When asked whether she found the press presentation of her 'quiet dignity' patronising, she responded:

> Well yes ... Because they [the media] always stereotype black people to be aggressive – always shouting and fighting for everything. And all of a sudden they've seen a family who doesn't do that. So they had to put a label on it. But there are thousands of people who are like that. I'm no different (Doreen Lawrence speaking on *Why Stephen?*, BBC 2, 16 February 1999).

From this perspective it can be argued that the *Daily Mail*'s true agenda was to promote its usual law and order message rather than advance an anti-racist message. Consequently, Law mirrors this process when he suggests that by

---

[6] The anti-racist agenda is reflected in the way that the Lawrence affair was seen as damaging in light of improved race-relations. The national press was keen to state that the violent actions of the five white suspects had a negative impact on the progress that the nation had made in recent years.

advancing the opinions of a black mother, the national press did in fact provide a sympathetic forum for the anti-racist message.

Therefore, Lawrence's transition from bad black (made evident by his parents and Duwayne Brooks' treatment by the police) to good black (seen from his media representation) is revealed by examining his identity rehabilitation following his death. Looking back to stories where ethnic minorities were the primary actor, such as that of Rolan Adams, the media audience is often led to believe that the victim somehow had a hand in their own violent treatment. Similar stories of racially motivated violence have appeared in the British press over the years, and for the most part they have received equally little attention to that of Adams. One example that outwardly parallels the Lawrence case is that of Asian man Surjit Singh Chhokar, who was beaten and stabbed to death outside his home in Lanarkshire, Scotland in 1998 (Dodd, *The Guardian*, 29 November 2000 and Seenan, *The Guardian*, 8 December 2000). Although this case received some limited nationwide publicity in the broadsheet press when an inquiry was opened into the failure to convict anyone for his murder, interest was lessened due to the gap between standard British identity and those of the victim and his family. Various news sources called this the Scottish Stephen Lawrence case; however, there were too few recognizable features in either the victim or his family (the family of Chhokar were Sikh and English was not their first language) for it to make any great impact. In this instance Chhokar's ethnic *difference* caused representational problems for the channels of publicity.

The reason for Adams' and Chhokar's exclusion and Lawrence's inclusion stem from several differential characteristics. Whereas other victims of racial violence have been discursively defined by their difference (i.e. the Adams family's association with radical black politics and the Chhokar family's cultural isolation), from the beginning Lawrence was defined by his similarity to the white centre. Even though initial newspaper reports into Lawrence's death were limited to a few column inches, in these stories he was invariably described in terms of his academic achievement and his strong family bond. Themes that highlighted the Lawrences' civic inclusion remained the focus of the national press:

> Stephen grew up with confidence in himself and others. Bright and determined, by the age of seven, he had resolved to become an architect. At 12 he was in charge of his own birthday party (*BBC News Online*, 19 February 1999).

> They [Doreen and Neville Lawrence] watched in pride as Stephen thrived at school. He also developed a keen interest in art, was an accomplished athlete, and had taken the first steps to realising his dream of becoming an architect (Dodd, *The Guardian*, 25 February 1999).

These quotes highlight the way that the media invented a discursive framework in which to position Lawrence. From the onset his identity attributes were clearly demarcated as identical to that of the reader of the middle-English press. A discourse of inclusion was taken up by journalists across the board, stressing the Lawrences' commitment to hard work, educational achievement and family unity in order to secure empathy from their white audience (for whom these were recognizable characteristics). In contrast to this process, the Adams family campaign, supported by the Socialist Workers Party, provided an antagonistic reference to structural inequality. For the majority right-wing press the ideology of such groups went against its stance on work and individual responsibility, and in effect was seen to accuse the social order of allowing their son to be killed. In this regard the Adams' mistake was to accuse the wider population of racism rather than focus on the individual perpetrators of the crime.

Insofar as getting their campaign taken seriously, the Lawrences (assisted by the ARA) realized that they needed to provide an identifiable presence in order to overcome the usual problems of representing black subjectivity. For this reason the ARA focussed on the stability of the Lawrence family and contrasted this with the irrational individual act of violence that led to Stephen's death. In this regard the press illustrated that the people guilty of killing Lawrence (on his own just another black victim of violence) were also guilty of destroying the family – the very symbol of middle-English morality. The Lawrences were presented to the press as hard-working, church-going, and educationally aspirational, characteristics that were readily consumed by the media, which needed to re-code Lawrence in order to present him as a sympathetic victim rather than a 'deserving' victim.

Harmit Athwal (2001) attends to this point of victim blaming in a review of the structural management of racism in the post-Macpherson report era. Pointing to the treatment of Duwayne Brooks by both the police and, paradoxically, the same media that turned Lawrence into a heroic victim, Athwal notes that Brooks was subject to suspicion and 'low-level police harassment' (Athwal, 2001: 116) which left him outside the sympathetic treatment meted out to Lawrence and his family. Like Adams' suggested involvement in gang culture, Brooks was presented as somehow leading Lawrence into trouble. Although they were both victims of the same racist attack, Brooks failed to achieve the same level of media support. For the media, who were keen to portray Lawrence as the embodiment of middle-English values, Brooks was too much like the kind of black man who would appear in their newspapers as a perpetrator of crime, rather than its victim. In order to negotiate this point the media stressed Brook's mental health problems (post-traumatic stress disorder). Re-coding Brooks' identity within a medical discourse enabled the media to re-establish his debased position in a more sympathetic manner, without giving him the iconic status attributed to Lawrence:

> The killers walk free and triumphant, leaving behind them not only the body of a bright and promising young man but the friend who was with him that night, Duwayne Brooks, who has needed psychiatric help ever since (Comment, *Daily Mail*, 15 February 1997).

This is a far cry from the media's speculation about Lawrence's character, which turned him into the heroic object of mass scrutiny. However, this process of re-codification can also be read in line with his particular identity attributes. It is easy to speculate that the media in Britain simply re-coded Lawrence as 'white' in order to present a sympathetic symbol to its mass audience. While I would suggest that this is a major part of the rehabilitative process, the remainder relies on his subjective characteristics. In other words, it was also his very blackness that allowed him to be re-coded from within a dominant framework. In this regard, Rattansi (1992) suggests that in order for members of the ethnic community to succeed in a white dominated society, they must work harder and have more positive qualities, in terms of educational achievements, family unity, and social mobility.

This idea suggests that part of Lawrence's (and his parents') appeal came precisely from their perceived embracing of the ideology of individualism as a marker for equality in multicultural Britain. In other words, they could be situated within a discourse of hard work, which overwrites cultural, ethnic or religious difference in favour of objective liberal value. This is reminiscent of the Thatcherite version of the work ethic, which states that a person's success is dependent on their willingness to accept the principles of market forces. By emphasising the Lawrence family's hard-working characteristics, the press were thus able to demonstrate their desire to be included in the dominant social order, rather than negotiate their exclusion from it on the basis of ethnicity. This process can be understood if the main facet in the portrayal of Stephen Lawrence, which revolved around his studying for 'A' levels and his ultimate desire to train to become an architect, is examined. In fact this point of reference took on so much significance in the organization of Lawrence's identity that his name and image have been used as the emblem for a charitable foundation related to youth employment and education in the 'art and science of architecture'.[7]

The iconography that surrounds Lawrence has been an important feature in turning him into an 'extraordinary ordinary' individual. For example, *BBC News Online* noted that the media impact of the Lawrence case was largely due to the symbolism manufactured around the Lawrence family. The emphasis on Stephen being 'just like us' was the very thing that rendered him as somehow special. Referring to its own Black Britain documentary shown on BBC 2, *Why Stephen?*, reporter Nick Higham states that the ARA's management of the publicity surrounding the case was what kept it within the public realm long after it should have disappeared from public consciousness. Here, ARA spokesperson Marc Wadsworth (a former television producer) claims that the group deliberately set this process in motion by 'saying to white society, Stephen Lawrence was like you' (cited in Higham, 19 February 1999). In addition to this effect the BBC news story notes:

> The image-making, he said, was not overt, but was highly effective because it
> played on the value systems of (white) newsdesks, politicians and public (Higham,
> *BBC News Online*, 19 February 1999).

---

[7] The Stephen Lawrence Trust was set up as a charitable organization to give young people from ethnic minorities an opportunity (through funding and expertise) to enter professions similar to the one Lawrence aspired to succeed in.

One can also understand this process of coding in terms of other representational constructions about Lawrence and the events surrounding the case. For example, although documentaries such as *Why Stephen?* highlight the discursive restraints placed upon him and his family by the popular media; they too maintain these structures of identification. Further evidence of this representational structure can be found in the myriad of public sphere images. For example, the Richard Norton-Taylor play based on the public inquiry started at a small theatre in London, but was subsequently transferred to the West End. The play went on to be published in 1999, appeared on British television screens a year later, and has gone on to be distributed to an international television audience.[8] This process of representational proliferation highlights the universal character of self/other modes of identification. In other words, the media management of Lawrence's identity as self/normal only worked if it was contrasted with the aberrant otherness of the white men accused of his murder. Although the racist structures of the dominant social order were temporarily inverted, the narrative of difference remained the same in order to protect white society. The self/other binary was subject to symbolic manipulation (a superficial postmodern strategy) in order to uphold the rule of racial identification.

The use of his person as the subject of documentaries, docu-dramas, plays, and to underwrite charitable trusts, means that Lawrence's representation has become synonymous with race relations in Britain. This is largely due to the way in which he has been transformed into a sign. Unlike O.J. Simpson and Rodney King, who were at once constructed as both sympathetic subjects and dangerous individuals, but not allowed to receive unconditional acceptance (because they did not complete the journey from body to sign), it was Lawrence's death that allowed him to escape the construction as dangerous black man. The continued existence of the black man, no matter how far related to white society, will always be perceived as dangerous by the white majority. In this regard the only way for the black man to achieve true integration into white society is to cease to exist: to undertake the complete transformation from body to sign.

From this perspective we can begin to understand why Brooks received such different treatment to Lawrence in the representational development of the case. For each different section of the British media, Lawrence was ideal symbol for the negotiation of narratives of justice. For example, the language and content of the tabloid press is always predicated toward sensation. As I have discussed, Lawrence's murder provided several key elements for the tabloids to exploit: the dangerous thugs, legal incompetence, and the destruction of a 'decent' family. However, although the traditional tabloid newspapers (e.g. *The Sun* and *Daily Mirror*) gave the incident some coverage, it was largely left to the 'quality tabloid' or middle-brow *Daily Mail* to take up the story. In this newspaper the Lawrences' campaign revolved around both the incompetence of the police and the miscarriage

---

[8] Together with the Richard Norton-Taylor play, there were several other documentaries and a docu-drama based on the case. These included the Granada television production 'The Murder of Stephen Lawrence' and the Channel 4 programme 'The Stephen Lawrence Story'.

of justice that saw their son's killers getting away with murder. However, the *Daily Mail*'s coverage centred on the individual act of violence by the alleged perpetrators and the incompetence of particular actors in the case, such as Police Commissioner Sir Paul Condon, rather than any structural injustice. This discursive realignment from social to individual culpability, together with the re-ordering of Lawrence's identity, meant that the *Daily Mail* could readily support the campaign without undermining its broader representational agenda.

Furthermore, although the broadsheet press presented the story in a less explosive manner, they delivered a similar line in editorials and reporting to that of the tabloids. However, even though the story still centred on the miscarriage of justice, there was a difference in representation between the right-wing and liberal press. The right-wing papers (*The Times, The Sunday Times* and *The Daily Telegraph*), although sympathetic to the plight of the Lawrences, maintained a law and order stance that mirrored that of the tabloids, while the liberal press (*The Guardian, The Observer* and *The Independent*) also developed a social critique. Similarly, as the campaign for justice increased, television news and documentary coverage mirrored the approach of the liberal press, questioning both the effectiveness of the legal system in this particular case and race relations in Britain. Interestingly however, the media failed to cover the story to any great degree until 1997, when an aspiring New Labour party announced their intention to initiate a public inquiry into the matter.

Spurred on by New Labour's election campaigning slogan, 'It's time for change', the British mass media seemed keen to embrace the new political climate. *The Sun* famously switched its long-term allegiance from Conservative to Labour during the 1997 general election campaign, claiming that the Tories no longer represented the wishes of the people.[9] Perhaps the renewed interest in the Lawrence case can be understood as a cynical attempt to promote New Labour's multicultural agenda. The action to initiate an inquiry was part of the process to show a commitment to social equality and the anti-racist agenda of past Labour parties, but with a new 'tough' policy on law and order issues. For the new government, the Lawrences were the epitome of modern Britain: they had embraced the ideology of personal growth, but also represented ethnic diversity – a multicultural success story destroyed by racial hatred.

This was the perfect case for image-conscious New Labour. The iconography of Lawrence developed over years of campaigning by his parents and affiliated groups suddenly took on greater significance; that of a campaigning tool for multiculturalism. In line with Lawrence's media rehabilitation, and in contrast to Brooks' (mis)treatment, Neville and in particular Doreen Lawrence provided the necessary ingredients for widespread recognition. Whereas Brooks' criticism of the police's handling of the initial investigation (and his treatment as a suspect) was read as a subjective critique of dominant structural law, Lawrence's parents were allowed to front the campaign for justice because their disapproval could be

---

[9] This was due to New Labour's increased emphasis on traditionally Conservative policies such as law and order and the economy, rather than a shift in the ideology of the right-wing press (Jones, 1997).

understood sympathetically as part of the grieving process of bereaved parents. Again this relates to the reversal of the bad black discourse. Here, the Lawrence family were set up as civilized black subjects.

Doreen and Neville Lawrence had both been born in Jamaica. Neville had come to Britain to find work in 1960, while Doreen was brought over by her mother as a child. Like many migrants to Britain, the Lawrences experienced a certain level of racism, the kind that would obstruct their ambitions, rather than one that would put them in any physical danger (Cathcart, 2000). On the whole, however, they managed their situation by adopting dominant structural codes, while retaining their cultural roots. Fanon (1952/1986) examines this negotiation of black identity by looking at the way the colonized are interpellated into the ruling social system. Doreen Lawrence in particular represented a symbol of post-colonial inclusion. Unlike Neville Lawrence, who had seemingly retained a greater level of black subjective identity due to periods of unemployment and the preservation of his Jamaican accent, Doreen characterized the possibilities of assimilation.

Relating back to the work of Said (1978/1995), Doreen Lawrence in particular provided the embodiment of the civilized other. She often acted as spokesperson for the couple, which was managed by the ARA, who suspected that Doreen would come across as more acceptable than Neville because of her greater inclusive identity attributes such as her late entrance into higher education and her representation as quiet, respectful, and unemotional. In terms of Fanon's thesis, the Lawrences were written as civilized blacks. Their positive characteristics were emphasized by mediators, and the media then exaggerated these attributes in order to present an over-determined vision of British blackness:

> The murder threw into the public gaze an ordinary family who had asked for nothing more than a quiet life. Neville Lawrence, a plasterer, and his wife Doreen, a teacher, came to Britain from Jamaica and built a life for their young family based on strong religious faith and a belief in the value of education (*Sunday Telegraph*, 16 February 1997).

Furthermore, the Lawrences were positioned as a positive marker against the cipher for black deviance, the Nation of Islam:

> To their credit, Stephen's mother and father both reacted with great dignity to this deplorable attempt by extremists to hijack the inquiry into the killing of their son (Leading article, *Daily Mail*, 30 June 1998).

However, regardless of the Lawrences' inclusive identity attributes, they would have remained outside the discursive remit of the British media had it not been for the greater need to outlaw the containers of the violent extreme. Nancy Fraser (1997) explains how such constructions work to reinforce dominant ideology in her examination of the Clarence Thomas/Anita Hill case. Here she suggests that the sexual harassment dispute between Thomas, an American Supreme Court candidate, and his employee Anita Hill, was resolved through racial coding despite the fact that both Thomas and Hill were black. Fraser argues that through a series of identity shifts, the situation eventually culminated in the exclusion of Hill and reinstatement of Thomas' dominant position. Fraser explains the development of dominant discourse according to the following moves:

1. *Gender* According to the public/private separation between Thomas (masculine, public office) and Hill (feminine, private sphere), Thomas was able to frame Hill's accusation in political terms. After Hill's initial attempt to confine her accusation to the private sphere, Thomas was able to control the public appearance of her claim.

2. *Race* In the next stage Thomas claimed that he was a victim of racial sexual stereotyping. He argued that Hill's claim against him referred to '...racial stereotypes of black men as having large penises and unusual sexual prowess' (Thomas quoted in Fraser, 1997: 108). Against Thomas as sexualized black man, Hill represented the hysterical 'white' woman (even though she was black), terrified by the primal sexuality of the black man.

3. *Class* Following the 'whitening' of Hill, the case referred to her middle-class status. Hill's roots in rural poverty were ignored in favour of her bourgeois academic status. Fraser's point is that Hill's situation was ordered in response to Thomas' early attempt to position himself as black working-class. Due to the imposition of this class lens (Hill's 'whitened' bourgeois status versus Thomas' working-class blackness), Fraser argues that the employer/employee power relation was largely ignored.

Fraser's example shows how public legal discourse is written out in terms of sociological categories which the media constructs through popular representations. In this instance, Thomas' representatives were able to manipulate standard modes of identification as a reaction against 'political correctness'. They were able to follow dominant modes of identification (his dominant political masculine position) by reading these through categories of subordinate identity positions (gender, race, class). The effect of this ideological procedure was that they were able to influence the representational outcome of the affair. In other words, Thomas' representatives were able to re-code the dispute and make their client appear to be a victim of liberal political correctness 'gone mad'.

The process of media codification highlighted by Fraser's model is important in understanding how the players in the Lawrence case were reconstructed in order to fit into existing discourse. For instance, Hall et al (1978) state that respectability in the face of adversity is an attractive trait in dominant representations of the other. This refers to self-discipline and the notion of self-control that keeps the subject within the law and order category. Repeatedly the Lawrences are depicted as 'stoical', 'unemotional', 'quiet' and 'dignified', but always with an underlying subtext of having to carry a great burden. Their very ordinariness (they appear to occupy the 'silent majority' against the idea that black people are 'always shouting and fighting') delivers them from stereotypes of blackness. However, the respectable characteristics of the Lawrences only work against the norm of mass deviance perceived in the stereotypical accounts of their 'race', i.e. the Nation of Islam. Like the woman who has to work twice as hard to 'make it' in a 'man's world', the ethnic other must be super-disciplined – extraordinary – in order to succeed (or, in fact, be ordinary) in white society. But like all such traits (as noted in the Thomas/Hill example) these extraordinary characteristics are always overwritten to emphasize racial categories that ultimately aim to uphold the dominance of law.

Looking at the Lawrence case, Arun Kundnani (2000) identifies the newspaper columnist as an agent who works to maintain 'solid' social order. He argues that columnists provide a stable presence and articulate an overarching discourse within often complicated news stories.[10] However, Kundnani claims that such writers do not actually form opinions; rather they act to sustain national myths and stereotypes in order to reassure their readership that 'right' and 'wrong' do indeed exist. The problem here lies in the over-determination of complex issues. By maintaining simplistic binary structures, the writer promotes the integrity of the existing socio-political order. In other words, journalists often reinforce society's pre-existing notions of right and wrong. In the Lawrence case this process, which seeks to renegotiate the law of the social order, led to the Lawrences being re-coded as middle-English. The effect of this move was to excuse British society of being racist. The media's representation suggested that British society could not be racist because (1) the Lawrences had 'made it' to the middle class (symbolically promoted from their structural position to the ideological notion of middle class), and (2) the media had taken their side and condemned the racism of a particular criminal element of British society. Stephen Glover writes in the *Daily Mail*:

> Why are we all to be condemned for Stephen's death? Like most people I feel desperately sorry for his parents, and sad that a promising young life should have been brutally and needlessly cut short. I feel some shame that such a thing could happen in this country, and a sense of outrage (though no great surprise) that the police should have bungled the investigation. But it is not my fault, and not yours either, unless you are one of the five white thugs who stabbed Stephen to death (Glover, *Daily Mail*, 26 February 1999).

This sentiment reveals that the identity transformation of the Lawrences was paradoxical in light of their overt criticism of the legal process. While the media wanted to defend the Lawrences by attacking the racism of Britain's white extremists, the Lawrences wanted to criticize British justice as a motivated institution for upholding social exclusion. In the media's effort to overwrite the Lawrence family's identity with positive middle-English-friendly attributes, they also attempted to re-code their criticism of the dominant social order, highlighted by the depiction of institutional racism. This analysis of the representational shifts of the Lawrences seems to show that the media were playing a dialectical game. The identity positions within the representations of the case were continually

---

[10] In this case it was the *Daily Mail*'s Lynda Lee-Potter that provided the rhetoric of inclusion on behalf of the Lawrences.

shifted to uphold the integrity of the dominant social order in the face of the criticism of institutional racism.

White Trash: Constructions of the Anti-Social

The notion of the dialectical game refers to the way that the mass media was able to transport the Lawrences from the category of dangerous blacks to middle-English folk. Following the logic which separated Martin Luther King from Malcolm X, the Lawrences became 'insider blacks': people who could be recognized by Britain's white population due to their middle-English values. By contrast Rolan Adams remained an outsider black, a casualty of the culture of criminality that includes both black and white outsiders. The specificity of the media's procedure of discourse construction, which saw the separation of insiders from outsiders, can be seen to refer to the wider social situation. Whereas Adams' murder was re-organized around notions of gang culture and working-class criminality, and the old-left campaign that sought to critique the dominant social order for its racism was ignored for its archaic socialism, Lawrence was re-made an insider to support the multicultural ideologies of New Labour policy. In line with new socialism, which jettisoned old Labour's social critique in favour of elements of Conservative ideology, the Lawrences became the multicultural others who could be included in the dominant social order. Due to their aspirational attributes (such as academic achievement, their loyalty to the nuclear family, which contradicted the stereotype of the deviant black family structure, and their positive attitude towards work, that saw Neville Lawrence maintain his work ethic despite periods of unemployment) the Lawrences became a symbol of successful British multiculturalism.

By contrast, the Adams campaign was blighted by its reference to old socialist values and its rejection of the dominant ideologies of middle-class aspiration, nuclear family organization, and hard work for institutional ends. In this regard Adams' campaigners failed to find media support because their ideology was past its sell-by date. In much the same way that Adams remained a reminder of Britain's past, the Lawrence case also had its own archaic left-over, the element that recalled the politics of class division: the white underclass. The alleged murderers of Stephen Lawrence came from a particular socio-economic sector of the community that has always suffered exclusion from political mandate and vilification by public discourse. Divorced from a sector of the working class in Britain that has gained status by virtue of its 'noble' or aspirational attributes, the underclass is seen as a threat both physically and ideologically. In this final section I will show how Jamie and Neil Acourt, Gary Dobson, Luke Knight, and David Norris became signifiers for a criminal element that is perceived to endanger decent moral society.

The examination of the media representations of the Lawrences revealed how they attained symbolic status due to their re-coding from black subjectivity to a decent working-class/aspirational middle-class position. Put another way, they were delivered from the fate of racist constructs by their identifiable inclusive characteristics. However, the same discursive re-coding that allowed the Lawrences to enter public sphere discourse at the level of undeserving victim also necessitated the creation of a new scapegoat that could excuse wider white society from blame. The transference of racist identity constructs to the white periphery has for a long time been a way of naturalising the idea of deviance in those on the margins of mainstream society. For example, Pearson (1983) explains that the representation of a hooligan element in Britain has existed as a response to the white underclass for centuries. The discursive re-ordering of those outside mainstream economic structures of society as 'thugs' is as much evidence of a fear of the unknown element in subcultural groups as it is a fear of real physical threat. In other words, people not defined by their commitment to the dominant ideology are treated as aberrant.

Mac an Ghail identifies the branding of white outsiders in Britain with the racism inflicted upon the black other. Referring to how the Irish were treated in Victorian Britain, he states that they were often subject to popular images that 'juxtaposed the dirtiness, drunkenness, laziness and violence of the alien Irish with the purity, industriousness and civilization of the English' (Mac an Ghail, 1999: 20). This happens for two reasons: first, in order to legitimate the rule of the colonizer; and second, to reinforce dominant capitalist ideology. In a similar manner the Irish were subject to racism as a colonized other. Throughout British colonialism, much like in other colonized countries, Ireland was largely stripped of its native language and culture. However, the Irish's similarity to their English rulers proved problematic because of the need to use them for cheap migrant labour, so it fell upon popular publications of the day such as *Punch* to portray the Irish as ignorant, lazy and dirty. This symbolic device allowed British parliamentarians to shift the blame of poverty onto the Irish people themselves. But it was Charles Kingsley, a mid-nineteenth century social observer, who epitomized popular anti-Irish racism in his observations about the Irish 'race':

> I am haunted by the human chimpanzees I saw along that hundred miles of horrible country. I don't believe they are our fault. I believe... they are happier, better, more comfortably fed and lodged under our rule than they ever were. But to see white chimpanzees is dreadful; if they were black, one would not feel it so much, but their skins, except where tanned by the sun are as white as ours (Kingsley cited in Lebow, 1976: 40).

It is my argument that a similar but updated form of racist imagery has been used to vilify the white periphery in Britain. In a comparable way to how black extremism becomes the signifier for *all* black subjectivity, the violent actions of a few individuals are related to the socially-excluded white population. For instance, Lydia Morris (1994) argues that the underclass in Britain are re-coded from their debased economic or cultural origins into a more damaging symbolization as deviant others. Similar to historical constructs of Irish characteristics, these representations often focus on attributes that would affect an individual's viable position in the market place, such as work ethic and family responsibility. She states that representations of the so-called 'dangerous classes' have been borne out of a temptation to blame those at the bottom of the social pile for their own exclusion. Matt Wray and Annalee Newitz support this argument in their examination of 'white trash' in the United States. They argue that the term white trash retains its usage and meaning because it points to the last visible group that the social is 'allowed' to blame for their own circumstances:

> In a country so steeped in the myth of classlessness, in a culture where we are often at a loss to explain or understand poverty, the white trash stereotype serves as a useful way of blaming the poor for being poor (Wray and Newitz, 1997: 1).

Wray and Newitz claim that such constructions of debased whiteness resonate with racist codes of otherness. They argue that with issues of race and gender leading the way for social reform, class has fallen foul of the machinations of political development. However, they believe that we should understand class in relation to both racial and gender exclusions. Wray and Newitz suggest that white exclusion can be traced back to pseudo-scientific constructs of deviance, i.e. the Eugenics movement, which sought to demonstrate genetic deficiency among the rural poor. Such movements across the United States and Europe aimed to legitimate the institutionalization of those 'afflicted' by this genetic deficiency, in order to waive the state's obligation to improve their structural conditions.

Since the failure of the legitimacy of pseudo-scientific disciplines such as eugenics, however, there has been a shift away from assuming genetic deficiency to a view that degrades the socially excluded for their perceived inability to seize equal opportunity. In Britain this ideology of individualism (blaming the individual) has been used in response to debates surrounding welfare state funding (Golding and Middleton, 1982). Against the true aim of the welfare state, which sought to redress the balance of structural inequality, critiques that pathologize the individual's cultural failure in order to justify reductions to state benefit, erode the social's responsibility for its least well-off members in favour of an every-person-for-themselves ideology. The ideological justification for this policy is that individual responsibility will encourage the least well-off to succeed within a meritocratic social order and contribute to social well-being through their own selfishness. However, instead of creating a more democratic base for social inclusion, notions of welfare dependency have seen 'council estate' poor become the cipher for deviance, where representations gloss over the possible influence of poor structural conditions in favour of a far more attractive proposition: personal delinquency (Roberts, 1999). Representations of the white men connected to Lawrence's murder highlight this argument if we consider the focus on their apparently intrinsic criminal traits:

> Few people on the Brook estate in Eltham are in any doubt about the identities of the racist savages who committed the crime. Yet two attempts at a trial had to be abandoned because of the climate of fear around the streets where members of the gang live. The Acourts in particular are notorious thugs. Neil Acourt's psychopathic hatred of blacks is graphically captured on a secret police video (Comment, *Daily Mail*, 15 February 1997).

Such representations of the five accused killers can be seen as an inversion of the characteristics found in Stephen Lawrence. For example Lawrence's educational achievements are abjectly mirrored by the emphasis on the five men's lack of schooling. Furthermore, the men are presented as being actively anti-educational. The stress on their being rule-breakers in school is a discursive tool employed in order to highlight the men's complicity in their own deviance:

> At the age of 14 the delinquent Jamie was permanently excluded and moved to Kidbrooke secondary to join his friend Luke Knight. But Jamie lasted only 10 months. Once he was found with a monkey wrench in his bag. Another pupil claims he brought in a replica hand gun, later found by the police at this home. He was finally thrown out after an assault on a black pupil (Pallister, *The Guardian*, 25 February 1999).

Linked directly to the five men's educational delinquency is their lack of work ethic. Articles from the *Daily Mail*, *The Guardian* and the *Daily Telegraph* highlight the suspects' joblessness and lack of career ambition. All described as 'unemployed' and having 'plenty of time on their hands' (Pallister, *The Guardian*, 25 February 1999), there is the added suggestion that idle hands make the devil's work. The representation of the suspects as ignorant, lazy and violent mirrored earlier constructions of white deviance and was presented as an inversion of the Lawrences' commitment to education, hard work, and religious faith. Additionally, in the instance of David Norris, the wealth of his family was understood to have come from organized crime. Against Neville Lawrence, who the media upheld as a hard worker who struggled through periods of unemployment, Norris' father was portrayed as an example of underworld crime, achieving wealth through 'ill-gotten gains'. It was Norris' father in particular that tied the thugs to the symbolism of the 1960s and the image of the violent underworld:

> Norris's father Clifford, a renowned local criminal, is in prison after being convicted of drug and gun offences. When his house was raided, police found a cache of Kalashnikovs (Ungood-Thomas and Harvey, *Daily Mail*, 14 February 1997).

Supporting the idea of underworld crime, Ungood-Thomas and Harvey continue to say that the suspects were said to 'model themselves on the Kray twins' (ibid.). This connection was highlighted by the *Daily Mail*'s depiction of the local community held 'under a reign of terror' by the suspects. Local people apparently failed to assist police by naming the men. In statements to reporters, unnamed residents said that the local community were 'struck dumb by fear' by the young mobsters: [11]

---

[11] In the days following Lawrence's murder several local residents came forward to both Mr and Mrs Lawrence and the police to provide the names of suspects, some of whom did not want to give evidence in court. In addition to this however, there were anonymous notes (with the names of the five main suspects) left on police car windscreens and in telephone boxes.

One woman, who had a long-running dispute with the Acourts was said to be under police protection at one stage, told the Daily Mail yesterday: 'I've been to hell and back and I don't want to do it again. I've got nothing to say'. Another resident said: 'People here are disgusted with the attack on Stephen Lawrence, but they don't want to say anything publicly against the Acourts and their gang' (Ungood-Thomas and Harvey, *Daily Mail*, 14 February 1997).

Arguably the wall of silence surrounding the five accused killers demonstrates the segregated existence of a community on the periphery, in other words those who live outside of structural law. This process can be seen at work when considering that media representations of the thugs were determined by the absence of the law of the father – both structural and biological. There is an obvious contrast to be drawn between Lawrence's father, who was regarded as an example of an upwardly-mobile ethnic, and the fathers of the thugs, who were either physically absent (the Acourt brothers), discursively missing (Dobson and Knight), or criminally deviant (Norris). While Neville Lawrence became a strong role model, who could teach his son the virtue of hard work and moral righteousness, the thugs' fathers came to represent lack of responsibility and a tendency to use criminal means to achieve material ends.

Akin to the differential representations of the fathers, the alleged murderers' mothers were also portrayed as failures in their parenting role. This is, of course, another sharp contrast to the media's depiction of virtuous Doreen Lawrence. The representation of the five men's mothers also suggests a link between the instability of the family unit and deviance. With regard to both historical and contemporary understandings of poverty, Morris explains that the mother's role is always of particular interest. Seen as the 'moral educator and budget manager', the mother is both the reason for success and failure in a family because her '...role [offers] a potential solution to poverty' (1994: 111). In this regard it was the structurally flawed origins of the suspects that were understood to be a symptom of their deviance. Moreover, it was their collective failure to overturn these debased economic circumstances (other than by criminal means) that was regarded as the real problem. Whilst the parents of Lawrence were seen to instil both moral and economic stability into their children, the mothers (and deviant/absent fathers) of the Acourts, Dobson, Knight and Norris, were understood to avoid parental responsibility and shift blame onto others. After a long period of absence from the discourse generated about their sons, the suspects' mothers gave an interview,[12] defending the innocence of their children and attacking the media for making them 'sacrificial lambs' (Hopkins, *The Guardian*, 20 February 1999). Written into the press coverage was an overarching rhetoric of accusation that the mothers failed (and continued to fail) to see what was plain to the media audience. The underlying suggestion was that the suspects' mothers had provided a corrupt role model,

---

[12] BBC Radio Four's *Today* programme, 19 February 1999. In this interview they defend the violent appearance of their sons in the police surveillance video, claiming that it was 'bravado' and 'play-acting'.

which was evidence of moral turpitude and an explanation for the delinquency of their children.

In this regard the process of individualization continues to organize the representations of the alleged murderers and their families. This shifts the blame from structural to individual, where the crimes of the children are seen to be the responsibility of the parents.[13] Here, the family is regarded to be the first level of socialization. After the dominance of the liberal ideology of individualism, the role of the state as mechanism of secondary socialization is minimal at best. Young (1996) notes this point in her discussion of the James Bulger murder. In this case the parents of the two boys found guilty of killing Bulger were from single-parent families (where the father was absent). Young states that the media's emphasis on parental delinquency reflects the political ideology of citizenship and individual accountability. In the Lawrence case the parents of the thugs are symbolically charged with 'lack of care'. The mothers' libellous defence of their criminal sons (stating that they did not know where their children were or what they were doing) supports the idea of parental deficiency. Therefore, the social order is defended by the notion of pathological deviance.

Although the *Daily Mail* took on the Lawrence campaign using his 'white' characteristics to promote its crusade, it only did so to any great degree after the white men accused of his murder were exposed as thugs. Essentially, Lawrence's features could only take on any significance after his positive identity attributes could be contrasted with the deviance of the white thugs. Such images of the alleged murderers' deviance were located in their violent appearance. For instance, one of the many representations that condemned the thugs in the public sphere was the undercover video footage that showed them making racist remarks and stabbing the air in a scene which was understood by many observers to be a re-enactment of the original Lawrence murder.

Such images of the thugs lend to the excessive representation of the general delinquency of 'council estate' inhabitants. By the time the suspects agreed to give a television interview to Martin Bashir[14] (who had previously interviewed Princess Diana and Louise Woodward); they had already been subject to debased identity rehabilitation. Whether guilty or not, the alleged murderers were turned into individual representations of the underclass, the horde or mass, that lives in a minimal culture of drinking and violence. In this regard, they are the terrifying representatives of the council (es)state of nature, a place where life is nasty, brutish and short.[15]

The sociology of deviance has been concerned with cataloguing evidence of constructions of moral panics against the inside outsider for many years. From Marx's proletariat, Becker's drug takers, and Cohen's mods and rockers, the

---

[13] The trend to punish parents for their children's delinquency has been highlighted by cases where mothers have been fined and imprisoned for their children's misbehaviour, e.g. truancy from school.

[14] This interview took place on 8 April 1999 on ITV's *Tonight with Trevor MacDonald*.

[15] This idea refers to the Hobbesian notion of the criminal and chaotic state of nature inhabited by the underclass (McClelland, 1996).

dominant social order is at pains to maintain power by creating an aberrant other. Marx told us that the crowd is subject to structural control to allow capitalism to function, but by the same token the individualized body of workers is liable to slip back toward mob formation (McClelland, 1996). The governing response to this revolutionary possibility is to construct a supplementary scapegoat to serve as warning of the inhumanity of crowd violence. As such, one can return to Foucault's (1984) idea of the dangerous individual which shows how the person who threatens to slip back towards animal un-differentiation becomes a criminal body made illegal to deter others from similar transgression. Foucault argues that the criminal's body is written through the definition of their transgression in order to re-structure the wider social order:

> Legal justice today has at least as much to do with criminals as with crimes. Or more precisely, while, for a long time, the criminal had been no more than the person to whom a crime could be attributed and who could therefore be punished, today, the crime tends to be no more than the event which signals the existence of a dangerous element – that is, more or less dangerous – in the social body (Foucault, 1984: 128).

According to this explanation, the 'thugs' represent the mob. They came to symbolize what might happen if law collapsed. Consequently, when the *Daily Mail* ran the 'MURDERERS' headline on 14 February 1999, which named and shamed the individuals it believed responsible for Lawrences' murder, it can be understood as an attempt to restate the law by individualizing the mass. Against legal controls that protect the identity of those perhaps suspected but not prosecuted of a crime, this front page story pictured the five men with the challenge 'The Mail accuses these men of killing. If we are wrong, let them sue us'. This illegal accusation can be seen as an attempt to discipline the mass. In this instance public sphere discourse sought to target the individuals who represent mob violence. For example, the rogues gallery depicted on the front page of the *Daily Mail* under the accusatory headline is comparable to a wanted poster or the contemporary equivalent: the representation of suspects on real crime television. Here, grainy video surveillance shots and photofit pictures are used to target individual criminals. In the same way, the *Mail*'s 'outing' of the five men sought to individualize the mob in order to bring it to justice by breaking its anonymity.

Against the civilized appearance of the Lawrences, the thugs accused of his murder literally stuck two fingers up at the law and consequently at the ordering system that sought to represent the situation. At the inquiry the suspects' antagonistic behaviour contributed to their being outcast by the middle-English press. The five men were already at the limits of representation because of their underclass status. As members of the underclass, they were a representation of 'old Britain'. In other words, the emblem of a racist past in a nation that wants to see itself as multicultural. But in its urgency to get rid of them, the liberal multicultural nation follows the same exclusionary system. The thugs are, therefore, the transparent logic of British multiculturalism. They (allegedly) stab blacks; whilst multicultural society excludes people who fail to uphold middle-class ideology.

Chapter Six

Criminal Justice and Society

Since his murder media representations of Stephen Lawrence have arguably defined the British view of race relations. Although the death of this young black man marked the fourth in a series of possible racial murders in that area of London, it is Lawrence who has since become a cipher for understanding antagonistic race relations in Britain. The events surrounding Lawrence's death, and the subsequent failure to secure a conviction for his murder, have caused intense speculation about the way the case was handled by the legal authorities. The victim's parents continue to claim that their son was a casualty of both race crime and institutionalized police/judicial racism. Their suggestion is that racial factors caused the authorities to investigate their son's murder with less conviction than a comparable assault on a white person. The police force responsible for the Lawrence investigation denied this criticism, stating that, on the contrary, they were determined to catch Stephen's killers. In this regard, it can be argued that police determination was augmented by the high incidence of racial crimes and British National Party activity in an area where racial tension was beginning to cause major embarrassment to a judicial system that was organized around the need to uphold the ideology of liberal multiculturalism advanced by successive British governments.

After several years of unsuccessful police activity, Lawrence's murderers remain at large. However, as a result of this apparent miscarriage of justice, Home Secretary Jack Straw commissioned *The Stephen Lawrence Inquiry Report* (1999), which led to the passing of the Race Relations (Amendment) Act in 2000. In it Sir William Macpherson made seventy recommendations. Among the suggestions was a request for a review of the double jeopardy rule and a proposal for the subjectivization of objective definitions of incidences of racial violence. Proposal 38, which can be seen to act as a critique of the double jeopardy rule, states that 'consideration should be given to the Court of Appeal being given power to permit prosecution after acquittal where fresh and viable evidence is presented' (Macpherson, 1999: 331). In the first instance, the proposition for alterations to the double jeopardy rule, which states that once acquitted the same person cannot be tried for the same crime again, can be seen to represent an attempt to create a space of undecidability within the law. In the Lawrence case the effects of the conventional version of double jeopardy, which led to the judgement that the accused could never again be prosecuted for Lawrence's murder, began to suggest a critique of the mechanisms that allowed the traditional objectivity of legal judgement to remain sealed to retrospective alteration. For this reason I will argue that Macpherson's recommendation to revise the double jeopardy rule became emblematic of an attempt to introduce a germ of subjectivity, or doubt, into the law by allowing for the possibility that legal judgement might be re-written at a later date.

In this chapter, therefore, I want to argue that Macpherson's critical assessment of the social order and attempt to allow room for subjective accusation against agencies of the state should be understood as the turning point in the Lawrence case. Before the inquiry Lawrence was written as a sympathetic symbol so that he could be read in terms of the British politics of inclusion. However, considering the media treatment detailed in chapter five, in this chapter I suggest that the representation of the events surrounding the murder of Stephen Lawrence can be read against a scapegoat model that shows how the social order sacrifices individuals in order to guarantee its own integrity. It is my assertion that the dominant representations of Lawrence enacted this scapegoat model at a symbolic level in order to avoid the possibility of structural critiques of ordinary racism. Here, I show how Lawrence's death has sparked such an enormously complicated set of debates about the British justice system, police procedure, and collective white western attitudes to ethnic minorities, that his individual attributes became obscured by wider socio-political motivations. Therefore, by examining the political and judicial debates resulting from the publicity of this racist murder, I want to argue that Lawrence has been consumed by his own representation. Mirroring postmodern notions of sign systems that exist independent of reality, the image of Lawrence is dominant over the reality of the murder. I will therefore show how the narrative developed by the media allowed the wider collective to consume the representation of the black man as victim. In this regard, Lawrence became an object of unified sympathy, rather than a symbol of racial hatred. This strategy of objectification turned Lawrence into a double sacrifice; first at the literal level and second at the level of representation.

After chapter five, where I demonstrated the symbolic means by which individual actors in the Lawrence case were re-coded to fit into existing discursive roles, this chapter will focus on the discourse surrounding the police, the legal system, and the Macpherson report. By adopting this perspective it is my suggestion that media representations of such public institutions followed a similar pattern to representations of the Lawrence family and the five suspects. Moreover, the chapter will show how the media narrative resulted in the following logic:

1. *Stephen Lawrence is murdered* This is quickly blamed on racist 'thugs' who are seen as peripheral to normal middle-English society. Their action is seen as the extreme logic of racist groups who feel marginalized in 'their own country'.

2. *Justice fails* The alleged killers go free and Lawrence's parents accuse the legal system and police of racism.

3. *Symbolic intervention* The media takes up the story, opposing the image of the racist thugs with that of a decent, law-abiding black family destroyed by a singular act of violence.

4. *Virtual justice* The Macpherson report supports the criticisms of the Lawrences. Recommendations follow the logic of the case: that British society is racist.

5. *White backlash* Macpherson's judgement is seen as an example of anti-white racism. As such, it provokes a hostile response from sections of the media. Macpherson is the final symbolic sacrifice. The status quo is maintained and perversely the racist thugs' original feeling of resentment/exclusion is upheld.

In terms of this argument the current chapter seeks to demonstrate the process by which the individual is sacrificed in order to restate the dominance of law. By referring to theorists such as Douzinas (2000) and Girard (1986; 1996), and reading them against the dominant legal narrative in the Lawrence case – the Macpherson report – I want to develop a method for recognising the politics of exclusion and show how this understanding can be used to extend an inclusive liberal justice.

Liberal Justice and the Double Jeopardy Rule

In recent times Britain's openness to the emergence of the nation state as a multicultural entity has been questioned by incidents of racial violence. For instance race riots in the north of England led to the British National Party's relative success in local election polls. Despite the regular occurrence of comparable events, British politics continues to suggest that racial tensions are anomalous to the emergence of a multicultural society. However, this notion of inclusion is set against continuing narratives of discrimination. These stories of exclusion have developed around the fear of the ethnic other. For example government clampdowns on cultural difference have become the overriding response to demonstrations of difference. Consequently, the contradiction between the idea of multiculturalism and the practicality of ordinary racism suggests that major party politics is concerned to view events like the Oldham or Bradford race riots as setbacks that should not cause unnecessary panic nor compromise our utopian vision of Britain as an egalitarian liberal democracy.

According to the liberal perspective, the persistence of racial antagonism should be seen as evidence of our violent past. Such conflicts are regarded as a left-over or remainder that should act as a reminder of the west's intolerant roots. Within many liberal democracies race is, therefore, seen as characteristic of an earlier stage of humanity that must be denied or repressed in order to ensure the continuation of non-violent social relations. This position sees racial identity as the lack of full subjectivity, or the difference between peoples, that encourages tribal violence. In this regard the motives of extreme fundamentalist groups are an archaic reminder of conflict politics and the idea of 'race' creates the space for racial antagonism and allows conflict to occur. In contrast liberal ideology assumes that the central role of racial politics should be to abolish racial difference and create a neutral, objective space for the emergence of an ideal model of communicative social interaction (Habermas, 1988; Seshadri-Crooks, 2000).

In order to critique this particular brand of multiculturalism, authors such as Žižek (1993; 1998) have argued against the liberal thesis, which regards race as a divisive aspect of identity formation that requires objective correction. Instead he asserts that multiculturalism must understand racial difference as the very condition of possibility of liberal democracy. Žižek argues that it is precisely through the attempt to deny racial identity that liberal democracy encourages the violence of racial antagonism. The destruction of racial categories, so that racial others conform to the dictates of liberal individualism, incites an increase in violent attempts to re-assert subjective difference as racial superiority (Boothby, 1991).[1]

In this regard Stephen Lawrence became representative of racial violence in contemporary Britain in a way that exceeded earlier cases such as Rolan Adams precisely because his murder was transformed into a media event. The result of Lawrence's symbolic representation was the exposure of the presence of racial antagonism to wider British society: that Lawrence's transformation into a media event was able to confront British society with an image of its own racial violence. It was precisely because of Lawrence's entry into the representative arena of the symbolic order that the events that followed his murder became so important for understanding both earlier and later instances of racial antagonism. From this point of view perhaps the major political outcome of the events surrounding the Lawrence murder was the production of the Macpherson report and in particular its judgement for assessing instances of racial antagonism (Holohan and Featherstone, 2003).

This specific judgement, which suggests that the victim of possible racial violence should have the power to define the crime committed against their person as either racial or non-racial, advances an important argument for the acceptance of the other *as* racialized subject. Proposal 12, which states that: 'A racist incident is any incident which is perceived to be racist by the victim or any other person' (Macpherson, 1999: 328), recommends that criminal definitions should be referred to the victim's own subjective (which includes racialized) identity position. This allowance for subjective assessment can be seen to enact a radical critique of traditional authority because its purpose is to under-cut standard legitimacy over objective judgement, which is usually given over to the police as the official representative of the state's authority over criminal definition. Here, Macpherson's judgement sees the responsibility for the definition of the specificities of criminal law pass from the arbiters of traditional authority to the racialized subject. Against the standard system for the production of criminal definition, whereby legal institutions attempt to produce an objective statement on racial violence that attempts to overwrite subjective understandings of difference/antagonism,

---

[1] This follows Richard Boothby's interpretation of Lacan's (1977) concept of 'aggressivity'. This states that inter-subjective violence is representative of a projection of intra-psychic alienation. As Boothby explains 'Lacan's notion of aggressivity restores the central point of Freud's view: aggressivity is a function of a primordial destructiveness *toward oneself*' (1991: 40).

Macpherson's recommendation re-opens a space for the re-emergence of racial difference. Whereas the official position of traditional authority is concerned with the erasure of subjectivity and the insurance that we all have the same view of what constitutes racial violence, Macpherson's judgement aims to empower the subject with the legal authority to decide upon their own subjective experience as victim.

Therefore the legalization of subjectivity may possess the ability to reduce instances of racial violence through its use as a device for the reduction of antagonistic attempts to rediscover racial difference/racial superiority as a condition of capital success. Macpherson's decision to accept the other *as* other may possess the potential to reduce the frequency of instances of racial violence. I would therefore argue that the central aim of the Macpherson report is its attempt to rehabilitate/legalize subjective difference. This objectivization of subjectivity both enables the construction of equivalent judgements and recognizes antagonistic social relations. As such, Macpherson's recommendation to allow the victim of crime to decide upon its racist intent creates space for the possibility of a legal judgement that evades the violent repression which forms the root of the traditional authority of the law.

Macpherson's proposal in favour of the subjective critique of the law can be understood within the following framework constructed from the content of the seventy recommendations in the inquiry report: (1) that British society (including its structural institutions) is racist; (2) that because of the ramifications of this ordinary racism, victims of crime should have the power to judge the racist intent of an incident; and (3) the law on double jeopardy should be changed to reflect the problems arising from points one and two.

Akin to Lord Scarman's report on the Brixton riots of 1981, Macpherson recognizes that racist crimes are often the effect of poor race relations in Britain. The discrepancy between the two reports is to be found in their different treatment of structural authority. Scarman implicated individual actors, rather than institutional considerations, as the cause of racial antagonism. He denied the existence of institutional racism, preferring instead to locate blame in some prehistoric germ that 'poison[s] minds and attitudes' (Scarman, 1981: 11). In contrast, Macpherson accepts the existence of the germ of racial antagonism. However, he was concerned to show how this root of violence remained active due to its role in the maintenance of structural legitimacy (Holdaway, 1999; Kushnick, 1999). In this regard the Macpherson report sought to explain that racism was not the privilege of individual agents but rather the condition of society at large:

> Racism, institutional or otherwise, is not the prerogative of the Police Service. It is clear that other agencies including for example those dealing with housing and education also suffer from the disease. If racism is to be eradicated there must be specific and co-ordinated action both within the agencies themselves and by society at large, particularly through the education system, from primary school upwards and onwards (Macpherson, 1999: 6.54, p33).

While the logic of Scarman's argument funds a return to the elimination of race in order to secure social cohesion, it individualizes the 'problem' of race, rather than attacking the system that keeps it alive. Contrary to Macpherson's conclusions, the Scarman report considered the Brixton riots to be the result of individual thuggery. In this regard Scarman was able to re-state the integrity of the traditional authority of the law by attributing the violence of racial antagonism to individual actors. For this reason Scarman's individualization of social antagonism is comparable to the media's attempt to scapegoat various agents for the murder of Stephen Lawrence. Against this position, one can see Macpherson's understanding of social racism as representative of a radical critique of the violence of contemporary British society.

While he criticizes the Scarman report for failing to implicate specific policies, Lee Bridges (2001) suggests that the Macpherson report performs a similar injustice. Bridges' argument is that Macpherson's critique of institutional racism supports the dominant social order through its failure to target specific institutions or individuals for their particular acts of racism. For example he refers to the controversial police policy on 'stop and search', which he argues continues to be directed at members of ethnic communities specifically due to policy wording. However, the value of Macpherson's assessment of social racism may reside in the very aspect of the report that Bridges critiques for its lack of definition. Against Bridges' demand for individual targets for reform, Macpherson looks to relationships between actors, agents or institutions: he is concerned to consider not the particular racist attributes of an individual or an institution, but the racism that might occur when an individual or an institution comes into contact with (an)other individual or institution of a different ethnic background.[2] While Bridges wants to focus on individuals to say that this or that individual or institution is by definition racist, Macpherson understands that racism resides in the power relation that exists between actors (at a microscopic level, between individuals, at a macroscopic level, between institutions, or various combinations of these two levels of political articulation).

This argument is mirrored by Floya Anthias (1999), who formulates a position similar to Patricia Hill-Collins' (1990) matrix of domination, when she argues that institutional racism is connected to a set of power relations that cut across race, gender and class. She contends, however, that this does not deny the permanence of the ideological reproduction of discriminatory ideas:

> The power of racist ideas, in this case ideas that do not emanate from solitary individuals but penetrate the hegemonic dominant ethnicity in British society, will be embodied in the words and actions of different individuals, in different ways in different contexts. The issue of power is not one about a power that is exercised by *all 'whites' over all 'blacks'* but is about the power of the dominant group represented in the state to reproduce its own values and practices on its own terms, despite the discontinuous and shifting nature of the processes (Anthias, 1999: 4.3).

Anthias argues that it is power that is institutionalized rather than racism. In this respect racism (like sexism or economic discrimination) is the effect not the cause

---

[2] Here, the term 'institution' relates to both structural organizations and social or cultural bodies such as religion or nationality.

of power relations. Therefore, the Macpherson report provides an attempt to move beyond the 'rotten apple' thesis that scapegoats individual actors, and replaces it with the idea of 'unwitting racism' (Kushnick, 1999). However, I would argue that unlike Scarman's version of unwitting racism, which was used to excuse institutions of racism, Macpherson's usage employed the term in order to critique structural authority. In this regard, the report accepts the Lawrences' criticism of the police, but also recognizes that the police are representatives of the law. Thus, in its refusal to scapegoat any one individual for the murder of Stephen Lawrence, the Macpherson report moves beyond the critique of individual blame towards an analysis of the power relations that are written into the law.

In this regard the inquiry report's proposal to revise the rule on double jeopardy was a way of subverting the power relation implicit in legal institutions. By introducing an element of doubt, and the possibility of retrospective alteration into the institutional notion of right, the law is open to challenge. In the specific case of Lawrence the alteration to the double jeopardy rule may have taken into account the poor handling of the incident in the early stages of the police investigation and given the Lawrences an opportunity to invite the judiciary to re-prosecute the suspects in the light of fresh or rediscovered evidence. However, the proposal to alter the double jeopardy rule was subject to much public debate. It was argued that if the double jeopardy rule was reviewed it would open the way for further miscarriages of justice. For instance writing in *The Guardian*, Madsen Pirie argues that the double jeopardy rule not only acts to protect people from persistent harassment by the authorities but also prevents the erosion of general principles of liberty. In this respect Pirie contends that a revision of double jeopardy would in fact extend the power of law:

> In the interest of bringing these low lifes to justice, the principles which protect the liberties of all of us are swept away. The precepts which have guarded society are destroyed to target particular groups of offenders. After all, we do not want them getting off, do we? In some cases, though, we might accept that. Preferring a few unsavoury individuals to walk free rather than compromise the foundations of which our liberties depend (Pirie, *The Guardian*, 9 February 2002).

The tension between double jeopardy and the law was highlighted by the media's treatment of the case after the publication of the Macpherson report. Prior to the report, the logic of double jeopardy was that it existed to prevent the law from running amok. In other words, the rule of double jeopardy *protects people from the law*. Pirie's position is that double jeopardy acts as a safeguard for human rights because it provides an internal limit to a law that may otherwise exceed the idea of neutral objectivity. Therefore, the liberal critique of the revision of the double jeopardy rule is concerned with the removal of counter-power that would seem to sanction legal absolutism.

The initial media campaign for justice resided in its support for the Lawrences rather than a criticism of structural law. However, because the Lawrences openly criticized the police and legal system, this too became part of the media discourse on the case. Here, the central question must be about the media's role. Was the media concerned to criticize racial prejudice or, on the contrary, to objectify racial subjectivity by siding with the Lawrences as middle-English folk? The danger of repealing the double jeopardy rule (understood as the judgement that seals legal authority by excluding the accused from future prosecution) referred to the influence that the media's treatment of the Lawrence case might have on legal objectivity. The defence of traditional legal authority would state that media coverage (like the *Daily Mail*'s 'MURDERERS' headline) could distort the neutrality of the legal process to such an extent that objective justice would become impossible. That is to say that in the event of a re-trial the media's influence would lead to a verdict based on popular opinion or mob justice rather than objective legal practice. In such circumstances the traditional authority of the law would be unable to dispense proper justice, because its authority would have been over-taken by the illegality of subjective, racial judgement. According to this situation, where the double jeopardy rule relates to the possibility that re-trials might be affected by the media's coverage of the initial judicial process, the role of the media is comparable to Macpherson's attempt to subjectify the objectivity of legal authority.

Therefore, the example of the double jeopardy rule allows us to see how the media performs a double function: (1) the institutions of the media seal the law, by forcing judicial authority to abandon the possibility of re-trials, and (2) compromise legal authority by suggesting that the ruling of the initial trial should be seen as a potential miscarriage of justice. It is precisely because of this understanding of the media as arbiter or supplement to judicial power that we need to argue against the interpretation of popular representations as critiques that might undercut the authority of the legal system (Žižek, 1993). This double function positions the media as a kind of overseer that criticizes objective judgement whilst supporting the ideology of the possibility of a just law.

One could, therefore, argue that newspaper coverage like the 'MURDERERS' headline is an attempt to criticize the double jeopardy rule as a synecdoche of the objective state of law. But this perspective, which sees the aim of such coverage as an attempt to undermine the traditional authority of the legal system, is misguided because it fails to understand how such representations of popular justice act to uphold the sustainability of the law. Therefore, while other commentators might argue that media representations can attack the traditional authority of the law by challenging dominant legal authority,[3] this attempt to circumvent legal objectivity can be understood as a device that supports the integrity of the law. In other words, the law depends on the existence of a germ of subjective judgement that is characterized by its illegal status, to sustain the authority of the legal sphere and the notion of objective justice (Derrida, 1990). In view of the necessary presence of subjective critique, the media's attempt to deal with racial antagonism is an activity that re-asserts the dominant ideology of liberal multiculturalism/ individualism. The media achieves this goal by endlessly repeating its double function. In other words, the media must challenge the progressive instinct of

---

[3] For instance Eric Gans (1997) states that symbolic expenditure is safer because it replaces the violence that can be the result of mob justice.

dominant legal authority (e.g. the Macpherson report) in order to protect the ideology of the law and the belief in an essential or objective truth.

The Backlash

The tabloid media's spontaneous move to criticize Macpherson's recommendations was understood by many to be a 'white backlash' to its progressive stance on racial antagonism. This sentiment was voiced in particular by right-wing newspapers after the publication of the Macpherson report. In defence of Britain as an egalitarian and tolerant state, *Daily Mail* columnist Stephen Glover expressed the stereotypical notion that young black men commonly commit trouble in this country:

> If I am walking alone at night in a badly lit London street I may be more disquieted by the sight of two black men coming towards me than of two white men. This is because I know that some 80% of muggings in London – not a figure you can generally quote without provoking uproar – are committed by young blacks, even though they form a small minority of the young population (Glover, *Daily Mail*, 26 February 1999).

Mirroring responses to ethnicity prior to the Lawrence campaign, this comment highlights the antagonistic relationship that continues to exist between ethnic groups and the press despite the appearance of tolerance. In a further piece in the *Spectator*, Glover tries to undermine the effects of the Macpherson report by saying that most people would see past its over-politically correct recommendations and continue to 'stumble on' through race relations (cited in Kundnani, 2000). Kundnani goes on to explain that: 'This, in a nutshell, was the Right's programme – the familiar English elite technique of integrating protest into a long-drawn-out process of reform which eventually results in the barest minimum of concessions' (Kundnani, 2000: 3).

Kundnani's critique of British legal reform highlights Douzinas' (2000) assessment of British common law. Explaining that, in contrast to American or European law, British law is 'commonsensical', Douzinas states that 18th Century philosophers such as Edmund Burke have defended British justice as the most perfect in the world. For thinkers such as Burke, the beauty of British common law resides in its evolutionary nature. From this perspective British law is a kind of quasi-organic system that evolves from out of its relationship to the community. Against the common law interpretation of the British model and its quasi-natural perfection, American and European law is seen as overly metaphysical. That is to say that the Burkean position would suggest that it is enacted from above the community and made by philosophers and theoretical lawyers.

Contemporary examples show how a residue of the Burkean position still permeates British legalism. Since the rise of the European Union and the global community (what Douzinas calls the human rights society), Britain has been critical of European legalism. Supporters of common law are critical of European attempts to enforce abstract philosophical arguments onto its own citizens, and since the rise of the human rights society, onto Britain. According to Douzinas, Britain has responded to this challenge by foregrounding the claims of traditional law. The defence of this position is that because common law depends on organic evolution to affect change, extremism is unlikely to occur and over-legalism is avoided. The revolutionary traditions of both Europe and America caused the instantaneous development of new legal orders, and opposed the British model of justice. From the perspective of common law, such revolutionary change is dangerous, as evidenced by the revolutionary terror in France, Stalinism's Soviet purges, and America's legal totalitarianism; justice is better served by organic modes of authority. In this sense common law is the institutionalization of natural law.

Following this logic, Glover's argument is that British justice is based on gradual reform of the status quo rather than massive revolutionary change. This conservative view of law is reflective of the media's treatment of the Lawrence case. The *Daily Mail* championed Lawrence so long as he remained fixed into a specific identity position (inclusive liberalism), but turned against the legalization of difference when it appeared to infringe the rights of the sealed individual. This effect was amplified by editorials by several *Daily Mail* columnists who accused the state among other things of 'politically correct McCarthyism' and of being 'Stalinist bullies' who threatened to damage the tolerant nature of British social relations (Lee-Potter, *Daily Mail*, 24 February 1999). This conviction was summed up by Andrew Alexander, who stated that 'beneath the benign face of do-gooders may lurk sinister totalitarian instincts of the sort normally associated with Stalin and Hitler' (Alexander, *Daily Mail*, 5 March 1999).

Therefore, while the initial media criticism of the law (for letting the thugs escape justice) appeared to call for the organization of a new legal order, its true aim was to shore up the dominant ideology of liberal multiculturalism. Consequently, the critique of institutional law, which suggested that legalism was failing with regard to its goal of justice, came from the space of a particular perspective (liberal individualism) rather than the open view of natural law. The media's intention was never to force the law to open to a more inclusive version of justice, but to secure the integrity of liberal individualism by criticising legalism for its inability to conform to its own ideological principles. Thus, the media's role in the Lawrence case was never about making the law sensitive to race, but to secure dominant ideology when the law failed to do so.

Evidence to support this interpretation of the media's position resides in the previous chapter's interpretation of the symbolic construction of the Lawrence case's key figures. Newspapers such as the *Daily Mail* were not concerned to open the law through the organization and representation of the Lawrences as middle-English characters. The law was seen to let down those at the very centre of British life, rather than those on the periphery of society. In fact these characters, who inhabit the pre-social (council es)state of nature, were condemned to their outlaw status. No attempt was made to rehabilitate the white trash. As the previous chapter has shown, this strategy, which sought to redefine the just nature of British multiculturalism in line with its own idea of itself, relied on particular discursive moves. The media's critique of the law appeared to endorse a radical critique of institutional justice. However, the fact that this criticism supported the cause of a black man (after his re-organization as virtual middle-class white man) and condemned the existence of ordinary racism as an exceptional transgression, shows that the media was really concerned to re-place the liberal veil of justice for a society that is beset by social inequality.

The totalitarian nature of this ideological system often produces its own transgressions. While problems within society are blamed on individual actors, who become containers for wider structural problems, it is predictable that individual actors who believe in the totalitarian vision of society as a coherent structure that is contaminated by aberrant others, will continue to enact their own violent attempts to confirm the totality of the law of the dominant ideology. By drawing a comparison between Timothy McVeigh (as representative of the excessive logic of the American ideology) and the thugs (as a symbol of the extreme right-wing in Britain), one can see how it was their very belief in the ideology of the coherent nation (American and British) that provoked their violent acts. For Gulf War veteran McVeigh, the realization that America failed to live up to its own ideology proved too much to bear. However, his attempt to attack structural authority (bombing the Oklahoma federal building) at once confirmed the American ideology (McVeigh was a maverick individual, the archetypal American) and threatened to exceed its own boundaries. By taking the myth of the frontier to heart, McVeigh threatened to over-reach the American ideology. Because he took the Constitution literally he was concerned to attack the representation of authority, rather than marginalized members of the community (e.g. the ethnic other, the standard target for the excluded). In contrast to McVeigh, the political arm of the far right in Britain – the BNP – provides a more established symbol of antagonism precisely because it fails to recognize structural considerations in favour of demonising the ethnic other.

Following 'End of History' declarations from Francis Fukuyama (1993), one can understand why the far right has become the popular alternative to third way politics. In Britain, France, Germany, Austria, Denmark, Holland, and America far right groups have achieved political support because their opposition to the dominant order avoids the structural critiques of the old Left in favour of the demonization of the other. In his *New Left Review* article 'Why We All Love to Hate Haider', Žižek (2000) has argued that the far right's re-emergence as a political force should be understood as a consequence of the Left's move to the centre. His theory is that socialist parties aimed to represent the poor (socially excluded). However, the need to gain power led these parties to move towards the centre of party politics. As such, socialism jettisoned its critique of the economy in favour of the politics of minor reform. In this regard, the acceptance of the capitalist economy as a quasi-natural force led to the acceptance of the figure of the liberal individual as a natural character. It is this foreclosure of structural politics that abandons critique to the far right and its demonization of particular individuals as ciphers for the problems of the social order:

... the moment we introduce the 'thriving multitude' what we effectively assert is its exact opposite, an underlying all-pervasive Sameness – a non-antagonistic society in which there is room for all manner of cultural communities, lifestyles, religions, sexual orientations. The reply of a materialist theory is to show that this very One already relies in certain exclusions: the common field in which plural identities sprout is from the start sustained by an invisible antagonistic split (Žižek, 2000: 39).

Insofar as the extreme right wing has become the voice of the man on the street, one can argue that BNP racism represents the excessive truth of *Daily Mail* common-sense rhetoric. That is to say that far right politics often mirrors middle-ground ideology. For example, the media's critique of British asylum policy is repeated in the BNPs' xenophobic attacks on ethnic others. As such, the Lawrence suspects' violent demonstration of their racist views exposes the excessive truth of centre politics. They are agents of the social order and their views derive from the media as arbiter of the collective social order. However, the suspects' problem is that their racism exceeds the exclusionary politics of state law. Even though their actions conform to the logic of the nation, they are illegal. This illegality is determined by their over-conformity. It is this over-identification that threatens to expose the exclusionary logic of the law of the nation state. In order to prevent such exposure the media is, therefore, required to abandon the men to the state of nature. While this activity confirms the state's exclusionary logic, it also restores the notion of the law as a fair institution in need of repair, and confirms the just nature of liberal ideology, by standing against the criminal excesses of right-wing extremism.

This last point goes some way to explain why the Lawrence case was subject to renewed political interest after almost five years of unsuccessful legal process. In a climate of political change sponsored by the possibility of a New Labour election victory, the Lawrences became a symbol of British multiculturalism (i.e. the dominant ideology of the inclusive nature of British society), while the suspects were cast out as an archaic reminder of working-class poverty and criminality (that bore no resemblance to the new middle-class exclusivity of New Labour). From this point of view the main problem with the suspects was that they came to represent evil insiders. This category of inside-outsider is more dangerous than that of the ethnic other (who can be grouped as deviant in an Orientalist discourse) because they remind us of the possibilities of our own apparently inclusive logic: violence. In other words, white transgression is seen to be more dangerous to the social order because it exposes the logic of dominant ideology. It shows how the ideology of liberal inclusion depends on its own form of exclusivity for survival.

Lawrence became important because the positive construction of a particular instance of black British identity (the middle-English attributes given to the Lawrences) allowed the press to define Britain as a truly inclusive state. However, this logic ignored the fact that to be included one has to first prescribe to certain middle-class ideals. The other side of this apparent inclusivity is represented by the suspects' racism. Working-class Britain – seen as a place which has never really caught up to the rest of the country – becomes a pole of intolerance that re-defines multicultural tolerance. The fact that this version of liberalism relies on the exclusion of otherness (white thugs and non-middle-English blacks), an activity that mirrors the suspects' own intolerance, remains hidden behind the rhetoric of liberalism that transforms outsiders (blacks) into insiders (middle-English) and insiders (working-class/underclass whites) into outsiders (dangerous criminals) in order to create the image of total inclusion (multicultural Britain). However, while the media's coverage of Lawrence sought to produce symbolic integrity and re-order dominant ideology as imaginary institution, the Macpherson report became the law's own answer to the need for reform. It is clear that the media coverage surrounding the Lawrence case produced the Macpherson report and that we should see this policy document as an attempt by the law to reform itself, to conform to its own image of justice. In this regard the law took into account those issues that the media had pushed to the foreground of British politics:

> We believe that the Stephen Lawrence Inquiry has provided such publicity and such awareness of the problems directly and indirectly revealed that there is now a signal opportunity to deal with specific matters arising from the murder and all that followed (Macpherson, 1999: 2.17, p4).

Yet, because the media was always concerned with the image of inclusion, Macpherson's policy document was seen to go too far. As my analysis of the Lawrence case representation shows, the media's notion of Britain as a multicultural state was qualified by particular conservative principles which never went beyond the demands of dominant ideology. As such, Macpherson's attempt to institute legal openness and build sensitivity to otherness into the law itself horrified the media, which understood the difference between imaginary inclusion and structural critique. Akin to McVeigh, therefore, who took American ideology to heart; Macpherson took the media's critique of legal closure too seriously. It was this failure to maintain the distance between what the ideology said and how society could look in practice that led to the media's backlash. That is to say that after supporting the principles of multiculturalism, the same media sources reversed their position to critique Macpherson.

Perhaps the media's criticisms of Macpherson's proposals can now be understood as something more than a 'white backlash'. Although the conservative and liberal press provided conflicting criticisms of the report's recommendations, they were equally against its attempt to open the law. For example critical argumentation would suggest that to abolish double jeopardy would be to open the law to subjectivity and otherness. Against the liberal media position, which was concerned with the image of undecidability, Macpherson's critique sought to de-limit the integrity of the law. While media sources such as *The Guardian* continued to critique the argument for the revision of double jeopardy on the grounds that the removal of limitations within the law itself could lead to the expansion of judicial power, they missed the point that the possibility of justice is unavoidably linked to the possibility of evil (Derrida, 1994). In other words, although the newspaper was right to argue that the abolition of double jeopardy could lead to the erosion of civil liberties (due to the fact that the law would gain expansive powers to try suspects an indefinite number of times) it was wrong to assume that this would be the natural outcome of legal openness. As Douzinas (2000) explains although the possibility of justice is marked by the problem of excessive legalism, this cannot lead us to abandon the utopianism of the natural law tradition that continues to push to open the law.

Methods of Maintaining Social Stability

From the perspective of liberal inclusion the Lawrence case can be recognized as a further example of the scapegoat mechanism that acts to reassert the dominance of law. To explain how the authority of structural law is upheld through representational shifts that at first appear to undermine its dominance, then move toward its reinstatement, Lawrence must first be understood as the cipher for narratives of law. The first stage of Lawrence's rehabilitation occurs when he is physically killed by a racist society characterized by the white assailants. They act out the violence of the originary scene, whereby the social system is arranged around the death of an alien other (Girard, 1986; 1996). In this instance Lawrence equals the other or scapegoat, sacrificed in order to guarantee internal (white) cohesion. Second, the media representation of Lawrence is itself a scapegoat. Because the text is consumed in the same way as Lawrence's body it re-balances the social system in much the same way as the actual murder. In the second instance we should understand that it is because we consume events from within the bounds of contemporary western liberal democracies that representations of the real must be constantly reorganized in order to obscure the harshness of the disordered system in which they actually exist. In other words, although Britain is popularly presented as a tolerant and generally non-racist society, the reality of its structure is illustrated by the aforementioned first level of sacrifice. As this proposition contradicts the idea of a democratic system it must be over-written by the more acceptable perception of singular acts of violence. In this regard, the five white men accused of murder constitute an extreme position, successfully concealing wider society's racism, in much the same way that Lawrence illustrates the victimary sign; the excessive consequence of brutal individuality.

Therefore, the rule against difference, which shapes the structural inequalities inherent within the ideology of liberal individualism, is over-written by agents of the social order who become containers for the system's racial prejudice. Due to this process of transference the real nature of the objectivity of the law remains obscure: the particular agents of the social order become the racist outlaws that save the ideological notion of liberal multiculturalism. Put another way, the racism of the outlaws allows them to become martyrs to the cause of the wider, racist socio-political system. Within this ideological complex the media's critique of the law acts to repress the otherness of the original victim (in this instance the subject of racial difference, Lawrence) and initially attack the faults of the judicial system. However, these representational attacks on the flaws of the legal process evade the issue of structural violence in order to concentrate on mistakes that are characteristic of a legal system that is subject to the possibility of human error.[4] In this regard, the 'Law' is no longer seen as being racist.

From this perspective it is clear how the double function of the media works in the Lawrence example. The media acts to repress subjective racial difference (because Lawrence is re-coded as an insider) and critique the law for allowing the five men (who have already become guilty of being racist outlaws) to escape the rule of law. The media's criticism avoids the question of structural racism and thus obscures the issue of the subjectivity of the social order. This is made apparent on the one hand by the backlash against Macpherson's consideration of a racist society, and on the other hand by recourse to the issue of the double jeopardy rule. That is to say that the double bind that surrounds the media's relationship with British racism and the double jeopardy rule pulls both examples back into the position that they are arguing against. Here, the *Daily Mail*'s assertion that Britain is not racist plays out the logic of the racist argument, and *The Guardian*'s criticism of double jeopardy, despite its overall support for Macpherson, undermines the call for subjective critique. Consequently, both positions act to re-stabilize the authority of law by evading the question of subjective critique and once again re-coding the suspects in the role of outlaw. The subjectivity of legal judgement is therefore dramatized by finding the racist outlaws guilty apart from the necessity of a guilty verdict.

It is precisely because of this understanding of the violence that occupies the centre of legal practice that Girard's (1986) theory of the scapegoat mechanism might illuminate my exploration of the Lawrence case. First, Girard's thesis tallies with the suggestion that Lawrence became representative of the sacrificial expenditure of a society organized around the endless expulsion of subjective otherness. By foregrounding a theory of structural determinism, Girard's theory also relates to the exploration of the five white men accused of the Lawrence murder as agents of the violence of the social order. Girard's assertion is that such agents might be seen as containers for the repetitious violence of the founding gesture of the social order. Here, the Lawrence murder is representative of an example of the expenditure that aims to guarantee future social cohesion. Second, my thesis about the violence that is done to textual signs is comparable to Girardian theory. In this instance, the idea of media objectivization can be compared to the model of the scapegoat myth. Girard defines these stories, which work to rehabilitate the status of the outlaw, as agents of ideological manipulation. In my exploration of the Lawrence case I have also considered the possibility that the media representations of the events surrounding Lawrence's murder might be similarly representative of a sacrificial text or mythology that aims to re-code the body of Lawrence as legal subject.

My argument about the role of the media has suggested that, because we consume events from inside the parameters of a particular form of social organization (liberal democracy), representations of the reality of the law require endless re-coding in order to obscure the harshness of the illegal system in which

---

[4] For instance legal process is subject to subjective interpretation by Judges, juries etc.

the events actually occur. In other words, although Britain understands itself as a tolerant, non-racist society, the reality of its structure is illustrated by the aforementioned first level of sacrificial violence. It is precisely because the nature of this reality contradicts the idea of a democratic, multicultural society that the media attempts to over-write the disorder of the social double bind with a more acceptable explanation of the nature of singular acts of violence. In order to achieve this acceptable understanding of violence, the media, as guarantor of symbolic security, saw the five white men accused of the Lawrence murder as racist thugs: they became representative of men who occupy the extremity of the outlaw position.

Against this interpretation of the outlaw as racist thug, the inclusive understanding of Lawrence, which sought to critique legal judgement and portray Lawrence as a sympathetic victim, saw the attempt to reorganize racial difference as an objective example of full citizenship in the state of liberal democracy. In other words the rehabilitation of Lawrence saw his transformation into disciplined black man/virtual white man. When the national newspapers eventually reported the murder, they discovered an erudite and respectable family behind an all-too-common case of racial hatred. By contrast to this version of the Lawrence family, the media then sought to present British society with an image of white extremism; of racist thugs making a mockery of the law. The accused killers became representative of the category of white trash. They were written into the role of the alien other, a situation that might be seen as the traditional territory of the black man as racial alien.

In ideological terms the importance of this move was to transfer the racism that is inherent to the state of liberal individualism onto the image of the murderous periphery. The five men accused of Lawrence's murder became emblematic of working-class criminality: they took on the role of the hidden sector of illegal subjectivity that haunts democratic society and problematizes its ideological coherence. In line with this perspective, Brian Cathcart speculates that because the suspects sought to debase the legal system by refusing to co-operate – by 'holding two fingers up to British Justice' (2000: 288) – they saw themselves as being above the law. The British media understood their symbolic value as deviant individuals. The effect of the construction of this position was to reorganize the authority of the law: the men became outlaws rather than subjects sympathetic to the rule of the society of ordinary racism.

By contrast to the demonization of the thugs, Lawrence was represented through religious iconography. The stained glass window bearing his image linked Lawrence to Princess Diana (who had also become a saintly figure) but more importantly to divine law and the Protestantism that backs capital accumulation (Weber, 1992). As a consequence Lawrence became a media-friendly martyr to postmodern capitalism. Girard shows that the person who is expelled from society for their difference is held up as the saviour of society. As such, Lawrence became the saviour of the liberal theory of multiculturalism even though he was murdered for his difference from the dominant ideology of white society. Weber's notion of the ordinary-extraordinary individual can also illuminate the logic at work in the Lawrence case. Lawrence was ordinary precisely because he was member of a capitalist society, but extra-ordinary because he became the other who was sacrificed for the sake of the social order. The tragic nature of Lawrence is written into every text that bears his image. From the media perspective he represents the heroic black man that might have made it in white society, who was murdered before he could achieve his goal in Britain's meritocratic society. However, from the critical point of view Lawrence was the outsider to British society, the black man who became a hero after his death.

According to this discrepancy between the two images of blackness (outsider black/heroic black) that defined Lawrence's identity as scapegoat, it can be understood how media institutions divide society into good and evil sectors and then exclude the individuals defined as evil in order to retain the legitimacy of the wider social system. Girard supports this view when he argues that society needs literal sacrifices to guarantee internal cohesion. He states that when a society is threatened with collapse (due to difficult or violent conditions such as social unrest, widespread disease, or war) the disordered masses need re-ordering to prevent total social failure. To achieve this form of collective order, society must unite against a common enemy. He proposes that a sacrificial victim acts as an object of mimesis or identification for the community acting out their aggression and fear. The scapegoat must be sufficiently like the perpetrators so that it can be recognized, but also must be different enough to indicate to the collective that it is outside normal moral society. This allows the community to sanction their actions against the sacrifice. According to this model, societies need and use scapegoats to project communal violence onto an external force. But to contain the evil within a sacrificial victim is unjust, says Girard, because it allows wider society to legitimate the innocence of the collective. When Lawrence campaigners and the Macpherson report accused the police force of institutional racism and the wider social order of being racist, individual actors were publicly scapegoated: police representative Metropolitan Police Commissioner Sir Paul Condon, and suspects Neil and Jamie Acourt, Gary Dobson, Luke Knight and David Norris. As such, the representation of Stephen Lawrence and the subsequent unfolding set of conditions provided the social with a continual scapegoat mechanism with which to absolve the collective from blame. As the following excerpt by *Guardian* writer Hugo Young understands, individual scapegoats appease the collective by attributing guilt to particular actors:

> Resignations by top people for misbehaviour by their subordinates are usually just symbolic: not proof of guilt but fulfilment of a ritual of accountability (Young, *The Guardian*, 23 February 1999).

Following this model we can see how the progressive scapegoat mechanism works through Girard's theory of mimetic desire. Here, Lawrence's role is dependent on the interaction of the two polar opposites: the alleged murderers and the police. The roles occupied by the polar opposites are interchangeable because they can be both guilty and innocent. The shifting of these roles alters the position occupied by Lawrence. Without the alleged murderers Lawrence is just another guilty victim, for example the victim of his own involvement in gang-related crime. However, due to media rehabilitation he becomes a martyr – a law-abiding 'A' level student, the victim of unjustified violence – while the suspects are re-ordered as evil racists, the exceptional element within a non-racist liberal democracy. The failure of the democratic society to convict the racists then leads to the scapegoat mechanism's accusation of the police as represented by the individual incompetence of certain officers. By focusing on the police in such a way, the scapegoat mechanism provides a critique of law and order without developing an explicit case against the British justice system as a whole. So, rather than recognising that the law itself is reliant on an unlawful violent foundation (in Benjamin's (1986b) terms, the police) this perspective would initially appear to accuse Condon for the corruption of an otherwise faultless judicial process. Despite the fact that the media is well aware that the police reflect society and do not uphold objective law, it was still concerned to find individual representatives of the law who could be found guilty for the failure of the wider institution. Mirroring the argument from the Macpherson report, Young acknowledges this process:

> The condition of the police, however, is only symptomatic. In the end, policemen mimic society. Working at the most jagged social frontier, their vices provoke most conflict, but the vices are not theirs alone. They have the greatest obligation to bury their racism, and need the most stringent rulebook to help them in this task (Young, *The Guardian*, 23 February 1999).

Despite this realization of the relationship between police and society, the media still required individual scapegoats. However, Condon's resignation did not provide adequate closure for the situation. He was sacrificed in order to create space for the critique of the Macpherson report, which suggested the corruption of tolerant British society. This is the final move of the scapegoat mechanism. Because the Macpherson report followed the friendly logic of the self/other thesis (that we need to allow the other to speak), and therefore speculated on the notion of an unjust society, it too had to be sacrificed in order to maintain the image of the Law.

Moral Deference

In the above sections I have shown how the retrospective objectification of Lawrence as representative of racial difference was the central purpose of the media's representation of the case. This was because the original state of the expenditure of Lawrence threatened to expose the illegal violence that both sustains and contradicts the possibility of the ideology of liberal individualism. This dangerous state was emblematic of the nature of the case before the discovery of the evil racism of the white working-class periphery. Prior to the arrest of the alleged murderers, Lawrence was representative of another guilty victim. However, because this vision of British race relations threatened to destabilize the image of the law by uncovering the obscene violence that conditions its very existence, Lawrence was re-made a racial martyr. He became representative of the black man as insider – encompassing the ideologies of family, education, and work – and the victim of anomalous racial violence. In order to further stabilize this vision of Britain as a liberal multicultural society, the five white thugs became evil racists, examples of the state of the exceptional periphery that stood against the rule of Britain as non-racist liberal democracy. Beyond this instance of scapegoating, whereby the five individual racists became responsible for the racism of the wider social order, the failure of democratic society to convict the racists led to the scapegoat mechanism's accusation of Sir Paul Condon as individual representative of wider police incompetence. By focusing on this particular case of police ineptitude, the media scapegoat mechanism was able to develop a critique of the law that avoided recourse to an explicit argument against the British justice system as a fallible method for dispensing objective judgements.

Thus, it can be understood how representation divides society according to insider/outsider social relations and then scapegoat the individuals defined as outsiders in order to retain the legitimacy of the wider social system (Girard, 1986). Following my definition of corporeal violence, this theory proposes that a sacrificial victim acts as a lost object of mimesis or identification for a community acting out the repetitious re-statement of its social order's founding gesture. In contemporary Britain this foundational gesture can be regarded as the re-staging of the exclusion of subjectivity that is required by the democracy of liberal individualism. In the works of Girard this sacrificial process, or *skandalon*, is regarded as definitive of the category of (a)social evil. He argues for this definition of evil because the skandalon's work dramatizes the nature of the social system that is based on the exclusion of otherness. Indeed, because this mode of violence allows wider society to legitimate the innocence of the social order, one can therefore argue for its ethical value. Despite the probability that the individual racist may be unaware of the social value of his/her violence, we can follow the Kantian definition of radical evil described by Copjec (1996), that reads violence as a coherent ethical activity. That is to say that while the individual racist remains oblivious to the philosophical or ideological ethic that underscores his/her actions, the social order provides the necessary structural coherence to his/her violence. In this regard the ideological position of society relates to the idea of radical evil: its function provides the ethic for the continuation of racial antagonism as a guarantor of the sustainability of the social order.

However, this position that sees the social order providing the rationale for racial violence, must evade the conclusion that racist individuals cannot be held responsible for their own activities (Salecl, 1996). On the contrary the ethic of racial subjectivity is about resistance to the ideology of liberal multiculturalism. In contrast to this political system – which I have argued both removes the subjectivity of racial difference and creates further agents of racism, as those who lose their racial subjectivity are re-coded into objective sameness – the argument in favour of subjectivity forms the central component of the theory of racial resistance. In order to organize this critical response to late capitalism, one can refer to several comparable sources. First, Girard's proposal for a Christian ethics, which points to the figure of Christ as a kind of originary victim, aims to over-code the scapegoat mechanism by exposing the violence that forms its core to the wider social order. Related to Girard's thesis of the ethics of the other, Laurence Thomas (1998) suggests the concept of moral deference as a secular version of the legalization of the other's subjectivity. According to Thomas, political theory should refrain from the temptation to speak *for* the other or objectify their situation. Instead, Thomas believes that politics should listen to the other's testimony and accept the element of difference that means that the self can never completely understand the other:

> Moral deference... is not about whether individuals are innocent with respect to those who have been treated unjustly... Rather, moral deference is simply about the appropriate moral attitude to take when it comes to understanding the ways in which another has been a victim of social injustice (Thomas, 1998: 359-360).

These two sources describe the ethical position of Macpherson's attempt to open the traditional authority of the law. First, Macpherson's ethical effort to centralize the position of the victim of racial antagonism appears to follow Girard's religious morality. However, because Macpherson's target is the reform of legal discourse, rather than refer to any form of religious morality, the notion of moral deference, which Thomas uses to define his attempt to legalize subjective experience, is a closer comparison to the particular secular politics of the Macpherson report's form of resistance. The aim of Macpherson's project is therefore the legalization of subjectivity as a means to the creation of a more inclusive social politics. The related effect of this effort might be to undercut the ethical nature of racial violence. That is to say that the opening up of the ideology of objectivity by the legalization of racial difference may lessen the frequency of occurrences of racial antagonism. This is a possibility precisely because the renewed ideological position of society will no longer serve to legitimate the attitudes or behaviour of racist individuals. Therefore, the effect of Macpherson's project is that the other becomes responsible for their own identity. This expansion of the ideology of individualism also represents the withdrawal of the exclusive politics of liberal individualism that acts as both the ideological support and philosophical alibi for the individual racist. In light of the withdrawal of the support of the racist society, the individual racist would, therefore, also become responsible for their own subjective beliefs and the ethical status of their own actions (Salecl, 1996).

   This political theory, which wants to claim ethical responsibility for the individual, differs from liberal individualism because it accepts racial difference (Žižek, 1998). While the politics of liberal individualism create a condition of (a)social introspection or social ignorance, the theory of racial subjectivity might thrust the individual outside itself towards the sphere of social intercourse: difference is the grounds for communication rather than a barrier to self/other relations. The acceptance of the lack of full subjectivity means that 'the man from nowhere' is unable to remain the self-sufficient ideal of the (a)social society. It is, therefore, my contention that people are more likely to accept responsibility for others when the 'politics of recognition' have become the ideological orthodoxy (Taylor, 1994; O'Neill, 2001). Following the legalization of subjectivity, and the popularization of a politics that views the greatest freedom of the individual in terms of the greatest freedom of wider society, we might be able to diminish the frequency of instances of racial antagonism and further the progress of the evolution of the inclusive society.

Conclusion

Toward an Ethics of Representation

My examination of the media's representation of the Louise Woodward and Stephen Lawrence cases has provided a way in which to understand how dominant narratives of law and order prevail in a world which recognizes the impact of media messages on social constructions of identity. Ever since authors such as Cohen (1972) and Hall et al (1978) wrote about the amplifying effects of the media on social concerns such as youth delinquency and the 'problem' of race, it has been understood that one of the functions of the media is to uphold dominant ideologies of social order. In addition to these contributions about the effect that the media has on society's relationship to the other, ideas of the consumer society and postmodern spectacle forwarded by theorists such as Baudrillard (1995) explain the anaesthetising effect of the media and the trivialising process of global communications technology. In this study it was my intention to consider these accounts on the relationship between media and society, and advance a discussion about current trends in media communications and public sphere debate. However, the process of examining my two cases in such depth has led me to consider the further implications of media discourse insofar as it relates to the social, political, economic, and legal arenas.

By considering ideas such as Foucault's genealogy of discipline and regulation and Girard's thesis on the scapegoat mechanism, I have shown how media narratives reflect the ideology of the society in which they exist. Cosmopolitan or multicultural considerations rarely enter the realm of popular media discourse, which continues to separate people based on the traditional exclusions of nation, race, gender, and class. This appears to be because it is the function of media discourse to maintain, rather than question, dominant ideology. Indeed, through my investigation of the Woodward and Lawrence cases I have found that even when it appears as though media representations are concerned to criticize authority in favour of the underdog, during the ensuing discursive battles the authority of the social order is more often than not preserved.

Such a reading would suggest a pessimistic view of public sphere communication. Nevertheless, it is also clear that the influence of the media can have a positive effect on legal process. This was reflected by the development of a more inclusive notion of justice represented by the Macpherson Report, which took as its starting point the high level of public concern sustained by the media. From this example one can recognize that the media is able to open up the space for discussion in order to challenge traditional authority. Problems occur, however, when an element of risk, or uncertainty, seeps into the process of criticism. When Macpherson took on the challenge to open the law to criticism, the media attempted to restore the state of theoretical closure. It is clear that this reaction occurred because it is difficult for western truth based societies to accept notions of open-endedness and undecidability. Consideration of the double jeopardy example may illuminate this situation. In the case of double jeopardy the argument for repeal is that guilty people who are found innocent may be tried again in order to reach an accurate verdict. The argument against the repeal of the double jeopardy rule is that legal power will be extended to the extent that it will be impossible to escape guilt, i.e. one will only be ever provisionally innocent. Therefore, the repeal of the act to achieve a more just, victim-centred, legal system involves a risk (the possibility of legal totalitarianism) that many commentators were unwilling to take. However, as authors such as Derrida (1994) and Douzinas (2000) have shown, the law must be open to risk in order to be just. One cannot dispense justice through theoretical calculations alone. True justice requires a faculty of judgment that cannot be systematized or ever made certain. As such, it may be the case that those critics who argued against the repeal of double jeopardy simply could not accept that the law makes mistakes.

In a broader sense one might suggest that such critics were also concerned to uphold the distinct balance between right and wrong insofar as these positions are reflected in the legal verdicts of guilt and innocence. In my other case, Zobel's judgment of Woodward's involuntary guilt served to close down the possibility of justice by casting the nanny as a child who could not be held responsible for her own actions. In this regard Woodward was made guilty in the eyes of the social order for her failure to conform to the ideal of male rationality. Against those who attempt to close down the space for critique almost as soon as it has been opened, my theory of victim centred justice suggests that the law should hold on to the space of undecidability even though this entails great risk. However, as authors such as Derrida and Douzinas have shown, it is only by taking this risk that the law will recognise that the positions of right and wrong, guilt and innocence, are not absolutes, but change according to specific contexts and alter according to particular perspectives. In the sense that the media criticizes legal process perhaps it seeks to undermine the domination of one particular perspective in favour of the spirit of opposition. This tendency supports my argument for an ethical, critical, mode of legal decision-making. However, through the process of writing the legal case in question, the media also seeks to impose its own dominant world view upon events. It is this representational form of decisionism that my work seeks to explore and expose. In the previous chapters I have considered processes of narrativization and social construction in action thorough an analysis of media representations. I have also sought to reflect upon these stories as symbols of wider social, political, economic, and cultural conditions.

Moving Images

In an effort to establish the similarity of the media treatment, and the comparability of the regulatory effects, of my two main cases one can refer to the television 'confessions' of Woodward and the 'Lawrence Five' given after the *legal* fact of their guilt had been decided. For Woodward the trial provided an uncontrollable public arena where she was castigated for her inappropriate courtroom behaviour. At first she appeared unemotional. This appearance was, to begin with, largely read to suggest that she was uncaring. However, many observers would later come to understand this response as illustrative of her youth and immaturity, rather than suggestive of her calculated callousness and potential monstrosity. According to Helena Kennedy (1992) the emotional output of female defendants is often an important feature of the trial, which can influence not only the opinion of the lay jury and public, but also of the lawyers and judge who are not immune to the demands of social and political pressure. In this regard Woodward had already been subject to identity constructions that (whether intended as positive or negative) put her in a difficult position. From the point of view of the law, and the media that covered the case, Woodward was a text that could be read for evidence of her guilt or innocence. Microscopic analysis of the defendant would surely betray her legal status.

Following such ocular examination it is easy to see why Woodward would want to tell her side of the story to the British public, who, she believed, had supported her plight. However, the *Panorama* interview conducted by Martin Bashir turned into a public relations nightmare for Woodward, who, in an attempt to assert her innocence, merely succeeded in reaffirming the element of doubt that had emerged from the initial legal decision. The interview itself was innocuous enough. Bashir's 'hard-hitting' questions cannot have come as a surprise to Woodward. What caused problems for her was the *fact* of the television *appearance*, rather than anything she said. The interview was recognized by media commentators as an attempt by Woodward to take control of her own representation. Picking up on insignificant details such as her stylish new haircut, make-up, and wardrobe, the newspapers that had once championed her cause proceeded to bring her down. Now that she had decided to manage her own appearance, it seemed as though she was concerned to nullify the gift of freedom given to her by the paternalistic social system and affirm her right to sovereignty beyond the authority of a legal decision that may have set her free *despite* the truth of her guilt. While the social, and in America the legal, order had given Woodward her freedom, despite the fact that they believed she was guilty of something, it was unacceptable for her to champion her own innocence. Because she wanted to assert her own innocence, rather than be given her freedom, she became fair game for re-trial by mediatized popular justice.

Woodward could not sustain popular innocence because the space of undecidability over the legal facts of the case was closed. She had been given her freedom on the premise of her abjection – her weakness as a woman – that rendered her subordinate to the dominant patriarchal social structure. As such, it was wholly unacceptable for her to try to break the terms of her contract with the social – freedom in exchange for abjection – by attempting to reassert her own personal dignity. She could be free only insofar as her freedom was given to her by the Judge (father) as representative of the social order. The men accused of the Lawrence murder occupied a similar position: their freedom was provisional upon silent acceptance of their guilt. That is to say that the Lawrence suspects could never be seen as blameless because of their long refusal to talk to both the law and media. Their apparent guilt, supported by their own refusal to suggest otherwise, became the condition of possibility of their freedom. Media commentators continue to ask: surely, if they were innocent they would speak out to clear their names? However, the media challenge to those involved in miscarriage of justice cases to speak out, to clear their name, leads back into the logic that seeks to condemn such figures for their very attempt to close down their own undecidability (they hope to turn the judgment that says 'innocent yet probably guilty' or 'guilty, but didn't mean it' to one that confirms 'wholly innocent'). Yet, rather than serving to prove their innocence, the representational order often seems to confirm the guilt of such people. While they may have slipped the net and escaped true legal judgment, the role of the media is to modify the original judgment and pass true sentence (guilty)[1] upon those who attempt to protest their innocence too strongly after grace from the legal system.

The idea of grace, whereby the social system allows the individual their freedom, and the confession, that places the subject in a relation of debt to the collective order, are strands that run through much of Foucault's work. He argues that modern society is geared around the search for an essential truth (the origin of things) that can only be exposed through the interrogation of the individual. The inter-relation between this search for truth and the disciplinary function of Enlightenment knowledge is, for Foucault, the essence of the modern period (Foucault, 1991). As such, the role of the confession is similar to that of the search for other forms of knowledge. Its aim is to discover the essence of the person who undergoes interrogation. Here, the very act of confession, the fact that the person has been placed in the situation where they are expected to confess, means that they must be guilty of some transgression or other. To suggest that one has nothing to say is no answer. This lack of response, or a response that uncovers nothing, simply defers the act of confession. That is to say that the guilty person simply does not know what they have to confess, or have not yet reached social age (i.e. they must still be a pre-social child). It is at this point that psychoanalysis enters the equation. The person who does not know their own mind (according to Freud nobody does) is encouraged to open their conscious mind to their own truth (the unconscious). Similarly, the media spectacle is another form of confession that seeks to gain knowledge of the person, who may or may not know their own truth, through processes of hyper-visibility. While psychoanalysis seeks to plumb the depths of the psyche for knowledge of the truth, the media spectacle aims, as the Woodward example was able to show, to capture the person in its gaze so that the truth will appear.

---

[1] This logic also works in the opposite direction, whereby people who are wrongly imprisoned can be found innocent by the media. The effect of this process is to modify legal judgment so that the law can bestow freedom upon those wrongly accused, thus closing down the space of undecidability – guilt/innocence – insofar as it relates to legal judgment. However, should such individuals continue to criticise the law for its original failure and not show sufficient gratitude for the law's reversal, they also become problematic characters.

While this panoptic process is primarily a disciplinary one, it may also be attractive to the individual who believes that they can tame the search for truth and prove their own innocence through its technologies. Consequently, after years of silence from the Lawrence suspects, during which time they refused to publicly declare either guilt or innocence, they attempted to manage their representation through an appearance on the *Tonight with Trevor MacDonald* programme. This action from the five men was regarded as a cynical attempt to use the media to assert their innocence only after the space for legal recourse had been closed. Although the programme-makers were widely criticized for giving the men a channel to speak, the interview in fact merely served to feed back into the popular representation of the men as 'thugs'. This act of defiance from the suspects undoubtedly upset the media that wanted an acceptable resolution to the Lawrence affair. Again, it is clear from the existence of such post-decision interviews that the purpose of the media is to interrogate the case further, to serve as a regulatory system that might close down the space of legal undecidability by attributing either guilt or innocence. In the Lawrence case the media was able to do this by transferring undecidability from the law onto the former suspects. In legal terms they are innocent – the law has done its job – but we never really know about their true status. Guilty or innocent, we are never sure. A person implicated in a crime is never really free from suspicion.

Nevertheless, the desire of the former suspects to 'set the record straight' makes them seek further media attention in the form of the television confession. They not only want to be structurally innocent, but also to be regarded as truly innocent: to be absolved. To achieve this effect former suspects often attempt to use the same media that oversaw their initial sacrifice to rescue their dubious reputations. They are concerned to clear their debt to the social system. They want freedom on their own terms, rather than have to accept the legal decision that they are innocent, though they may be guilty. In theoretical writings this desire for wholeness (the former suspects want to be wholly innocent) has a long tradition. According to the structuralist tradition the failure to be whole is what defines the human condition: to be human is to be split between the self and the other inside the self. In his psychoanalytic writings Freud was able to explain the lack of wholeness in terms of the split between the id and the ego that occurs when the child undergoes socialization. He showed how in order to become human (rather than animal) we must repress the desires of the id to the unconscious, whilst internalizing social regulation and therefore becoming ego-centric. While this split allows us to be social, in that we do not act on our repressed desires (e.g. to kill), the desire to rediscover the unity of the self remains intact. This desire, Freud argues, is the defining principle of human life, which runs through religious and secular society and problematizes civilization (Freud, 1939/1991).

The will to rediscover the unity of the self may therefore lead a person to explore the possibility of their lost innocence that is understood to be found in childhood or, before then, in the pre-Oedipal stage of development. However, it is inevitable that in maturity this desire for wholeness will run up against the law – either religious law when we ask God for forgiveness, or secular law when we attempt to prove our innocence to the social/legal system – because it is this very paternal edifice that split the self in the first place. When we are reminded of our split self (that is both innocent like a child and guilty for feelings of incest that provoked the wrath of the paternal law in the first place) we look to the law for approval. The law recalls both our lack before the father (that he knew our disobedient thoughts) and promises a lost sense of wholeness that we can never rediscover (because the law scolds us, we believe it can absolve us of the guilt caused by our endless desire for wholeness, incestuous reunion with the mother). However, the rediscovery of wholeness is impossible because we continue to desire a return to source. Even desires that run through sublimation contain a germ that is incestuous. It is, therefore, unlikely, if not impossible, for the law to find us wholly innocent. From a Freudian point of view we are always guilty before the God/law. It will never give us its complete approval, even though it might tolerate us like a wayward child who can be given their freedom on condition that they remember their scolding.

It is, therefore, apparent that subjects can never be wholly innocent because the desire to be seen as innocent depends on approval from the social order – i.e. innocent in the eyes of the father. This is the paradox of the confessional appeal (a declaration of innocence) to the wider social order: the desire for self-unity requires a return to the innocence of a pre-social state of being – a return to the state of nature – that necessitates being involved in social communication. Thus, the relationship between individual and society is always one of lack, guilt, or splitting. To become an individual we have to enter society. To enter society we have to lose our sense of wholeness. To be an individual – contrary to notions of self-sufficiency or individualism – is to rely on others (especially the social system) for one's sense of value. After our fall from wholeness, we ask the other to make us whole, to declare our innocence. When we ask to be made whole apart from the other (or, in the case of Woodward and the Lawrence Five, to be wholly innocent) we are, therefore, in violation of the social pact. We no longer want to rely on the other for our sense of self, even though we have to ask for its approval through media channels, because we have decided that we are whole apart from its decisions. It is this desire that the law rallies against because it violates the principle of the social order through which the desire is articulated in the first place. As such, the very nature of individuality, or what psychoanalysts call the subject, is that it harks back to a state of nature that is always impossible to attain from within the bounds of the speaking, social, subject.

On the side of the social order, this reading can also reveal that society has an ambivalent relationship toward the other. While vilified others struggle for wholeness before the law, the will to transgress fascinates those who are largely unaware of their split selves. As such, as an audience we were fascinated by Woodward and the Lawrence Five precisely because they provided a glimpse into the pre-social state of nature that we would all sometimes like to go back to, but repress because we fear the consequences of our risk. This ambivalence toward crime and deviance terrifies us. We want to know what it is like to act out our desires, but are afraid that the result of this might be our own social abjection. As a result we accept self-repression/social-regulation, but only if in return we can oppress those who have acted out their desires. Thus, if the act of structural oppression fails to suppress our interest in the other, (i.e. the law does not provide adequate closure) the other is regulated by alternative means. Here, the media's role is to reconstruct the hero/villain in more acceptable (less ambivalent) terms. Consequently Louise Woodward's *Panorama* re-birth as a stylish, in-control *woman*, put into question the public/media support for an immature, unaccountable child. It appeared as though she had duped us.[2] Similarly, the Lawrence Five had for years refused to speak, which left them open to construction. Their silence had legitimated our belief that they were asocial, confined to the state of nature. But their television appearance brought them uncomfortably close to us. Suddenly we could recognize the possibility of their alleged actions in ourselves.

Saints and Sinners

The idea that we do not, and possibly cannot, truly know whether a person suspected of wrong-doing is actually guilty, reveals the ambiguous relationship between social and legal control. We want to believe that the law is infallible, but inconclusive outcomes to high-profile cases lead us to question the integrity of structural justice. Foucault argues that in order to compensate for the fallibility of the law, modern systems of justice inscribe control and regulation via alternative social mechanisms. Following authors such as Hall et al it has been my assertion that the media acts as one such structure. By stepping in when the law is seen to fail, the media act to shore up any visible cracks in the social system. According to Girard, however, such symbolic identity constructions enact violence upon an individual who is sacrificed in order to satisfy the social demand for internal cohesion.

The role of the law in this mechanism is to be seen as an impartial system of justice. The law must be at once above popular (mob) justice, but must also be seen to uphold its demands. This bind is exemplified by the commonsensical approach employed in British judicial systems (Douzinas, 2000). In other words, British justice responds to 'man on the street' demands to exclude individual deviants, rather than alter the social system to enable a more just legal process, even though its argumentation elevates common sense reactions to the level of abstract legal theories. Following this logic Foucault argues that social regulatory mechanisms turn people into case studies rather than treat them as individuals in order to uphold the dominance of the social system. Thus the violence of self/other antagonism is elevated to the level of abstraction where it can be safely played out in the realm of legal objectivity. Consequently this process objectifies the victim in much the same way as it does the alleged perpetrator. Instead of asking the victim for a subjective interpretation of the crime, the social system operates to construct a set of representations about the events that work to sustain dominant ideology.

In an attempt to identify space for a more just system for passing judgments I have critiqued media representations of legal decisions and explored the objective

---

[2] This also refers to Woodward's re-birth as a law student, regarded as a cynical attempt to cash-in on her infamy.

nature of the legal system. Against the Foucauldian motif of regulation, which I have suggested characterizes normal legal process, my argument is that one should search for a mode of justice that can take into account subjectivity distorted by media/legal discourse. In their book *Justice Miscarried* (1994) Douzinas and Warrington refer to the Greek tragedy of Antigone in order to sketch their theory for a legal system that can dispense (an)other justice. My study attempted to discover the seeds of (an)other form of justice in the contemporary world. My analysis of two high-profile cases – Louise Woodward and Stephen Lawrence – has been an effort to theorize the tension between objective construction and subjective deconstruction at work in the legal world. In my first example – the Woodward/Eappen case – Judge Zobel appears to subjectify the law in a way that precedes my later analysis of the Macpherson judgment. By overturning the jury's decision, it is clear that Zobel shows that the legal *process* is fallible. Instead he is forced to impose what he considers the correct legal outcome onto the case, rather than allow popular justice to be enacted. However, a deeper analysis of this judgment shows how Zobel was never concerned to emancipate Woodward from the confines of objective construction. Rather, Zobel's aim was to uphold the dominance of abstract law and defend the court against popular justice. Through this course of action he was able to critique the notion of the unsuccessful family from an ideological point of view that re-routed popular conservative criticism through the objective position of legal theory. As such, although Zobel's decision might have appeared to open the law, the opposite was the case. Legal closure was achieved by overturning the jury's decision in the name of abstract right. Through all of this Woodward remained a construction. Zobel's final decision did nothing to free her from the bounds of objectivity. From killer nanny to irresponsible child, she was never allowed to express her own identity. In contrast, the Macpherson decision to empower the victim paved the way for the expression of subjectivity. In contrast to the abstraction of legal texts, a victim centred law would allow for a more ethical space for justice.

Against symbolic structures such as the law and the media, which write the other through discourse, perhaps we can regard the Macpherson Report as an effort to provide a model for inclusive justice by authorising the victim's subjective experience. While the two criminal legal cases provide a basis from which to argue that representation (media and legal) acts to objectify the subject (both victim and perpetrator) in order to uphold the dominance of the social order, to escape this cycle of representational violence, my argument is that subjects must be allowed to speak for themselves. However, perhaps more importantly, this speech act must be recognized by the dominant social order as legal currency.

Akin to Laurence Thomas (1998), who advances the concept of moral deference in order to suggest that those who judge the victim must privilege the subjective thoughts of that person, rather than make recourse to some neutral, textual, rule about legitimacy, Macpherson's report made recommendations for legalising the subjectivity of the racial other. While Macpherson advises the police to communicate with the other, to listen to their thoughts, Zobel became the author of Woodward's subjectivity. In order to excuse the social system from the feminist critique that exposes the capitalist double standard that women should be both mother and worker, Woodward is rehabilitated as a child, rather than a killer, and the Eappen family was disciplined and absolved. In this respect Zobel's decision was critical of the notion of the working mother insofar as it compromises the place of father and compromises the care of the child, even though capitalism itself pushes women into the difficult position of mother/worker. In order to manage this problematic relation between material demands (that women should work) and ideological concerns (that the father should head the family, while the mother should raise the children), Zobel's judgment described a tragic situation whereby the family collapsed without the steady hand of the father to guide its progress. As such, Woodward became a child, while Deborah Eappen started to look like a hysterical failure and Sunil Eappen a weak, castrated, peripheral figure.

After this symbolic reconstruction, it was no longer necessary to paint Woodward as a vicious child killer. In fact, the very nature of the tragic episode made it preferable that each actor became a fallen figure, an abject failure deserving of sympathy, rather than a dangerous individual. In terms of Woodward herself, the function of her visible breakdown in court was to illuminate the point of tragedy, the moment when the villainous nanny became a fallen hero. But as my discussion of the *Panorama* interview shows, this symbolic position enacted violence upon Woodward. She understood that she had been abjectly written by the case and attempted to author her own version of events. This was unacceptable for the social order.

My second case – Stephen Lawrence – follows the same pattern. Throughout the drama that followed their son's murder, the Lawrences wanted to maintain a critique of society rooted in their subjectivity. This resistance to construction involved an exposition of the ordinary racism of British society and a refusal to surrender to the ideology of multiculturalism that would have otherwise packaged Stephen's death as an aberration of racial violence in an otherwise peaceful ethnically diverse society. But the payoff for this resistant stance is that normal society has an uneasy relationship with the Lawrences. Even though they have avoided the suspicion, and eventual indifference, that surrounded Rolan Adams and Manjit Basuta, perhaps Neville Lawrence is still too black (political) for British society. As Douzinas (1994 [with Warrington]; 2000) shows in his works on justice and otherness, society continues to exclude those who do not conform to the prerequisites of insider identity. For these others any kind of justice, institutional or otherwise, is a difficult thing to achieve.

Given this critique of law, it is clear that the value of the Macpherson Report is that it tries to make subjectivity legal. For this precise reason the report was met with a cool response upon its issue. In the same way that Zobel was attacked by American commentators for freeing Woodward and thus failing to uphold American justice, Macpherson was scapegoated for his attack on institutional law and the British social order. His assertion that Britain is racist was unacceptable to a society concerned to advance an ideology of racial inclusion.

Yet, despite the popularity of such multicultural sentiment it remains clear that Britain is not yet open to otherness. Continual moral panics over citizenship status and the 'floods' of asylum seekers entering the UK highlight contemporary Britain's sensitivity to issues surrounding boundary policing: the need to protect self and nation from outside infiltration. However, due to processes of globalization, which continue to transgress such boundaries in the name of postmodern capitalism, we must ask ourselves whether symbolic strategies that seek to separate self from other are still viable. In a world seeking to promote global expansion, the determined pursuit of self/nation isolation results in violent antagonism between rich insiders and poor outsiders. In this respect a more equal legal system, which can recognize the other on its own terms would serve to equalize political, economic, and social inequalities. Beyond the consideration of abstract legal theory, this justice system would be about preserving the dignity of the other. As such, it would both reflect, and contribute to, the birth of a true multicultural society and, as Derrida (2001) has explained in his recent work on cosmopolitanism, maintain the space for the future negotiation of difference in the contemporary world.

Bibliography

Adorno, T.W and Horkheimer, M (1944/1997) *Dialectic of Enlightenment*, trans. J. Cumming. London: Verso.

Althusser, L (1970/1993) *Essays on Ideology*. London: Verso.

Anderson, B (1983) *Imagined Communities: Reflections on the Origin and Spread of Nationalism*. London: Verso.

Anthias, F (1999) 'Institutional Racism, Power and Accountability' in *Sociological Research Online*, Vol. 4(1).
<http://www.socresonline.org.uk/socresonline/4/lawrence//anthias.html>

Anthias, F and Yuval-Davis, N in association with Cain, H (1992) *Racialized Boundaries: Race, Nation, Gender, Colour and Class and the Anti-Racist Struggle*. London: Routledge.

Athwal, H (2001) 'The Racism that Kills', *Race and Class*, Vol. 43(2): 111-123.

Barker, M and Petley, J (1997) 'Introduction: From Bad Research to Good – A Guide for the Perplexed' in M. Barker and J. Petley (eds), *Ill Effects: The Media Violence Debate*. London: Routledge.

Barnett, R.C and Rivers, C (1996) *She Works/He Works: How Two-Income Families are Happier, Healthier, and Better-Off*. San Francisco: HarperCollins.

Baudrillard, J (1983) *Simulations*. New York: Semiotext(e).

Baudrillard, J (1988) *The Ecstasy of Communication*. New York: Semiotext(e).

Baudrillard, J (1995) *The Gulf War Did Not Take Place*, trans and intro P. Patton. Sydney: Power Publications.

Baudrillard, J (1970/1998) *The Consumer Society: Myths and Structures*, London: Sage.

Beck, U and Beck-Gernsheim, E (1995) *The Normal Chaos of Love*. Cambridge: Polity Press.

Becker, H (1963) *Outsiders: Studies in Sociology of Deviance*. New York: Free Press.

Benjamin, W (1986a) 'The Work of Art in the Age of Mechanical Reproduction' in *Illuminations*, ed and intro H. Arendt. New York: Schoken Books.

Benjamin, W (1986b) 'Critique of Violence' in *Reflections: Essays, Aphorisms, Autobiographical Writings*, ed and intro P. Demetz. New York: Schoken Books.

Benyon, H (1999) 'A Classless Society?' in H. Benyon and P. Glavanis (eds), *Patterns of Social Inequality*. London: Longman.

Benyon, J and Solomos, J (1987) *The Roots of Urban Unrest*. Oxford: Pergamon.

Bhabha, H (1994) *The Location of Culture*. London: Routledge.

Bobo, L (1997) 'Race, Public Opinion, and the Social Sphere', *Public Opinion Quarterly*, Vol. 61: 1-15.

Boorstin, D (1961/1987) *The Image: A Guide to Pseudo-Events in America*. New York: Vintage Books.

Boothby, R (1991) *Death and Desire*. London: Routledge.

Bridges, L (2001) 'Race, Law and the State' in *Race and Class*, Vol. 43(2): 61-76.

Brooker, P (1992) 'Introduction: Reconstructions' in P. Brooker (ed), *Modernism/Postmodernism*. London: Longman.

Butler, J (1993) 'Endangered/Endangering: Schematic Racism and White Paranoia' in R. Gooding-Williams (ed), *Reading Rodney King, Reading Urban Uprising*. New York: Routledge.

Cathcart, B (2000) *The Case of Stephen Lawrence*. London: Penguin.

Chibnall, S (1977) *Law and Order News: An Analysis of Crime Reporting in the British Press*. London: Tavistock.

Cohen, P (1992) '"It's Racism What Dunnit": Hidden Narratives in Theories of Racism' in D. James and A. Rattansi (eds), *'Race', Culture and Difference*. London: Sage.

Cohen, S (1972) *Folk Devils and Moral Panics: The Creation of the Mods and Rockers*. London: Heinemann.

Collins, P. Hill (1990) *Black Feminist Thought: Knowledge, Consciousness and the Politics of Empowerment*. London: Routledge.

Collins, P. Hill (2001) 'Like One of the Family: Race, Ethnicity, and the Paradox of US National Identity' in *Ethnic and Racial Studies*, Vol. 24(1): 3-28.

Copjec, J (1996) 'Introduction: Evil in the Time of the Finite World' in J. Copjec (ed), *Radical Evil*. London: Verso.

Corner, J (1996) *The Art of Record*. Manchester: Manchester University Press.

Dahlgren, P (1995) *Television and the Public Sphere: Citizenship, Democracy and the Media*. London: Sage.

Debord, G (1967/1994) *The Society of the Spectacle*, trans D. Nicholson-Smith. New York: Zone Books.

Deleuze, G and Guattari, F (1984) *Anti-Oedipus*. London: Athlone.

Delphy, C and Leonard, D (1992) *Familiar Exploitation: A New Analysis of Marriage in Contemporary Western Societies*. Cambridge: Polity Press.

Derrida, J (1990) 'The Force of the Law: The Mystical Foundation of Authority' in *Cardozo Law Review*, Part 2: 919-1045.

Derrida, J (1994) *Spectres of Marx: The State of Debt, the Work of Mourning and the New International*, trans P. Kamuf, intro B. Magnus and S. Cullenberg. London: Routledge.

Derrida, J (1978/1995) *Writing and Difference*, trans and intro A. Bass. London: Routledge.

Derrida, J (1998) *Of Grammatology*, trans G. Chakravorty Spivak. Baltimore: Johns Hopkins University Press.

Derrida, J (2001) *On Cosmopolitanism and Forgiveness*. London: Routledge.

Douzinas, C (2000) *The End of Human Rights*. Oxford: Hart Publishing.

Douzinas, C and Warrington, R (1994) *Justice Miscarried: Ethics, Aesthetics and the Law*. London: Harvester Wheatsheaf.

Du Bois, W.E.B (1903/1994) *The Souls of Black Folk*. New York: Dover.

Du Bois, W.E.B (1920/1999) *Darkwater: Voices From Within the Veil*. New York: Dover.

Dubofsky, M (1980) 'Neither Upstairs, Nor Downstairs: Domestic Service in Middle-Class American Homes' in *Reviews in American History*, Vol. 8(1): 86-91.

Eco, U (1967/1986), *Travels in Hyperreality*. San Diego: Harcourt Brace & Co.

Engels, F (1987) *The Origin of the Family, Private Property and the State*, intro E. Burke Leacock. London: Lawrence and Wishart.

Entman, R.M (1990) 'Modern Racism and the Images of Blacks in Local Television News', *Critical Studies in Mass Communication*, Vol. 7: 332-345.

Entman, R.M (1992) 'Blacks in the News', *Journalism Quarterly*, Vol. 69(2): 341-361.

Ericson, R.V, Baranek, P.M and Chan, J.B.L (1987) *Visualizing Deviance: A study of News Organization*. Milton Keynes: Open University Press.

Ericson, R.V, Baranek, P.M and Chan, J.B.L (1989) *Negotiating Control: A Study of News Sources*. Milton Keynes: Open University Press.

Ericson, R.V, Baranek, P.M and J.B.L Chan (1991) *Representing Order: Crime, Law and Justice in the News Media*. Milton Keynes: Open University Press.

Fanon, F (1952/1986) *Black Skin, White Masks*. London: Pluto Press.

Fanon, F (1961/1990) *The Wretched of the Earth*. London: Penguin.

Featherstone, M (2000) 'Speed and Violence: Sacrifice in Virilio, Girard and Derrida', *Anthropoetics*, Vol. 6(2). <http://www.anthropoetics.ucla.edu>

Folbre, N (1994) *Who Pays for the Kids? Gender and the Structures of Constraint*. London: Routledge.

Forrester, J (1991) *The Seductions of Psychoanalysis: Freud, Lacan and Derrida*. Cambridge: Cambridge University Press.

Foucault, M (1973/1993) *The Birth of the Clinic*. London: Routledge.

Foucault, M (1977/1991) *Discipline and Punish: The Birth of the Prison*. London: Penguin.

Foucault, M (1978/1990) *The History of Sexuality, Volume One: The Will to Knowledge*. London: Penguin.

Foucault, M (1984) *Theories of the Political: History, Power and the Law*. London: Routledge.

Foucault, M (1988) 'The Dangerous Individual' in *Politics Philosophy Culture: Interviews and Other Writings 1977-1984*, ed and intro L. D. Kritzman. London: Routledge.

Foucault, M (1991) *The Foucault Reader*, ed and intro P. Rabinow. London: Penguin.

Fraser, N (1997) *Justice Interruptus: Critical Refelctions on the "Postsocialist" Condition*. New York: Routledge.

Freud, S (1939/1991) *The Penguin Freud Library, Vol. 12: Civilization, Society and Religion*. London: Penguin.

Freud, S (1950/1994) *Totem and Taboo*. London: Ark.

Fukayama, F (1993) *The End of History and the Last Man*. London: Penguin.

Gans, E (1997) *Signs of Paradox*. Stanford: Stanford University Press.

Gilroy, P (1987) *There Aint No Black in the Union Jack*. London: Hutchinson.

Gilroy, P (1992) 'The End of Antiracism' in D. James and A. Rattansi (eds), *'Race', Culture and Difference*. London: Sage.

Gilroy, P (1993) *The Black Atlantic*. London: Verso.

Girard, R (1979) *Violence and the Sacred*, trans P. Gregory. Baltimore: Johns Hopkins University Press.

Girard, R (1986) *The Scapegoat*, trans Y. Freccero. Baltimore: Johns Hopkins University Press.

Girard, R (1996) *The Girard Reader*, ed J. G. Williams. New York: Crossroad Herder.

Glasgow University Media Group (1976) *Bad News*, intro R. Hoggart. London: Routledge, Kegan & Paul.

Glasgow University Media Group (1980) *More Bad News*. London: Routledge & Kegan Paul.

Golding, P and Middleton, S (1982) *Images of Welfare: Press and Public Attitudes to Poverty*. Oxford: Blackwell.

Goode, E and Ben-Yehuda, N (1994) *Moral Panics: The Social Construction of Deviance*. Oxford: Blackwell.

Gramsci, A (1971) *Selections from the Prison Notebooks of Antonio Gramsci*, ed Q. Hoare and G. Noell-Smith. London: Lawrence and Wishart.

Grant, L, Simpson; Layne A.; Xue Lan Rong and Peters-Golden, H (1990) 'Gender, Parenthood, and the Work Hours of Physicians' in *Journal of Marriage and the Family*, Vol. 52 (February): 39-49.

Gronbeck, B.E (1997) 'Character, Celebrity, and Sexual Innuendo in the Mass-Mediated Presidency' in J. Lull and S. Hinerman (eds), *Media Scandals*. Cambridge: Polity Press.

Habermas, J (1988) *Legitimation Crisis*. London: Polity.

Habermas, J (1989) *The Structural Transformation of the Public Sphere: An Inquiry into a Category of Bourgeois Society*, Cambridge, Massachusetts: The MIT Press.

Habermas, J (1992) 'Modernity – an Incomplete Project' in P. Brooker (ed), *Modernism/Postmodernism*. London: Longman.

Hall, S (1992a) 'The Question of Cultural Identity' in S. Hall, D. Held and T. McGrew (eds) *Modernity and Its Futures*. Cambridge: Polity and Open University Press.

Hall, S (1992b) 'The West and the Rest: Discourse and Power' in S. Hall and B. Gieben (eds) *Formations of Modernity*. Cambridge: Polity and Open University Press.

Hall, S and Jacques, M (1983) 'Introduction' in S. Hall and M. Jacques, *The Politics of Thatcherism*. London: Lawrence and Wishart.

Hall, S; Critcher, C; Jefferson, T; Clarke, J and Roberts, B (1978) *Policing the Crisis: Mugging, the State, and Law and Order*. London: MacMillan.

Hariman, R (1990) 'Performing the Laws: Popular Trials and Social Knowledge' in R. Hariman (ed) *Popular Trials: Rhetoric, Mass Media, and the Law*. Tuscaloosa: The University of Alabama Press.

Harris, C (1999) 'Secular Religion and the Public Response to Diana's Death' in T. Walter (ed), *The Mourning for Diana*. Oxford: Berg.

Heyzer, N; Lycklama, A; Nijeholt, G; and Weerakoon, N (eds) (1994) *The Trade in Domestic Workers: Causes, Mechanisms and Consequences of International Migration*. Kualar Lumpa: Asian and Pacific Development Centre.

Hine, C (2000) *Virtual Ethnography*. London: Sage.

Hitchins, P (2000) *The Abolition of Britain*. London: Quartet.

Hobsbawn, E (1983) 'Falklands Fallout' in S. Hall and M. Jacques (eds), *The Politics of Thatcherism*. London: Lawrence and Wishart in association with Marxism Today.

Hoggart, R (1958) *The Uses of Literacy*. London: Penguin.

Holdaway, S (1999) 'Understanding the Police Investigation of the Murder of Stephen Lawrence: A "Mundane Sociological Analysis"' in *Sociological Research Online*, Vol. 4(1). <http://www.socresonline.org.uk/socresonline/4/ lawrence/holdaway.htm>

Holohan, S and Poole, E (2002) 'Race, Representation and Power: The Experience of British Muslims' in *Intersections: The Journal of Global Communications and Culture*, Vol. 2(3/4): 79-88.

Holohan, S and Featherstone, M (2003) 'Multiculturalism, Institutional Law, and Imaginary Justice' in *Law and Critique*, Vol. 14(1): 1-27.

Holt, L (1998) 'Diana and the Backlash' in M. Merck (ed), *After Diana: Irreverent Elegies*. London: Verso.

Howitt, D (1998) *Crime, Deviance and the Law*. Chichester: John Wiley & Sons.

Jackson, B.S (1998) 'The Louise Woodward Trial: The Distinction Between Murder and Manslaughter'. <http://www.legaltheory.demon.co.uk>

Jacobs, R.N (2000) *Race, The Media and the Crisis of Civil Society: From Watts to Rodney King*. Cambridge: Cambridge University Press.

Jameson, F (1991) *Postmodernism, Or, the Cultural Logic of Late Capitalism*. London: Verso.

Jones, N (1997) *Campaign 1997: How the General Election was Won and Lost*. London: Indigo.

Jones, N (1999) *Sultans of Spin: The Media and the New Labour Government*. London: Victor Gollancz.

Kafka, F (1992) 'In the Penal Colony' in *The Transformation and Other Stories*. London: Penguin Books.

Kellner, D (1989) *Jean Baudrillard: From Marxism to Postmodernism and Beyond*. Cambridge: Polity Press.

Kennedy, H (1992) *Eve Was Framed*. London: Verso.

Kidd-Hewitt, D (1995) 'Crime and the Media: A Criminological Perspective' in D. Kidd-Hewitt and R. Osborne (eds), *Crime and Media: The Postmodern Spectacle*. London: Pluto Press.

Kundnani, A (2000) '"Stumbling on": Race, Class and England', *Race and Class*, Vol. 41(4): 1-18.

Kushnick, L (1999) '"Over Policed and Under Protected"': Stephen Lawrence, Institutional and Police Practices' in *Sociological Research Online*, Vol. 4(1).
<http://www.socresonline.org.uk/socresonline/4/1/kushnick.html>

Kymlicka, W (1995) *Multicultural Citizenship: A Liberal Theory of Minority Rights*. Oxford: Clarendon Press.

Kymlicka, W (2001) *Politics in the Vernacular: Nationalism, Multiculturalism and Citizenship*. Oxford: Oxford University Press.

Lacan, J (1977) *Écrits*. London: Routledge.

Law, I (2001) *Race in the News*. London: Palgrave.

Lea, J and Young, J (1995) 'The Drift to Military Policing' in S. Caffrey with G. Munday (eds), *The Sociology of Crime and Deviance: Selected Issues*. Greenwich: Greenwich University Press.

Lebow, R.N (1976) *White Britain and Black Ireland: The Influence of Stereotypes on Colonial Policy*. Philadelphia: Institute for the Study of Human Issues.

Lévy, P (2000) *Collective Intelligence: Mankind's Emerging World in Cyberspace*. New York: Perseus Books.

Lloyd, A (1995) *Doubly Deviant, Doubly Damned: Society's Treatment of Violent Women*. London: Penguin.

Lull, J and Hinerman, S (1997) 'The Search for Scandal' in J. Lull and S. Hinerman (eds), *Media Scandals*. Cambridge: Polity Press.

Lyotard, J-F (1984) *The Postmodern Condition: A Report on Knowledge*. Manchester: Manchester University Press.

Lyotard, J-F (1992) 'Answering the Question: What is Postmodernism?' in P. Brooker (ed), *Modernism/Postmodernism*. London: Longman.

Mac an Ghail, M (1999) *Contemporary Racisms and Ethnicities: Social and Cultural Transformations*. Buckingham: Open University Press.

Macpherson, Sir W (1999) *The Stephen Lawrence Inquiry: Report of an Inquiry*. London: HMSO.

McClelland, J.S (1996) *A History of Western Political Thought*. London: Routledge.

Memmi, A (1957/1990) *The Colonizer and the Colonized*. London: Earthscan.

Morris, L (1994) *Dangerous Classes: The Underclass and Social Citizenship*. London: Routledge.

Nietzsche, F (1961) *Thus Spoke Zarathustra*. London: Penguin.

Norton-Taylor, R (1999) *The Colour of Justice*. London: Oberon Books.

O'Neill, J (1995) *The Poverty of Postmodernism*. London: Routledge.

O'Neill, J (1998) *Millennial Madonna: Is There a Third Way for Britain?* Paper presented at Goldsmiths College, University of London, 16 March.

O'Neill, J (2001) 'Oh My Others, There is No Other!' in *Theory, Culture and Society*. Vol. 18(2/3): 77-90.

Oliver, K (1994) *Reading Kristeva: Unravelling the Double-bind*. Bloomington: Indiana University Press.

Oliver, K (1997) *Family Values: Subjects Between Nature and Culture*. London: Routledge.

Pearson, G (1983) *Hooligans: A History of Respectable Fears*. London: MacMillan.

Postman, N (1986) *Amusing Ourselves to Death*. London: Methuen.

Rattansi, A (1992) 'Changing the Subject? Racism, Culture and Education' in D. James and A. Rattansi (eds), *'Race', Culture and Difference*. London: Sage.

Reik, T (1961) *The Compulsion to Confess: The Psychoanalysis of Crime and Punishment*. New York: Grove Press.

Reineke, M.J (1997) *Sacrificed Lives: Kristeva on Women and Violence*. Bloomington: Indiana University Press.

Reiner, R (2002) 'Media Made Criminality: The Representation of Crime in the Mass Media' in M. Maguire, R. Morgan and R. Reiner (eds), *The Oxford Handbook of Criminology*. Oxford: Oxford University Press.

Roberts, I (1999) 'A Historical Construction of the Working Class' in H. Benyon and P. Glavanis (eds), *Patterns of Social Inequality*. London: Longman.

Robertson, B.C (2000) *There's No Place Like Work: How Business, Government, and Our Obsession with Work Have Driven Parents from Home*. Dallas: Spence Publishing Company.

Rogin, M (1988) *Ronald Reagan, the Movie: And Other Episodes of Political Demonology*. Berkeley: University of California Press.

Romero, M (1992) *Maid in the U.S.A.* New York: Routledge.

Said, E.W (1978/1995) *Orientalism: Western Conceptions of the Orient*. London: Penguin.

Salecl, R (1993) 'Crime as a Mode of Subjectivization: Lacan and the Law' in *Law and Critique*. Vol. 4(1): 3-20.

Salecl, R (1994) *The Spoils of Freedom: Psychoanalysis and Feminism after the Fall of Socialism*. London: Routledge.

Salecl, R (1996) 'See No Evil, Speak No Evil: Hate Speech and Human Rights' in J. Copjec (ed) *Radical Evil*. London: Verso.

Scannell, P (1992) 'Public Service Broadcasting and Modern Life' in P. Scannell, P. Schlesinger and C. Sparks (eds) *Culture and Power: A Media, Culture & Society Reader*. London: Sage.

Scarman, Lord (1981) *The Brixton Disorders, 10-12 April 1981, Report of an Inquiry*. London: HMSO.

Schuetz, J (1994) *The Logic of Women on Trial: Case Studies of Popular American Trials*. Carbondale: Southern Illinois University Press.

Scollon, R (1998) *Mediated Discourse as Social Interaction: A Study of News Discourse*. London: Longman.

Seshadri-Crooks, K (2000) *Desiring Whiteness: A Lacanian Analysis of Race*. London: Routledge.

Smart, C (1977) *Women, Crime and Criminology: A Feminist Critique*. London: Routledge & Kegan Paul.

Solan, L.M (1998) 'The Louise Woodward Trial: Why Louise Woodward Was Convicted'. <http//:www.legaltheory.demon.co.uk>

Soothill, K; Peelo, M; Francis, B; Pearson, J and Ackerley, E (2002) 'Homicide and the Media: Identifying the Top Cases in *The Times*', *Howard Journal of Criminal Justice*, Vol. 41(5): 401-421.

Sparks, C (1992) 'The Popular Press and Political Democracy' in P. Scannell, P. Schlesinger and C. Sparks (eds) *Culture and Power: A Media, Culture & Society Reader*. London: Sage.

Stacey, J (1996) *In the Name of the Family: Rethinking Family Values in the Postmodern Age*. Boston: Beacon Books.

Surette, R (1998) *Media, Crime, and Criminal Justice: Images and Realities* (second edition). Belmont, California: West/Wadsworth.

Taylor, C (1994) *Multiculturalism*, ed A. Gutman. Princetown: Princeton University Press.

Thayler, P (1994) *The Watchful Eye: American Justice in the Age of the Television Trial*. Westport, Connecticut: Praeger.

Thayler, P (1997) *The Spectacle: Media and the Making of the O.J. Simpson Story.* Westport, Connectitut: Praeger.

Thomas, L (1998) 'Moral Deference' in C. Willett (ed), *Theorizing Multiculturalism: A Guide to the Current Debate.* Oxford: Blackwell.

Todorov, T (2000) 'Race and Racism' in L. Back and J. Solomos (eds), *Theories of Racism: A Reader.* London: Routledge.

Tomlinson, J (1997) '"And Besides, the Wench is Dead": Media Scandals and the Globalization of Communication' in J. Lull and S. Hinerman (eds), *Media Scandals.* Cambridge: Polity Press.

Virilio, P (1999) *Politics of the Very Worst.* New York: Semiotext(e).

Walter, T (1999) 'The Questions People Asked' in T. Walter (ed), *The Mourning For Diana.* Oxford: Berg.

Weber, M (1992) *The Protestant Ethic and the Spirit of Capitalism.* London: Penguin.

West, C; Lazar, M.M. and Kramarae, C (1997) 'Gender in Discourse' in T.A. van Dijk (ed), *Discourse as Social Interaction.* London: Sage.

Willet, C (1995) *Maternal Ethics and Other Slave Moralities.* London: Routledge.

Williams, R (1981) *Culture.* London: Fontana.

Wray, M and Newitz, A (1997) 'Introduction' in M. Wray and A. Newitz (eds), *White Trash: Race and Class in America.* London: Routledge.

Young, A (1996) *Imagining Crime: Textual Outlaws and Criminal Conversions.* London: Sage.

Žižek, S (1993) *Tarrying With the Negative: Kant, Hegel and the Critique of Ideology.* Durham: Duke University Press.

Žižek, S (1997) 'Multiculturalism, or, the Cultural Logic of Multinational Capitalism' in *New Left Review,* 225: 28-52.

Žižek, S (1998) 'Love Thy Neighbor? No, Thanks!' in C. Lane (ed) *The Psychoanalysis of Race.* New York: Columbia University Press.

Žižek, S (1998) 'Why Does the Law Need an Obscene Supplement?' in P. Goodrich and D.Gray Carlson (eds) *Law and the Postmodern Mind.* Ann Arbor: The University of Michigan Press.

Žižek, S (2000) 'Why We All Love to Hate Haider' in *New Left Review* 2: 37-45.

Zobel, Judge H.B (1997) Commonwealth v Louise Woodward.

Index

press 82, 83, 95, 107, 113, 126
Mimetic desire/rivalry 14, 37, 58, 61, 62-
    4, 66, 67-9, 74, 143
Mob, the 59, 126, 134
Mob violence 58, 75, 99, 105-6, 126
Moral deference 144-6, 155
Moral panic 3, 61, 69, 76, 104, 126, 156
Morris, L. 121, 124
Mother
    abject 23, 56, 124-5
    absent 16, 35
    child relationship 70, 72-3, 77
    good 34, 39
    model of mimetic desire 60-1, 62-6,
        67-8
    see also Oedipus complex
Multiculturalism 1, 8, 10, 88-91, 95, 148
    liberal justice 129-30, 134, 136,
        140, 145, 156-7
    UK politics 81-5, 101, 114, 116,
        120, 126, 127, 138-9, 142
Myth/mythology 39, 41, 45-6, 88-9, 119,
    137, 141
    function of 6, 58-60, 62, 69-71, 76

Nation of Islam 85, 108-10, 117, 118-9
National Front 91, 108, 109, 110
New Labour 36, 38, 38n2, 39, 116, 120,
    138
Nietzsche, F. 70
Norton-Taylor, R. 115, 115n8

Oedipus complex 58-9, 60, 61, 72-3,
    74n7
Oliver, K. 65, 70-1, 72, 73n6, 74n7
O'Neill, J. 36, 39, 73-5, 146
Orientalism 9, 94, 96, 99

Panopticon 55, 75
Patriarchy
    and the family 20-4, 61
    and society 33, 58, 74, 77-8, 150
    see also father
Pearson, G. 101, 121
Police 16, 65, 99, 113, 128
    and society 55, 98-9, 123-4, 144,
        155
    criticism of 8, 37, 110, 116-7, 119,
        127, 133, 145
    powers 5, 110, 132

race relations 84, 85-6, 102, 107,
    127-8, 130, 143
Postman, N. 13
Postmodern
    condition 2, 7, 75-7
    media 52-3
Postmodernity
    criticism of 73-4
Princess Diana 36, 37-40, 42, 48n5, 49,
    50n8, 78, 125, 142
Public sphere 4, 20, 32, 38, 68, 71, 73,
    75, 115, 121
    democratic 7, 42, 111
    forum for debate 5, 14, 25, 35, 37,
        39, 54, 148
    production of knowledge 2, 3, 6, 19,
        58, 77, 125-6

Race relations
    and the media 111
    in UK 10, 84, 103, 115-6, 127, 131,
        144
    Macpherson report 135
    under Margaret Thatcher 85
    see also anti-racism and police
Rattansi, A. 91, 114
Reik, T. 53, 53n11, 55
Reineke, M.J. 74, 76
Reiner, R. 4
Riots 8, 87
    1980s 81, 86, 87, 88
    Brixton 131-2
    North of England 81, 129
Roberts, I. 123
Robertson, B.C. 16, 18-9
Rogin, M. 105
Romero, M. 26-7, 29

Sacrifice
    and law 60
    originary scene 58-9
    scapegoat mechanism 61-2, 64, 68-
        70, 74-5, 82, 97-8, 140, 143-4
    symbolic 14, 34-5, 38-9, 43, 47, 57,
        66-7, 128-9, 154
Said, E.W. 9, 82, 91, 94, 96-7, 99-100,
    111, 117
Salecl, R. 49n7, 60, 145, 146
Scandal 4, 40, 48, 66
    political 36, 42, 49
    and scapegoat mechanism 62

Scannell, P. 2
Scapegoat mechanism 10, 37, 58, 60-4,
  69, 74, 75-7, 140-1, 143-5, 148
Scarman report 131-3
Schuetz, J. 48, 56
Scollon, R. 4
Seshadri-Crooks, K. 92, 130
Sharpton, Al 107-8
Simpson, O.J. 13, 36-7, 40-1, 42, 43-4,
  47, 48, 49, 52, 54, 55, 115
Skandalon 58, 62, 145
Smart, C. 34, 56
Solan, L.M. 15n3
Solomos, J. 85
Soothill, K., Peelo, M., Francis, B.,
  Pearson, J. and Ackerley, E. 8
Sparks, C. 2
Spectacle 1, 2, 13-4, 31, 36-43, 47-50,
  52, 55, 56, 58, 66, 148, 151
Stacey, J. 20-1
Subjectivity 70, 87, 91, 94-5, 97, 128,
  129, 131, 141, 145
  and law 131, 139, 141, 142, 146,
  155, 156
  black 106, 110, 113, 121
  ethnicity 10, 83, 95, 134
  victim 154, 155
  white 57
Sun, The
  anti-Eappen sentiment 29, 56
  nationalism 16, 21, 47-8, 50n9
  political allegiance 116
Surette, R. 52

Taylor, C. 7, 88, 89, 146
Thatcherism 85-8, 94, 101, 103, 104, 114
Thayer, P. 37, 40-1, 52
Thomas, Clarence / Hill, Anita 117-8
Thomas, L. 146, 155
Tomlinson, J. 49
Tonight with Trevor Macdonald 125n14,
  152

Undecidability of law 127, 139, 149-52
Underclass 17, 120-1, 126, 139

Victim
  centred justice 149, 155
  innocent 48, 58, 81
Virilio, P. 38n3

Walter, T. 36, 37
Watts uprisings 105, 105n2
Weber, M. 38, 39, 49, 142
West, C., Lazar, M.M. and Kramarae, C.
  56
White backlash 82, 129, 135, 139
White trash 120, 122, 136, 142
Willett, C. 70, 72-3
Williams, R. 50-1
Woodward, Louise
  as childlike 35, 36, 56, 156
  courtroom appearance 16, 33, 53-4,
  66-7
  Panorama interview 16, 48n5, 58,
  78, 150, 154, 156
  regulation of 56-7, 69-70, 77, 156
  relationship with Deborah Eappen
  9, 33-5, 56, 62-4, 68
Work 2, 22, 104
  domestic 19, 21-2, 24, 25-31, 68,
  70, 77
  ethic 100, 113-4, 120, 122-4
  woman's 71, 155-6
Working class 10, 17, 23, 26, 95, 120-1,
  138, 139, 142, 144
Working mothers 9, 17-24, 35, 44, 56,
  61, 64, 66-7
Wray, M. and Newitz, A. 122

X, Malcolm 105, 108, 120

Young, A. 6, 48, 70, 71, 125

Žižek, S. 59, 90, 130, 134, 137-8, 146
Zobel, Judge H.B. 9
  decision 9, 14, 15n3, 16, 31, 36, 67,
  149
  popular justice 155-6
  regulation 55-6, 57,
  scapegoat mechanism 77-8